Detecting Lies and Deceit

Wiley Series in

The Psychology of Crime, Policing and Law

Series Editors

Graham Davies
University of Leicester, UK

and

Ray Bull
University of Portsmouth, UK

The Psychology of Interrogations,
Confessions and Testimony
Gisli Gudjonsson

Children as Witnesses
Edited by Helen Dent and Rhona Flin

Paedophiles and Sexual Offences against Children
Dennis Howitt

Psychology and Policing in a Changing World
Peter B. Ainsworth

Offender Profiling: Theory, Research and Practice
Edited by Janet L. Jackson and Debra A. Bekerian

Crime, the Media and the Law
Dennis Howitt

Psychology, Law and Eyewitness Testimony
Peter B. Ainsworth

Investigative Interviewing: Psychology and Practice
Rebecca Milne and Ray Bull

Detecting Lies and Deceit: The Psychology of Lying and the
Implications for Professional Practice
Aldert Vrij

Detecting Lies and Deceit
The Psychology of Lying and the Implications for Professional Practice

Aldert Vrij

Department of Psychology, University of Portsmouth, UK

JOHN WILEY & SONS, LTD

Chichester • New York • Weinheim • Brisbane • Singapore • Toronto

This publication is designed to provide accurate and authoritative information in regard to the subject
matter covered. It is sold on the understanding that the Publisher is not engaged in rendering
professional services. If professional advice or other expert assistance is required, the services of a
competent professional should be sought.

Other Wiley Editorial Offices

John Wiley & Sons Inc., 111 River Street, Hoboken, NJ 07030, USA

Jossey-Bass, 989 Market Street, San Francisco, CA 94103-1741, USA

Wiley-VCH Verlag GmbH, Boschstr. 12, D-69469 Weinheim, Germany

John Wiley & Sons Australia Ltd, 33 Park Road, Milton, Queensland 4064, Australia

John Wiley & Sons (Asia) Pte Ltd, 2 Clementi Loop #02-01, Jin Xing Distripark, Singapore 129809

John Wiley & Sons Canada Ltd, 22 Worcester Road, Etobicoke, Ontario, Canada M9W 1L1

British Library Cataloguing in Publication Data

A catalogue record for this book is available from the British Library

ISBN 0 471 85316 X

Typeset in 10/12pt Century Schoolbook by Saxon Graphics Ltd, Derby
Printed and bound in Great Britain by Antony Rowe Ltd, Chippenham, Wiltshire
This book is printed on acid-free paper responsibly manufactured from sustainable forestry
in which at least two trees are planted for each one used for paper production.

Contents

PART II   VERBAL CHARACTERISTICS OF DECEPTION

PART III   PROFESSIONAL DETECTION OF DECEPTION

About the Author

Aldert Vrij (born 1960) is Reader in Applied Social Psychology in the Department of Psychology at the University of Portsmouth. He has published extensively on deception, particularly the relationship between non-verbal behaviour and deception. His recent work has also concentrated on speech content and deception. Over the years he has held several research grants. His current research on suspects' behaviour during police interviews is funded by the Economic and Social Research Council, and he holds sponsorships from the Leverhulme Trust and the Economic and Social Research Council for his research on the relationship between speech content and deception. Aldert has been recognized by courts as an Expert Witness.

Series Preface

The Wiley Series on the Psychology of Crime, Policing and Law publishes concise and integrative reviews on important emerging areas of contemporary research. The purpose of this series is not merely to present research findings in a clear and readable form, but also to bring out their implications for both practice and policy. The series will be useful not only to psychologists, but also to all those concerned with crime detection and prevention, policing and the judicial process.

In this book Aldert Vrij provides an overview of research on the detection of deception, which includes his own now extensive series of studies, for which he has acquired an international reputation. The book is divided into three parts. The first part examines non-verbal indicators of deception. Studies of how people actually behave when either lying or truth-telling have revealed that there is not a simple dichotomy. The difference in behaviour when being deceptive as opposed to truthful varies between individuals. It also varies within a person across situations and contexts. No wonder observers are not good at detecting deception from their observations of behaviour! However, many people (including relevant professionals, such as police officers) believe that they are good at detecting deception from behavioural cues. This book's overview of research on people's beliefs about behavioural cues to deception, including the author's own work, demonstrates that while people seem to have strong beliefs and largely concur with each other in these beliefs, those beliefs are mistaken. Many of the cues which they believe to be useful are not in fact so.

What liars say forms the focus of the book's second part. The use of Statement Validity Assessment which originates from pioneering work in Germany, does seem—when used by properly trained people—to offer promise as a way of helping to determine whether a person is describing a genuinely experienced event. It began as a procedure for use with children who may have been abused, and its possible usefulness in adults is also now being researched. Of course, if some of the criteria by which it examines statements are indeed found by research to be reliable indications of truthfulness, liars who become aware of such research findings may then try to include certain information in their deceptive accounts. The same could happen for the recently researched 'reality monitoring criteria'.

The third part of the book is concerned with physiological activity in the truth-teller's or liar's body. These psychological responses (e.g. palmar sweating and heart rate) may indeed increase when some people tell lies (e.g. unskilled, inexperienced liars.) However, approaches based on examining this physiological activity, which is often referred to as polygraphic lie detection, must note that people's physiological activity will change due to a whole range of reasons. For example, an innocent married person may be very nervous when the police put questions to him or her about the murder the previous day of his or her secret lover. Aldert Vrij explains very clearly that what is crucial to this approach is the nature of the questions put to the person who is taking 'the test'. Even with appropriate questioning, a liar could use countermeasures to attempt to deceive the polygrapher.

This book presents a well-written and comprehensive overview of research. It also marks a step forward in bringing in more relevant theory, something which much of the research literature lacks.

At the very end of the book, Aldert Vrij poses the reader a question. We are sure that he was telling us the truth when he told us he would welcome receiving your reply to that question!

During the two days in which we were writing this preface, a discussion occurred on the most esteemed national radio station (BBC Radio 4) about whether liars could be detected by their behaviour. It seemed that in London a training programme for personnel officers was telling them that they could detect liars at interviews by examining their behaviour. Those who read this overview of the relevant research will be in a very good position to determine who is really deceiving these personnel officers!

RAY BULL
and GRAHAM DAVIES

June 1999

Preface

In 1997, Jonathan Aitken, an English Conservative politician at that time, was accused by the British newspaper *The Guardian* and by *Granada Television* of staying at the Ritz Hotel in Paris in 1993 while he was serving as Minister for Defence Procurement, at the expense of a Saudi Arabian businessman. Aitken denied this allegation and sued *The Guardian* and *Granada Television* for libel. Was the accusation indeed wrong, or was Aitken lying?

There are, in principle, three different ways to detect a lie. The first way is by observing people's non-verbal behaviour (the movements they make, whether or not they smile or show gaze aversion, their vocal pitch, speech rate, whether or not they stutter, and so on). The second way is by analysing speech content—that is, by analysing what is being said. The third way is by examining physiological responses (blood pressure, heart rate, palmar sweating, and so on).

This book examines all three aspects of lie detection. In particular, the following two issues will be addressed. First, are there systematic differences between liars and truth-tellers in non-verbal behaviour, speech content and physiological reactions? Secondly, to what extent are observers able to detect deceit when they examine someone's non-verbal behaviour, speech content and physiological responses?

The first part of this book focuses on non-verbal behaviour and deception. In Chapter 2, non-verbal behaviours that are typically displayed by liars will be addressed. Included is a discussion about how a suspect—who was later convicted for murder on the basis of substantial evidence—behaved during police interviews in which he denied having committed the crime. This chapter will demonstrate that the relationship between deception and non-verbal behaviour is complicated, because different types of people show different behaviours when they are lying. Moreover, a liar's behaviour depends on the situation in which the lie takes place. Chapter 3 discusses how accurate untrained lay people and professional lie detectors (e.g. police officers and customs officers) are in detecting lies when they examine someone's behaviour. Their ability to detect deceit while judging someone's behaviour is generally low, while several misconceptions exist among both lay people and professional lie detectors as to how liars generally behave.

The second part of this book focuses on what liars actually say. Early research was not very systematic, but did reveal insight into verbal indicators of deception. Chapter 4 discusses the early research. Systematic research into the relationship between deception and verbal behaviour is relatively new, having started approximately a decade ago. The German forensic psychologist, Udo Undeutsch, has described several content criteria to assess the credibility of statements made by alleged victims of sexual abuse. Based primarily on his work, Statement Validity Assessment—a method to assess the veracity of written statements—has been developed. To date, Statement Validity Assessment (SVA) is the instrument most widely used to assess the veracity of verbal behaviour. SVA assessments are accepted as evidence in several courts in the USA and in courts in several Western European countries such as Germany and The Netherlands. Statement Validity Assessment will be described in Chapter 5. Research has indicated that SVA assessments are a useful tool for discriminating between liars and truth-tellers. The assessments, however, are not as accurate as one would wish them to be. In an effort to improve the accuracy of lie detection by analysing speech content, an alternative method has recently been introduced, called Reality Monitoring. Chapter 6 discusses this new method.

The final part of this book deals with physiological responses to deception. Throughout history it has been assumed that lying is accompanied by physiological activity within the liar's body, and several methods have been developed to measure physiological reactions. The modern method of detecting physiological activity in liars involves using a polygraph, also known as a lie detector (although this labelling is misleading, as will be discussed in Chapter 7). The use of the polygraph is widespread in several countries, including the USA and Israel. Polygraph results have been accepted as evidence in several court cases in the USA. Western European countries are more sceptical about the use of polygraph tests. The working of the polygraph and the accuracy of polygraph tests in detecting deceit will be discussed in Chapter 7. A review of the scientific literature, discussed in that chapter, reveals that lies can be detected with polygraph tests, but that the polygraph is not as accurate as some people suggest.

Analyses of verbal behaviour and physiological reactions are sometimes accepted as evidence in court; analyses of non-verbal behaviour should never be presented in court cases, as interpretations of non-verbal behaviour are complicated and therefore not always reliable. Despite this lack of authority concerning examinations of non-verbal behaviour, the relationship between non-verbal behaviour and deception will be thoroughly discussed in this book. The first reason for this is that observers have more opportunities to examine non-verbal behaviours than to examine verbal behaviour or physiological reactions. For analyses of verbal behaviour and physiological responses, it is necessary for the potential liar to say something. A verbal response is not required for analysis of a person's behaviour, and such analyses can take place even when a person decides to remain silent. Secondly, unlike analyses of verbal behaviour and physiological reactions, analyses of non-verbal behaviour can take place immediately and do not require any equipment. Examinations of verbal behaviour require written transcripts of statements, and physiological reactions can only be investigated with the use of technical equipment. This implies that analyses of verbal behaviour and physiological responses are not possible in situations in which immediate observations are required, as is so in the majority of cases. Obviously parents would never ask their children to perform a polygraph test in order to find out whether they smoke secretly. Nor will customs officers transcribe the conversations they have with customers and decide on the basis of analyses of these transcripts whether or not to search someone's luggage. In most situations, observers are therefore dependent on analyses of non-verbal behaviour to find out whether someone is lying. Obtaining insight into the relationship between non-verbal behaviour and deception is therefore particularly useful.

Chapter 8, the concluding chapter of this book, summarizes the psychology of lying and detecting deceit. Hopefully this chapter can be used as a guide for those who want to improve their skills in detecting lies. However, one warning should be given. Detecting lies is difficult. Therefore, reading this book will not necessarily improve your skills in catching a liar. Rather, it is designed to increase your knowledge of deception, which will benefit you in detecting deceit.

Before discussing the non-verbal, verbal and physiological aspects of deception and detecting deceit, some general information about deception will be presented.

ALDERT VRIJ

Acknowledgements

I am grateful to Professor Tony Gale, Professor Günter Köhnken, Professor Ray Bull and Samantha Mann for their useful comments on previous drafts of this book. I also wish to thank those institutions who have funded my research over the years, namely the Dutch Organisation for Scientific Research (NWO), the Dutch Ministry of Justice, The Leverhulme Trust, The Economic and Social Research Council (ESRC) and the University of Portsmouth. Without their financial support I could not have carried out my research and would not have written this book. Police officers were participants in a substantial part of my research. I greatly appreciate their willingness to participate, and would like to thank various police forces in both the UK and The Netherlands for allowing me to include their officers. Finally, I am grateful to John Wiley & Sons for the opportunity to publish this book.

CHAPTER 1

The Social Psychology of Lying and Detecting Deceit

Deceiving others is an essential part of everyday social interaction. A man says that he is pleased with his birthday presents, although in fact he does not really appreciate them; the host receives compliments about his cooking, although the food was not really that good; a pupil watching TV tells her dad that she has completed her homework; an adulterous man denies having an affair with another woman; a smuggler tells the customs officer that she has nothing to declare; and a murderer systematically denies that he has committed the crime. These are only a few examples from an almost inexhaustible source of possible lies. Lying is a daily life event, as research has indicated. We try to dupe others more than once each day, and we often try to find out whether others are deceiving us. Sometimes deception has major consequences. The world would be entirely different today, had people been fully aware of Hitler's real intentions before World War II broke out. Despite the fact that we are confronted with deception every day, and that deception sometimes has severe consequences, there are many misconceptions about how liars present themselves and how they can be detected. The aim of this book is to give more insight into deception. I shall discuss how liars present themselves, and what a lie detector should do to detect lies. Before discussing these aspects, some general information about deception will be presented. This includes reasons why people are generally not good at detecting lies, a definition of deception, and information about how often people lie, why they lie, the different types of lie that exist, and which people lie most. This chapter will challenge the stereotypical view that 'lying is bad'. As will be shown, lying is an important phenomenon in social relationships and we often like the company of people who lie frequently.

POOR LIE DETECTORS

If someone asked you the following two questions 'Are you good at lying?' and 'Are you good at detecting lies?', what would you answer? You would probably answer that you are not such a good liar, but that you generally notice when someone is trying to dupe you. This book shows that the opposite is more likely to be true. Generally, people are rather good at lying, but not very good at detecting lies. One reason why people are not good at detecting lies is that they have poor knowledge about how to catch a liar. However, this is not the only reason. Lies also go undetected because often the observer is not motivated to catch the liar. A third reason is that some people are very good liars, which makes it very difficult to discover their lies.

As far as motivation is concerned, some lies go undetected because observers *do not want* to detect a lie, because it is not in their best interests to learn the truth. People generally like it when others compliment them about their body shape, their hairstyle, the way they dress, what they have achieved, and so on. So why bother trying to discover whether those who make these compliments actually mean what they are saying? A spouse will not always try to find out whether his partner is having an adulterous affair for this very reason. As soon as the husband tells his adulterous wife that he has found out about her and her lover, she may feel compelled to choose between him and the other man, possibly resulting in a divorce, which may be something he does not want. In short, communicating what he has discovered may have undesirable consequences for him and, on realizing this, he may decide not to investigate this issue.

Sometimes people do not want to detect lies because they would not know what to do if they were to know the truth. For instance, most guests will not try to find out whether their host actually likes the present, because of the dilemma of what to do if the present is not appreciated. More serious lies may also go undetected for the same reason. Many children smoke cigarettes, despite the fact that their parents have forbidden them to smoke. Their smoking often goes unnoticed, because their parents do not try to find out whether they are smoking. As soon as they discover that their children do smoke, they will have to take some action. But what can they do? Many parents are unclear about what to do in such a situation, and therefore prefer to remain ignorant. And suppose that the husband's wife in the example mentioned above decides not to leave him. What should he do then? Leaving her is perhaps appropriate, but for various reasons it may not be something that he wants to do.

President Clinton's personal secretary, Betty Currie, tried to avoid learning details of the relationship between President Clinton and

Monica Lewinsky. On one occasion, Lewinsky said (to Currie) of herself and the President: 'As long as no one saw us—and no one did—then nothing happened.' Ms Currie responded: 'Don't want to hear it. Don't say any more. I don't want to hear any more.' Indeed, it is difficult to see any benefits for Ms Currie in knowing about the affair, and that is why she probably preferred to remain ignorant.

George Stephanopoulos, once President Clinton's political adviser, was labelled by journalists as a hypocrite, arguing that he must have known about Clinton's affair with Lewinsky. Stephanopoulos said that he might not have looked hard enough because he did not want to know the truth.

After the scandal with Lewinsky broke, President Clinton told his aides in the White House that he did not have a sexual relationship with Monica Lewinsky. Erskine Bowles, the White House Chief of Staff, was more than willing to believe him. This is how he described that moment to the grand jury: 'All I can tell you is, this guy who I've worked for looked me in the eye and said he did not have sexual relationships with her. And if I didn't believe him, I couldn't stay. So I believe him.'

Ekman (1992, 1993) suggested that the ex-British prime minister Chamberlain did not want to know the truth when on 15 September 1938 he held talks with Hitler with the aim of preventing the Second World War. Hitler intended to invade Czechoslovakia, but his army was not yet fully prepared. If he could restrain the Czechs from mobilizing their army, his own army would be ready to spring a surprise attack in a couple of weeks. Hitler therefore concealed his real intentions in his meeting with Chamberlain, and assured Chamberlain that he would not attack Czechoslovakia, on condition that the Czechs would not mobilize their army. Chamberlain did not discover Hitler's lie, and tried to persuade the Czechs not to mobilize as long as the negotiations with Hitler continued. After his meeting with Hitler, Chamberlain wrote in a letter to his sister: 'in spite of the hardness and ruthlessness I thought I saw in his face, I got the impression that here was a man who could be relied upon when he had given his word' (Ekman, 1992, pp.15–16). In Parliament, Chamberlain said that he was convinced that Hitler did not try to deceive him. It therefore seems that Chamberlain really trusted Hitler. According to Ekman, Chamberlain did trust Hitler because he had no other option than to do so. If he admitted that Hitler was hiding war plans, he would also have to admit that his reconciliation policy had failed, and that this policy had brought Europe and the UK into real danger.

Sometimes the situation is different. The potential purchaser wants to know whether the second-hand car is really as good as the salesperson suggests; the employer wants to know whether the candidate is indeed as capable as the candidate claims to be; the customs officer wants to know whether the traveller really has nothing to declare; and the police detective wants to know whether the suspect is telling the truth when claiming to be innocent. Even when people try to detect lies, they often fail to do so. Research has indicated that even professional lie catchers, such as customs officers and police officers, often make mistakes when detecting lies, and that their ability to detect lies does not exceed that of lay people. However, the literature used by police officers, reveals remarkable confidence among the police in their ability to detect deceit, and provides sometimes detailed descriptions of how liars supposedly present themselves. This literature often demonstrates inadequate knowledge of deception research.

The following three examples illustrate this. The debate about the use of the polygraph as a lie detector is heated, as will be explained later on in this book. Belief in the accuracy of the polygraph among practitioners is strong. For example, Charles Honts, an American psychology professor and leading practitioner in the field of the polygraph, recently said: 'I've tested many psychopaths and killers, and when they lie, they all flunk the test' (Honts, cited in Sleek, 1998, p.30). However, strong faith in the accuracy of the polygraph can be questioned on the basis of literature reviews of polygraph studies.

Inbau, Reid and Buckley (1986) wrote an influential handbook about interrogation tactics and techniques. They also claimed to provide insight into how suspects usually behave when they are lying. According to Inbau and colleagues, behavioural clues to deception include posture changes, gaze aversion, self-manipulation (stroking the back of the head, touching the nose, straightening or stroking the hair, pulling at threads on clothing, and so on), placing a hand over the mouth or the eyes when speaking, and hiding the hands (by sitting on them) or hiding the feet (by pulling them under the chair). In particular, the belief that liars place their hands over the mouth and eyes is frequently mentioned in the police literature (Brougham, 1992; Kuhlman, 1980; Walkley, 1985; Walters, 1996; Waltman, 1983). However, this behavioural clue to deception, as well as the other behavioural clues mentioned by Inbau are not identified as such in the existing literature concerning the relationship between non-verbal behaviour and deception.

On the other hand, the former Dutch chief police commissioner Blaauw suggested that valid non-verbal cues to deception are virtually non-existent, and that behavioural cues should therefore be disregarded. This view was probably appropriate in 1971—the year in which Blaauw published his article—but nowadays there is much more to discuss about the relationship between non-verbal behaviour and deception, as a result of research conducted over the past 25 years.

However, we cannot always blame observers for making inaccurate judgements when they try to detect lies. Sometimes lies are not detected because the lie is not detectable—that is, the liar did not give anything away. This is especially likely in liars who do not find it cognitively difficult to lie, and who do not experience any emotions when they are lying. These are very good liars, and their lies are very difficult—if not impossible—to detect, as will be discussed throughout this book.

A DEFINITION OF DECEPTION

Deception can be defined in many ways. Mitchell's (1986) definition is probably one of the most remarkable. He defines deception as 'a false communication that tends to benefit the communicator'. Mitchell's definition implies that not only humans but also animals and even plants might lie. Some psychologists, such as Bond and Robinson (1988), agree with this. They describe how the orchid *Ophrys speculum* dupes male wasps with the illusion of sexual contact. The orchid produces an odour that mimics insect sexual pheromones to attract and arouse male wasps. Males are drawn to the centre of the flower, because its colouring resembles that of a female wasp. In the centre of the flower the male finds thick, long hairs which resemble the hair found on a female wasp's abdomen. The male wasp believes he has found a mate, and so a pseudo-copulation takes place. The wasp then moves on to another orchid, and the orchids are thus cross-pollinated in the process.

Mitchell's definition is controversial, but not because of the assumption that non-humans can lie, as we know that they can. DeWaal (described in Bond & Robinson, 1988) gives some examples of sophisticated animal deceit, including a case about chimpanzees bluffing. Male chimps use mutual bluff displays to find out which of the two is the strongest. Sometimes chimps show involuntary teeth-baring during these displays, which is a sign of fear. Obviously, teeth-baring would undermine a chimp's bluff, if the sign was perceived. Chimps therefore tend to turn their back before baring their teeth, and resume their bluffing once the expression has gone. In one instance, DeWaal even observed that a chimp quickly used his fingers to push his lips back over his teeth. Mitchell's definition is controversial because it implies that unconsciously and mistakenly misleading others should also be classified as deception. A sales assistant who has not been informed by her boss that a product's price has been reduced, and who therefore asks for too much money, is a liar according to Mitchell's definition. Many people do not agree with this, and believe that deception is an act of deliberately not telling the truth. Following Krauss (1981), many researchers therefore define deception as 'an act that is intended to foster in another person a belief or understanding which the deceiver considers to be false'.

Lying is an intentional act. Someone who does not tell the truth by mistake is not lying. A woman who mistakenly believes that she was sexually abused in her childhood and who therefore goes to the police to report this abuse, has given a false report, but she is not lying. The schizophrenic man who believes that he is Napoleon is not lying in his claims. It is obvious that he is not telling the truth, but he believes his own story and so does not have the intention of deceiving other people.

According to this definition, sarcastic remarks are not lies either. Indeed, someone who makes a sarcastic remark deliberately does not tell the truth, but this form of lie-telling is not intended to foster a false belief in another person. On the contrary, the deceiver wants the deception to be uncovered, and will try to make this clear to another either by facial expressions or by changing their tone of voice (Zuckerman, DeFrank, Hall, Larrance & Rosenthal, 1979).

Lying does not necessarily require the use of words. The athlete who fakes a foot injury after a bad performance is lying without using words. It is also possible to lie by hiding information, although again this must happen intentionally. Someone who forgets to give information by mistake is not lying. Taxpayers who deliberately do not report a particular source of income on their tax return are lying, whereas those who (for whatever reason) simply forget to give this information are not lying. The man who tells his wife who was present at the dinner party and accidentally forgets to mention that his secretary was there is not lying. However, he is lying when he deliberately does not mention her.

In my view, Krauss' definition is not entirely satisfactory. It ignores another aspect of deception which has been highlighted by Ekman (1992). He argues that people are only lying when they do not inform others in advance about their intention to lie. Magicians are therefore not lying during their performance, as people in the audience expect to be deceived. Ekman therefore defines deception as 'a deliberate choice to mislead a target without giving any notification of the intent to do so'.

In my view, Ekman's definition is not complete either. Liars sometimes do not succeed in misleading targets although they have a clear intention to do so. For example, the target may know that the information which the liar wants him or her to believe is untrue. In these cases, the attempt to deceive the target has failed, but such unsuccessful attempts can still be classified as lies. I therefore prefer to define deception as *'a successful or unsuccessful deliberate attempt, without forewarning, to create in another a belief which the communicator considers to be untrue'*.

People sometimes fool themselves—a process which is called self-deception. After failing an examination, students often delude themselves into believing that they could not motivate themselves enough to revise thoroughly for the exam, instead of acknowledging that they do not understand the topic very well. Self-deception has both positive and negative features (Lewis, 1993). People can ignore or deny the seriousness of several bodily symptoms, such as a lump in a breast or a severe pain in the chest during physical exertion. This can be life-threatening. On the other hand, self-deception may serve to protect self-esteem. After being rejected on a date, people may convince themselves that they were not interested in dating this person after all, instead of admitting that this person was not interested in them. According to my definition, deception is an act which involves at least two people. This definition excludes self-deception, which will not therefore be further discussed in this book.

WHY DO PEOPLE LIE?

The most comprehensive analysis to date of naturalistic deception is the work of Bella DePaulo and her colleagues. (DePaulo & Bell, 1996; DePaulo & Kashy, 1998; DePaulo, Kashy, Kirkendol, Wyer & Epstein, 1996; Kashy & DePaulo, 1996). They asked their participants (American college students and community members) to keep a diary for 7 days and to record all of their social interactions and all of the lies they told during those interactions. A social interaction was defined as an exchange with another person that lasted for 10 minutes or longer. Brief encounters such as greetings in the morning were therefore ignored. The study revealed that lying is a daily life event. On average, people lied almost twice a day or in one quarter of interactions with others. Of all the people they interacted with over the week, they lied to 34%. Some people they interacted with they lied to frequently. They told fewer lies to people to whom they felt emotionally closer. They told one lie in every 10 social interactions they had with spouses. Participants reported that they generally did not feel uncomfortable when lying, and were successful in most cases. Only 18% of the lies were detected by others. However, they felt relatively uncomfortable when they told lies to the people to whom they felt emotionally close, and lies were more often discovered by people to whom they felt close. Although people tend to lie less to those to whom they feel close, there were two exceptions. First, people lied relatively often to their romantic partners who were not their spouses (once in every three social interactions). One possible explanation for this is that people wondered whether their 'true self' was lovable enough to attract and keep these partners, and they therefore presented themselves as they wished they were instead of how they actually were (DePaulo & Kashy, 1998). Secondly, students often lied to their mothers (in almost half of their conversations). A possible explanation for this is that they are still dependent on their mothers (for example, with regard to money) and sometimes have to lie to secure their resources. For example, one student lied about the price she had to pay for her typewriter so that her parents would send her more money (Kashy & DePaulo, 1996). Another explanation is that they still care about what their mothers think of them. For example, one student told his mother that he did not drink beer at college (DePaulo, Kashy, Kirkendol, Wyer & Epstein, 1996).

How often people lie also depends on the situation. Robinson, Shepherd and Heywood (1998) interviewed undergraduate students, of whom 83% said that they would lie in order to get a job. They said that it was wrong to lie to best friends but not to potential employers. They saw nothing wrong in lying if this secured the job, and they thought that employers expected candidates to exaggerate qualities when applying for jobs. In Rowatt, Cunningham and Druen's (1998) study, 90% of the participants admitted being willing to tell at least one lie to a prospective date.

People lie for several reasons. First, they lie in order to make a positive impression on others or to protect themselves from embarrassment or disapproval. One girl in DePaulo's diary study told her friend that a particular boy still fancied her, although she knew that this was no longer the case. She felt ashamed that he had lost interest in her, and she did not dare tell this to her friend. When President Clinton admitted for the first time on television to the American people that he had had an 'inappropriate relationship' with Monica Lewinsky, the first reason he gave for having misled people was 'a desire to protect myself from the embarrassment of my own conduct.'

Secondly, people lie in order to obtain advantage. For example, applicants may exaggerate their current income during a selection interview in order to secure a higher income in their next job.

Thirdly, people lie to avoid punishment. For example, children may not tell their parents that they took a biscuit, in order not to be penalised. The lies mentioned so far are *self-oriented*, and are intended to make the liar appear better or to gain personal advantage. DePaulo's diary study revealed that approximately half of the lies which people told were self-oriented.

People also lie to make others appear better or lies are told for another person's benefit. For example, a pupil tells the teacher that her friend is ill, although she knows that her friend is playing truant. A girl in DePaulo's diary study told her friend that she (the friend) would soon find another boyfriend. She said this to boost her friend's self-confidence after being abandoned by her previous boyfriend. These lies are *other-oriented*. Approximately 25% of the lies that people tell fall into this category (DePaulo, Kashy, Kirkendol, Wyer & Epstein, 1996). A relatively large number of other-oriented lies are told to people to whom the liar feels close. This was also found in an experiment conducted by Bell and DePaulo (1996), in which participants discussed pictures painted by art students they liked or disliked. The findings revealed that participants communicated more kindly, but also more deceitfully, to the artist they liked than to the artist they disliked, particularly by making more flattering comments to the artist they liked.

Fifthly, people tell what I call 'social lies'. They lie for the sake of social relationships. Conversations could become awkward and unnecessarily rude, and social interactions could easily become disturbed when people tell each other the truth all the time. In order to maintain an appropriate relationship with colleagues, it is better to say that you are busy when they invite you for lunch than to say that you don't like them and therefore don't want to go out for lunch with them. Similarly, a husband would do better to refrain from explicitly criticizing his wife's dress when he knows that she bought it in a sale and that she cannot return it to the shop. Social relationships may improve when people pay each other compliments now and again. Most people will probably appreciate it when others make positive comments about their latest haircut. Making deceptive but flattering remarks might therefore benefit mutual relations. Social lies serve both self-interest and the interest of others. For example, liars may be pleased with themselves when they please other people, or tell a lie to avoid an awkward situation or discussion. DePaulo's diary study revealed that 25% of the lies that people tell serve both self-interest and the interest of others.

An alternative method of investigating the lies that people tell in daily life involves asking people to write down the last lie they told. This method, recently used by Backbier and Sieswerda (1997), revealed findings similar to those of DePaulo and her colleagues. Most of the lies that the participants (college students) told were self-oriented lies (69%), and most lies were told to their mother (29%). In most cases (80%) their lies went undetected.

If people are asked how often they lie, do they then realize that they probably lie every day? My own research has shown that this is the case (Vrij, 1997a,b). Participants were asked to indicate in a questionnaire how often they thought they lied in a week, how many of these lies were self-oriented and other-oriented, how uncomfortable they generally felt when they lied, and how many lies usually went undetected. Most of the findings were similar to those of DePaulo. Participants thought that they told on average 1.5 lies a day, they did not feel uncomfortable when they were lying, and they estimated that about 75% of their lies went undetected. The only difference to DePaulo's study was related to self-oriented and other-oriented lies. Participants in my study estimated that most of their lies were other-oriented, whereas DePaulo found that most lies were self-oriented. There are two possible explanations why people tend to underestimate the number of self-oriented lies that they tell. It is possible that people either do not want or do not like to admit that they often tell self-oriented lies. Alternatively, it may be that people do not realize that they tell many self-oriented lies. Perhaps people believe that they should not tell self-oriented lies, and therefore they do not want to think about it and try to forget the incident when they tell such lies.

DIFFERENT TYPES OF LIE

Apart from the distinction between self-oriented and other-oriented lies, a distinction is usually made between outright lies, exaggerations and subtle lies (DePaulo, Kashy, Kirkendol, Wyer & Epstein, 1996). Outright lies (also referred to as falsifications; Ekman, 1997) are total falsehoods—lies in which the information conveyed is completely different or contradictory to the truth. A guilty suspect who denies any involvement in the crime is telling an outright lie. Applicants who claim in a selection interview that they are happy in their present job, but want a change after being in that job for so many years, are telling an outright lie when the real reason for their application is that they have been sacked. When he testified in the Paula Jones case, President Clinton told an outright lie when he said that he could not remember whether he had ever been alone together with Monica Lewinsky in the Oval Office. DePaulo's study revealed that most of the lies (65%) which people tell are outright lies (DePaulo, Kashy, Kirkendol, Wyer & Epstein, 1996). A similar percentage (67%) of outright lies was reported in Backbier and Sieswerda's (1997) study.

Exaggerations are lies in which the facts are overstated or information is conveyed that exceeds the truth. People can exaggerate their regret for arriving too late at an appointment with a friend, can embellish their remorse for committing a crime during a police interview, or can present themselves as being more diligent than is in fact the case during an application interview.

Subtle lying involves telling literal truths that are designed to mislead. President Clinton was telling such a lie when he said to the American people that he 'did not have sexual relations with that woman, Miss Lewinsky.' The lie was subtle, because it suggests that nothing sexual happened between Clinton and Lewinsky, whereas he meant that they did not have actual sexual intercourse. Another type of subtle lying involves concealing information by evading the question or omitting relevant details. The homosexual man who tells a colleague about his sexual experiences without mentioning that he is referring to sex with men is concealing information if he knows that his colleague is assuming that he is talking about sex with women. Someone who does not like the picture painted by a friend can conceal her opinion by saying that she likes the bright colours used in the painting.

An alternative distinction can be made by looking at lie complexity and consequences (Ekman, 1992; Ekman & Frank, 1993; Vrij, 1998b). Some lies are more difficult to tell than others. For example, lying is more difficult when the other person has some form of evidence that a person may well be lying. Consider a 12-year-old boy who smokes despite his parents forbidding him to do so. When his parents ask him outright whether he smokes, it is more difficult for him to deny this when they have found an empty cigarette packet in his room than if they do not have any evidence to prove his smoking habits. Lying is also more difficult if the other person is suspicious. The adulterous wife will have more difficulties in hiding her secret affair if her husband is suspicious than if he is not. Finally, a lie is easier to tell when the liar has the opportunity to prepare the lie. It is easier for a girl to lie about why she does not want to go out with a particular boy, if she has already expected his request for a date, and has therefore prepared an excuse, than if his request took her by surprise and she had to lie spontaneously.

Moreover, the consequences of getting caught in a lie are not always the same. They are more serious for a murderer who, during a police interview, denies having committed the crime, than for a girl who exaggerates the number of CDs she possesses in a conversation with friends. The consequences are also more serious for smugglers if customs officers discover that they tried to smuggle heroin than if they were in possession of too much alcohol.

A classification on the basis of lie complexity and consequences is useful because liars behave differently in different situations, as will be explained in Chapter 2. That is, liars display different behaviour when they are telling a complicated lie to when they are telling an easy lie, and their behaviour is also different when they are telling high-stake lies compared to low-stake lies.

INDIVIDUAL DIFFERENCES IN TELLING LIES

Gender Differences

The diary study of DePaulo and her colleagues revealed gender differences in lie-telling (DePaulo, Kashy, Kirkendol, Wyer & Epstein, 1996).

Although no gender differences were found in the frequency of lying, it was noted that men and women tend to tell different lies. Men tell more self-oriented lies, whereas women tell more other-oriented lies, particularly with regard to other women. In conversations between two women, nearly half of the lies were other-oriented.

A second study, conducted by DePaulo and Bell (1996), also showed gender differences. Participants were asked to choose the two paintings that they liked the most and the two paintings that they liked the least from 19 paintings that were displayed. After making their choice, they wrote down what in particular they liked and disliked about each of the four paintings they had nominated. The participants were then informed that they would be meeting an art student with whom they would discuss their opinions about the four paintings. They were told that the art student might have actually painted some of the paintings herself, and that she would tell the participant if she had done so. They were also told that the art student did not know which paintings they liked most and which they liked least. In reality, the art student was a confederate (a helper of the experimenter) who did know which paintings the participants liked and disliked. For each of the four paintings, the art student asked the participant what they thought of the painting overall, what they specifically liked about it and what they disliked about it. As she opened the discussion about one of the paintings that the participant liked, and about one that the participant disliked, the art student mentioned that the painting was one that she had painted herself. This created four different situations for each participant. In one discussion, they had to give their opinion about a painting they liked and which was not painted by the art student. In a second discussion, they discussed a painting which they did not appreciate and which was not painted by the art student. In a third discussion, they had to talk about a painting that they liked and which was painted by the art student, and in a fourth discussion they talked about a painting which they did not like and which was painted by the art student. The order in which the discussions took place was systematically changed. Obviously, the most awkward discussion was the discussion in which the participants were forced to discuss the art student's painting which they did not like. The findings revealed gender differences in this situation in particular. The women exposed more positive feelings about the painting than did the men, especially by exaggerating their liking for those aspects of the painting that they really did like. Gender differences also emerged when participants were discussing the art student's painting which they liked. Women exaggerated their liking of the painting to the artist more than men did. Similar to DePaulo's diary study, this study revealed that women tell more other-oriented lies than men do.

Saarni (1984) has demonstrated that the female tendency to tell more other-oriented lies is already present in young children. Children aged 7 to 11 years received presents that they liked (such as sweets and money) as a reward for helping an adult with her work. Shortly after this, they were asked to help again, but this time the present they were given was boring and more suitable for younger children. Girls showed their disappointment to a lesser extent than boys, and responded more enthusiastically when they received their dull present.

It has been shown that, in their interactions with others, women are usually more open, intimate and emotionally supportive than men. As a result, both men and women appreciate conversations with women more than conversations with men (DePaulo, Epstein & Wyer, 1993; Reis, Senchak & Solomon, 1985). Reis, Senchak and Solomon (1985) have offered several explanations for this phenomenon. However, the finding that women tell more other-oriented lies than men—that is, they make more flattering comments and more frequently avoid saying things which may hurt the other person—may also be a reason for this.

Finally, there is some evidence that women and men cope differently with lying. Women become somewhat more uncomfortable when telling lies than men do (DePaulo, Epstein & Wyer, 1993; DePaulo, Kashy, Kirkendol, Wyer & Epstein, 1996; Vrij, 1997b). DePaulo and Kirkendol (cited in DePaulo, Epstein and Wyer, 1993) asked men and women about the most serious lie they had ever told to anyone, and the most serious lie that anyone had ever told them. These serious lies had a greater impact on women than on men. When talking about situations in which they were the ones who told a serious lie, women described themselves as more guilty, anxious and fearful than men. When thinking about the times when they were the ones who were fooled, women described themselves as being more embittered than men. The lie had a more detrimental effect on their relationship with the liar for women than for men, and the matter was more often on women's minds than on men's minds.

Age Differences

Children start to tell other-oriented lies at an early stage. Lewis (1993) cites an example of a 3-year-old girl who responded with great enthusiasm when she received a present from her grandmother, although in fact she did not like the present. Children are encouraged by their parents to tell these types of lies. If the girl had not spontaneously responded in such a positive way, her mother might have encouraged her to do so. Children also notice that others (for example, their parents) tell these types of lies, and they then start to imitate this behaviour.

We also learn in early childhood to lie in order to avoid punishment (Lewis, 1993). Children not yet 3 years old were left alone in a room for a while and were instructed not to turn around and look at the toy that was being set up. The children were secretly videotaped. When the experimenter came back after 5 minutes, she asked each child 'Did you peek?'. Although the videotapes showed that 90% of the children did look, only 38% told the truth and admitted that they had done so. A similar experiment in which the age of the children was varied showed that the older the children were, the less likely it was that they admitted any wrongdoing. For example, none of the 5-year-old children who had looked at the toys admitted to having done so.

Lewis (1993) also describes the process whereby children learn to lie in order to avoid punishment. For example, a 2-year-old girl is told not to eat a cookie. Later, when the mother asks the girl whether she has eaten the cookie, she admits that she has done so. Her mother then becomes angry and punishes her. After only a few interactions like this, the child learns that if she admits to any wrongdoing, she will be punished. Therefore, she starts to lie in order to avoid punishment. Sooner or later, however, the child will find out that some of her lies will be detected by her parents. The parent will then tell her that it is bad to lie and that she will be punished if she tells a lie. Now the child faces a difficult problem. If she tells the truth about her wrongdoing she will be punished, and if she lies she will be punished as well. She will soon find out that her parents do not detect all of her wrongdoing. It is therefore better for her to conceal any wrongdoing, and to admit such behaviour only when it is detected.

Personality Traits

Research findings suggest that different types of people deal with deception in different ways. I shall distinguish four different types of people, and will call them manipulators, actors, sociable people and adaptors.

Manipulators

A stereotypical view of liars is that they are selfish, crafty and manipulative. This is partly true (Hunter, Gerbing & Boster, 1982; Kashy & DePaulo, 1996; Vrij & Holland, 1999; Wilson, Near & Miller, 1998). Manipulators—people who score high in Machiavellianism or social adroitness—frequently tell self-oriented lies, tend to persist in lying when they are challenged to tell the truth, do not feel uncomfortable when they lie, do not find lying cognitively too complicated, view others cynically, show little concern for conventional morality, and openly admit that they will lie, cheat and manipulate others in order to get what they want. The term Machiavellianism is derived from the Italian statesman and writer Machiavelli (1469–1527). In 1513 he published his book *Il Principe* (The Prince), in which he made a plea for a united Italy with a powerful ruler to protect the national interest. This can be done by all necessary means, including those which are not morally justifiable. In his book *l'Arte Della Guerra (Art of War)*, published in 1520, he outlined several possibly effective means.

Interpersonally, manipulators are scheming but not stupid. They do not exploit others if their victims might retaliate, and they do not cheat if they are likely to get caught. In conversation, they tend to dominate, but they also seem relaxed, talented and confident. They are usually liked more than people low in manipulative skills, and are preferred as partners (Kashy & DePaulo, 1996). In contrast to these findings, Wilson, Near and Miller (1998) found negative evaluations of people who scored high in Machiavellianism. They asked people who scored either high or low in Machiavellianism to write a story about what they thought would happen after they found themselves shipwrecked on a deserted island with two other passengers. These stories were evaluated by readers. Compared to low-Machs, high-Machs were perceived to be more selfish, uncaring, judgemental, overbearing, untrustworthy, aggressive, undependable and suspicious. These findings are perhaps not surprising given the stories written by low-Machs and high-Machs. For example, a low Mach wrote: 'The two other passengers and I seem to get along pretty well...it's funny how we immediately began to trust each other' (p.210), whereas a high-Mach wrote: 'The two other passengers are cold bitches who constantly complain...when I got really hungry I wondered how I could cook them with the limited cooking equipment we had' (p.210). However, these examples make clear the fact that the negative evaluation of high-Machs was unrelated to their tendency to lie more often.

Actors

Some people are more skilled in regulating their verbal and non-verbal behaviour than others. The four constructs emotional control, social control, acting and social expressivity deal with this issue. Emotional control refers to the ability to regulate emotional communications and non-verbal displays (i.e. ability to conceal true feelings—for example, being good at maintaining a calm exterior, even when upset). Social control includes role-playing ability, regulation of verbal behaviour, and self-presentation skills. Acting also refers to someone's role-playing ability, while social expressivity includes skill in verbal expression, and verbal fluency. Obviously, all of these skills will be helpful in deceiving others. Research findings support this view (Vrij & Holland, 1999). Compared to non-actors, actors persisted more in lying when challenged, felt more comfortable when lying, and found it less difficult to lie.

Sociable People

Given the fact that lying happens in social interactions every day, it seems reasonable to suggest that those who enjoy more social interactions are particularly good at lying. Extraverted and sociable people are especially attracted to social life. Extraverts like being with other people, are not shy, and are confident in social interactions. Sociability refers to the tendency to affiliate with others and to prefer being with others rather than remaining alone. On the other hand, some people are typically reserved in social contexts. This is either because they prefer their own company and prefer to focus themselves on thoughts and reflections that deal solely with the self (people who are high in private self-consciousness), or because they are socially anxious (i.e. feel discomfort in the presence of others) or shy (i.e. feel awkward and tense when with others). This difference in social involvement has an impact on deception skills. Sociable people lie more often than socially withdrawn people (Kashy & DePaulo, 1996), feel more comfortable while lying (Vrij & Holland, 1999), and persist longer when they are lying. The latter finding was reported in a study conducted by Vrij and Winkel (1992b). A police officer interviewed participants about the possession of a set of headphones. Although all of the participants were given a small set of headphones prior to the interview (a fact which was unknown to the police officer), they were all requested to deny this possession. The police officer thoroughly interviewed each participant about possession of the headphones. Personality traits were measured with a questionnaire. Almost half (46%) of the socially anxious people admitted during the interview that they had the set of headphones in their pockets, whereas only 19% of those who were not socially anxious admitted that they had them.

Adaptors

People who are anxious and feel insecure in social interactions do not necessarily avoid lying. Some people (those who have high levels of public self-consciousness or other-directedness) have a special way of coping with their insecurity, namely by adapting themselves to other people. These 'adaptors' are highly motivated to make a positive impression on others. Kashy and DePaulo (1996) found that one way in which they do this is by lying. Evidence that adaptors feel relatively relaxed when they are lying was found by Vrij and Holland (1999). In their experiment, college students were thoroughly interviewed by a police detective about the course they were studying. Although none of the participants studied psychology, they were all asked to pretend that they were studying this subject. The police detective asked questions such as 'Can you tell me what topics you have recently studied?', 'Can you tell me something about these topics in more detail?', Tell me about your coursework titles', 'What do your exams cover?', 'Name three famous psychologists', and 'What did they do then?'. Personality traits were measured with a questionnaire. The findings revealed that, compared to their counterparts, adaptors persisted more in lying when they were challenged, felt more comfortable when lying, and found it less difficult to lie.

This chapter clearly demonstrates the complicated role of lying in daily interactions. The conventional view that lying is necessarily bad is simply not true. Conversations could become awkward and unnecessarily rude, and social interactions could easily become disturbed, if people told each other the truth all the time. We tell lies even to people to whom we feel close. We tell many lies at the beginning of a romantic relationship, and we make many untruthful flattering remarks to people we like. Manipulators lie often, but are preferred as partners. Sociable people are considered to be socially skilled, but they lie frequently. Socially withdrawn people are considered to be somewhat socially awkward, possibly due to the fact that they are honest. We do perhaps notice that they rarely make flattering remarks, which other people tend to make more often.

We do not always appreciate lying. The viewer wants to know whether the politician is telling the truth when she denies any involvement in a bribery scandal; the general wants to know whether he can trust his opponent before he signs the truce agreement; the teacher wants to know which pupil played a trick on him; the mother wants to know whether her daughter really has finished her homework; and the police detective wants to know whether the suspect's alibi is correct. How lies can be detected will be one of the topics covered in this book.

PART I

NON-VERBAL BEHAVIOUR AND DECEPTION

CHAPTER 2

Non-Verbal Behaviour During Deception

THE IMPORTANCE OF NON-VERBAL BEHAVIOUR IN CREDIBILITY ASSESSMENTS

Suppose you are a member of a selection board interviewing a female applicant. By coincidence you know her neighbour very well. The neighbour has told you that the applicant told him that she wants to leave her current job because she had a huge argument with her present employer. During the interview you ask the applicant, who does not know that you know her neighbour, about her relationship with her current employer. What would you pay most attention to if you wish to find out whether she gives a truthful answer? Would you focus on what she is saying or how she is behaving? You would probably pay most attention to what she is saying, and would check whether the information she gives is consistent with what she told her neighbour. You would probably do this because, in this situation, it is easier to check whether someone is lying by listening to the speech content than by observing their behaviour. Now suppose that you do not know her neighbour and do not have any prior information about the applicant. In this case you would probably pay more attention to her non-verbal behaviour than to her speech content in order to detect deceit (Stiff, Miller, Sleight, Mongeau, Garlick & Rogan, 1989). In these cases, in which there is no information to verify, people rely more on non-verbal behaviour than on the speech content to find out whether someone is lying. When they start their investigations, police officers sometimes have little information about the crime they are going to investigate, and therefore do not yet know whom to suspect of having committed the crime. Therefore they may decide to interview a number of people who live in the area where the crime took place. In such cases, it is likely that the non-verbal style of presentation of these people will determine whether they will be considered as serious suspects and will be invited for a second interview (Greuel, 1992; Kraut & Poe, 1980; Rozelle & Baxter, 1975; Vrij, Foppes, Volger & Winkel, 1992; Walkley, 1985; Waltman, 1983). Observers pay more attention to non-verbal behaviour when there is no information to verify, because they assume that it is more difficult for people to control their non-verbal behaviour than their verbal behaviour (DePaulo, Rosenthal, Eisenstat, Rogers & Finkelstein, 1978; Hale & Stiff, 1990; Kalbfleisch, 1992; Maxwell, Cook & Burr, 1985; Stiff, Hale, Garlick & Rogan, 1990; Vrij, Dragt & Koppelaar, 1992). They assume that it is more likely that non-verbal cues will 'leak' the information that a person is trying to hide. These intuitions are correct. Individuals are less able to control some aspects of their non-verbal behaviour than their verbal communication (DePaulo & Kirkendol, 1989; Ekman, 1992; Ekman & Friesen, 1969, 1974). Freud (1959, p.94) suggested this when he wrote: 'He who has eyes to see and ears to hear may convince himself that no mortal can keep a secret. If his lips are silent, he chatters with his finger-tips; betrayal oozes out of him at every pore.' Detecting deceit on the basis of non-verbal behaviour, however, is not as easy as Freud suggested, as will be discussed in Chapter 3.

Suppose that a heroin smuggler is asked by a customs officer at the airport to say what is in his suitcase. It is rather easy for this man not to mention the heroin, but it is probably more difficult for him to behave normally and to avoid raising any suspicion in his conversation with the customs officer. Nor will it be difficult for the student to tell the invigilator that her lecture-notes which he found on the floor during the examination do not belong to her, but it will be more difficult for her to stay calm.

There are at least four reasons why it is more difficult to control non-verbal behaviour than verbal behaviour (DePaulo & Kirkendol, 1989; Vrij, 1996).

- There are certain automatic links between emotions and non-verbal behaviours (Ekman, 1992), whereas automatic links between emotions and speech content do not exist. The moment people become afraid, their bodies jerk backwards and their faces contort in a certain way almost automatically. However, people do not automatically say certain things when they are afraid. Suppose that a girl is watching television instead of doing her homework, and that she tells her father that she has just finished her homework when he enters her room. Having said that, she becomes afraid because she realizes that he might want to check this. In order not to show her fear, she has to somehow override the automatic non-verbal links associated with fear, whereas she does not have to bother about automatic verbal links.

- We are more practised in using words than in using behaviour, and this practice makes perfect. We are more practised in using words because the latter are usually more important in the exchange of information than is behaviour. When people are asked to describe their activities of that day, they probably choose to use words to describe what they have done instead of using gestures. However, there are exceptions. For example, it is sometimes easier to describe the shape and size of objects (e.g. the shape of a lamp, the size of a CD) and the location of an object (e.g. the ball is there) with hand movements than with words.

- The fact that words are more important than behaviour in the exchange of information makes people more aware of what they are saying than of how they are behaving. A teacher would probably know what he said during his lecture, but will be less aware of how he actually behaved during that lecture. Unless someone tells him, he probably does not realize that he focused most of his gaze on one particular point at the back of the classroom. A suspect during a police interview and an applicant during a selection interview will probably know afterwards what they have said. However, it will be more difficult for them to indicate exactly how they behaved—that is, which hand movements they made, whether they moved their feet, how often they looked away during the interview, what their voice tone was like, and how their facial expressions appeared.

Being aware of behaviour is essential when effectively controlling behaviour. People cannot control their behaviour properly when they do not know how they normally behave. That is, if people are trying to show the behaviour that they normally display, they can only achieve this if they know how they normally behave. It is similar when someone's photograph is taken. How many people will be told 'not to look so silly' just before the picture is taken? The whole situation puts them in an awkward position—they want to look natural, but they do not know how they normally look.

- People cannot be silent non-verbally. Suppose that a suspect realizes during her police interview that the police know more than she thought they did about her involvement in the crime. This probably implies that she has to give a different story to the story she had planned to tell. Verbally she can afford a little rest and can think of an appropriate response in this awkward situation. Non-verbally, however, there is no possibility of taking a rest. She will display behaviour throughout the entire interview, even when she remains silent, and the police officers will observe and interpret this behaviour.

Given the difficulties involved in controlling it, non-verbal behaviour might be a valuable source of information to use in detecting deception. However, three issues are important. (i) Are there systematic non-verbal differences between liars and truth-tellers? (ii) Are observers aware of these differences? (iii) Are observers able to detect deception when they pay attention to someone's body language? The first issue refers to *objective* or *actual* indicators of deception—that is, non-verbal behaviours which have been found to be associated with deception. The latter two issues (i.e., (ii) and (iii) above) refer to *subjective* indicators of deception—that is, non-verbal behaviours that observers associate with deception, regardless of whether such behaviour is a manifestation of actual deception. The actual indicators will be discussed in this chapter, and the subjective indicators will be addressed in Chapter 3. The term 'actual indicators' is somewhat misleading, as it suggests that deception is related to a unique pattern of specific behaviours. This is not the case. There is nothing like Pinocchio's nose. In other words, typical deceptive behaviour does not exist. For example, it is simply not true that as soon as people start to lie they raise an eyebrow, move a finger, develop a trembling voice, shuffle their feet or look away. However, some behaviours are more likely to occur than others during deception. Which behaviours we can expect to observe will be discussed in the following section.

PROCESSES WHICH LIARS MAY EXPERIENCE DURING DECEPTION

Liars may experience three different processes during deception, namely emotional, content complexity and controlling processes (DePaulo, 1988, 1992; DePaulo, Stone & Lassiter, 1985; Edinger & Patterson, 1983; Ekman, 1992; Köhnken, 1989; Vrij, 1991; Zuckerman, DePaulo & Rosenthal, 1981). Each process may influence a liar's behaviour and emphasizes a different aspect of deception and deceptive behaviour. I shall therefore call them approaches. Before I discuss the three approaches, it is important to emphasize that the distinction between them is artificial. Lies may well feature all three aspects, and the three approaches should not be considered as different camps.

The Emotional Approach

The emotional approach proposes that deception can result in different emotions. The three most common types of emotion associated with deceit are guilt, fear and excitement (Ekman, 1989, 1992). Suppose that a politician has secretly accepted a large sum of money from a company in exchange for lobbying. A journalist becomes suspicious and asks the politician about his links with the company. While denying any wrong-doing, the politician might feel *guilty*, either because of the fact that he accepted illegal money, or because he realizes that it is wrong to deceive the journalist. He might also be *afraid*, because he might be worried that the journalist will find out that he is lying, which would probably result in the end of his political career. Alternatively, he might become very *excited* because he enjoys the opportunity to fool the journalist. The strength of these emotions depends on the personality of the liar and on the circumstances under which the lie takes place (Ekman, 1992; Ekman & Frank, 1993). Some people will feel less guilty than others when lying. As mentioned earlier, lying for manipulators is a normal and acceptable way of achieving their goals, and they therefore probably do not feel guilty when lying. The amount of guilt someone experiences also depends on the circumstances. A liar will not feel guilty if the lie can be morally justified. A spy, for instance, is trying to protect the national interests of her country and therefore finds it entirely acceptable to lie, and few people experienced moral objections when lying to German soldiers while their countries were occupied in the Second World War.

Neither will a liar feel guilty if he believes that it is legitimate to lie. A salesman considers it to be part of his job to emphasize the favourable aspects of the product he is trying to sell, and will therefore not experience guilt when doing this. A liar will also feel less guilty if he thinks that the negative consequences are not serious for the person he is duping. The hotel guest who deliberately does not mention to the hotel owner as she checks out that she made an international telephone call will probably feel more guilty if she made a lengthy call than if it was only a brief one.

The amount of fear that liars experience depends on several circum-stances as well. First, it depends on the person to whom the lie is told. If a liar thinks that this person is very good at detecting lies, the liar will experience more fear than if he thinks it is easy to dupe that person. Secondly, it depends on how good the liar thinks he or she is at lying. Some people are very good liars and they know it. By experience they have learned that it is easy for them to fool others and that they hardly ever get caught. This will increase their self-confidence and decrease their fear when lying. Finally, the liar will experience more fear if the stakes are high—that is, if the consequences of being caught are high. The negative consequences were much greater for President Nixon when he lied to the American people about Watergate than they would be for a child who denied having taken some biscuits.

The excitement which accompanies lying—so-called duping delight—will increase if the person to whom the lie is told is known to be difficult to deceive. The excitement will also increase if there are onlookers at the time when the duping takes place. The girl who tries to fool her teacher will be more excited if other pupils are in the classroom than if she is alone with the teacher.

Guilt, fear and excitement may influence a liar's behaviour. Guilt might result in gaze aversion because the liar does not dare to look the target straight in the eye while telling a wicked lie. Fear and excitement might result in signs of stress, such as an increase in movements, an increase in speech hesitations (mm's and er's) and speech errors (stutters, repetition of words, omission of words) or a higher-pitched voice. The stronger the emotion, the more likely it is that some of these behaviours will reveal deceit.

The Content Complexity Approach

Apart from emotions, thinking processes may play a role when lying, as is emphasized in the content complexity approach. Lying can be a cognitively complex task. A liar has to think of plausible answers, should not contradict him- or herself, should tell a lie that is consistent with everything which the observer knows or might find out, and should avoid making slips of the tongue. Moreover, they have to remember what they have said, so that they can say the same things when someone asks them to repeat their story. It is therefore sometimes much easier for a suspect to present his alibi if the alibi is real than if it is fabricated.

Evidence has suggested that people engaged in cognitively complex tasks make more speech hesitations and speech errors, speak more slowly, pause more, and wait longer before giving an answer (Goldman-Eisler, 1968). Cognitive complexity also leads to fewer hand and arm movements and to more gaze aversion (Ekman, 1997; Ekman & Friesen, 1972). The decrease in hand and arm movements is due to the fact that a greater cognitive load results in a neglect of body language, reducing overall animation. Gaze aversion (usually to a motionless point) occurs because looking at the conversation partner distracts thinking too much. It is easy to examine the impact of content complexity on movements and gaze aversion. Ask people what they ate 3 days ago, and observe their behaviour while they try to remember what they have eaten.

Obviously, lying is not always a cognitively complex task (McCornack, 1997). Sometimes it is easier to lie than to tell the truth. Suppose a friend gives you a present for your birthday which you don't like. In this case it is probably easier to pretend that you like the present than to say that you don't like it. In the latter case you would need to explain why you don't like it, you might become involved in an argument with your friend, or you might even run the risk of destroying your friendship.

The Attempted Behavioural Control Approach

So far, the predictions of how liars behave have been straightforward. A liar may experience emotions or may find it difficult to lie, and this will result in behavioural signs of emotion and content complexity. However, the situation is more complicated than this. Liars may be afraid that signs of emotion or content complexity will give their lies away, and therefore try to suppress such signs in order to avoid getting caught. This is emphasized in the attempted behavioural control approach. Liars may worry about making a dishonest impression on others, and may be particularly keen to make an honest impression, perhaps even more so than when they are telling the truth. Someone who tries to smuggle something is probably more keen on making an honest impression on customs officers than someone who does not smuggle, because the stakes of getting caught are much higher for the smuggler than for the non-smuggler. It will not harm the non-smuggler much if a customs officer asks her to open her suitcase. She might be annoyed about the time it takes and the delay it causes but, other than that, there are no negative consequences. The smuggler, however, will be in trouble if a customs officer wants to check his luggage.

In summary, liars will put more effort into behaving 'normally' or in making an honest impression than will truth-tellers. However, this is not easy. They should suppress their nerves effectively, should mask evidence that they have to think hard, should know how they normally behave, and should be able to show the behaviour that they want to show. The attempted behavioural control approach predicts that many liars will not manage when lying to show the behaviour that they normally display when telling the truth.

The attempted control approach predicts that some behaviours will give the lie away despite liars' efforts, most likely those behaviours which are the most difficult to control (Ekman & Friesen, 1969, 1974). The face should be easier to control than the body (this reasoning refers to gaze aversion and smiling, and excludes micro-expressions of emotions which are much more difficult to control, as will be discussed later). The face is important in the exchange of information. Via facial expressions people can make clear whether they are interested in someone's conversation, whether they feel happy or sad, whether they understand what someone is saying, and whether they want to say something (Ekman, 1992). The great communicative potential of the face means that people are practised at using and therefore controlling it. The body, on the other hand, is a channel that may not be salient in communication and is less often attended to and reacted to by others. We are therefore less practised in making movements and less good at controlling them. It may well be the case that, when controlling their behaviour, liars may exhibit a pattern of behaviour that will appear planned, rehearsed and lacking in spontaneity. For example, liars may believe that movements will give their lies away, and will therefore move very deliberately and tend to avoid those movements which are not strictly essential. This will result in an unusual degree of rigidity and inhibition, because people normally make movements which are not essential (movements of the hands, arms and fingers, movements of the legs and feet, and so on). Like the face, the voice has a great communicative capacity, is salient and is a channel that other people comment on. For example, by raising our voice we emphasize what we are saying or we make clear that things are serious and that we want others to do what we are asking them to do. Therefore it should also be a controllable channel. In fact, however, tone of voice is much more difficult for senders to control than are facial expressions (Ekman, 1981), as the automatic nervous system controls the relevant features of the voice at moments of high stress (Hocking & Leathers, 1980).

Like most movements, vocal characteristics such as speech hesitations, speech errors and pauses between sentences and words are usually made unintentionally and are not important in the exchange of information. We may therefore assume that people do not often practise controlling these behaviours, and are not very good at controlling them. It is likely that liars will think that the use of speech hesitations, errors and pauses will make them sound suspect. Therefore they will try to avoid such non-fluencies. However, this may result in a speech pattern which sounds unusually smooth, as it is normal for most people to make some errors in speech.

In summary, the attempted control approach predicts that liars will show behaviour that looks on the one hand rather planned or rigid (similar to how people behave when their photograph is taken) or on the other hand 'too smooth'. This will emerge in particular from their movements and speech. Liars will tend to avoid making movements and will speak smoothly with relatively few hesitations, errors and pauses.

People's efforts to make a convincing impression are called *impression management*. President Clinton showed a clear example of impression management when he testified before the grand jury about his alleged sexual affair with Monica Lewinsky (Vrij, 1998c). Betty Currie (Clinton's personal secretary) went to Monica Lewinsky's home to collect the presents Lewinsky had received from President Clinton. The question is whether or not President Clinton instructed her to do this. This is an important question, as it would be a clear sign of 'obstruction of justice' if Clinton indeed gave such instructions. Prosecutor Kenneth Starr's team asked Clinton twice whether he gave Betty Currie these instructions. Clinton denied doing so both times, but each time he showed remarkable behaviour. Both times he sat up, did not move and looked straight into the camera. The first time, especially, his behaviour was striking. He denied quickly, even before the interviewer had completed his question, and continued his rigid behaviour and looking into the camera during the period of silence that followed after his denial. It looks as if he expected more questions about this issue. However, more questions were not asked by Starr's team. I am not saying that Clinton was lying during this part of the interview. I cannot say this because I do not know whether he was lying. All I am saying is that he really wanted to make an honest impression on Kenneth Starr's team and the grand jury during that particular part of the interview.

Different Approaches, Different Predictions

The three approaches predict different and sometimes even contradictory behaviours during deception. For example, the emotional approach predicts an increase in movements (signs of nervous behaviour), whereas both the attempted control approach and the content complexity approach predict a decrease in movements during deception. However, the reasoning is different. The attempted control approach predicts a decrease in movements caused by overcontrol, whereas the content complexity approach predicts a decrease in movements as a result of neglecting the use of body language. The emotional and content complexity approaches predict an increase in speech hesitations and speech errors due to nervousness and cognitive load, respectively, whereas the attempted control approach predicts that liars will attempt to suppress these speech disturbances.

The emotional approach and the content complexity approach also predict an increase in gaze aversion as a result of nervousness and cognitive load. The attempted control approach predicts that liars will be good at controlling their gaze behaviour, and that there would therefore be no difference between liars and truth-tellers in gaze aversion.

Which behaviours do liars in fact usually exhibit? I shall provide the answer below. Before describing these objective indicators of deception, two comments have to be made. First, the approaches only suggest that the presence of signs of emotions, content complexity and overcontrol *may* be indicative of deception. None of these approaches claim that the presence of these signs *necessarily* indicates deception. The following examples will make this clear. A man is seen by a police officer trying to break a bicycle lock with a screwdriver. This means that there are at least two possible explanations for this behaviour. The man might have lost his key, or he might be trying to steal the bike. The officer asks the man whether the bike belongs to him. The man then starts scratching his head and answers 'Yes' with a high-pitched and weak voice. Is he lying? That is impossible to say. Apparently he shows nervous behaviour, but it is unclear why he is nervous. He may be nervous because he is trying to steal the bike. However, he may show nervous behaviour *even when he is telling the truth*—for instance, because the presence of a police officer makes him nervous, or because he is afraid that the policeman will not believe him when he says that he lost his key.

Suppose that a suspect stops fidgeting as soon as she starts to mention an alibi. It is possible that the suspect stops fidgeting because she is lying and is afraid of getting caught. However, she may also stop fidgeting if she is innocent, because of fear that the police will believe that fidgeting indicates lying.

Suppose that a woman at the airport avoids any eye contact with a customs officer when she passes by. There is evidence that people avoid eye contact when they do not want to be approached. When people do not want to be accosted in a street by a charity collector, the best they can do is to avoid any eye contact with the collector, as they run the risk of being approached by the collector as soon as their eyes meet the collector's eyes. Therefore it is likely that, when she desperately tries to avoid the officer's gaze, the woman does not want to be approached by the customs officer. This might make a suspicous impression on the officer, but it does not necessarily mean that the woman is trying to smuggle. An alternative reason is that she is in a hurry and does not want to be stopped because she knows that her husband is waiting for her at the airport.

Suppose that a girl remains silent and looks depressed as soon as her father comes to her room and notices that she is watching television instead of doing her homework. One explanation for her silent and depressed behaviour is that she realizes that she has been caught by her father and that she can now expect punishment. However, the same behaviour might occur if she has already finished her homework. An alternative explanation for her behaviour is that she feels sad because her father has come to check on her and apparently does not trust her.

In summary, *the behaviours shown by these people make them appear suspicious (and may be an indicator of deception), but do not necessarily indicate that they are lying*. I believe that police officers are not sufficiently aware of this. In discussions with police detectives, they often come up with statements like: 'I am sure that he is lying, because he does not dare to look me straight in the eye when we discuss the crime.' It is too premature to draw this conclusion on the basis of the suspect's behaviour. It may well be the case that something is going on when a suspect continuously looks away while talking about the crime.

However, it is impossible to say whether or not the suspect is lying. Even innocent suspects may display gaze aversion when they are interviewed about a crime—for instance because they find it hard to accept that they are suspected by the police. Someone has to undertake further action, such as asking more questions or checking the information that the interviewee has provided, in order to find out whether that person is lying. Drawing conclusions about deception solely on the basis of someone's behaviour is often not reliable.

Secondly, signs of emotion, content complexity and attempted behaviour control may only become visible if a liar experiences emotions or content complexity. That is, if a liar does not experience any fear, guilt or excitement (or any other emotion), and the lie is not difficult to fabricate, behavioural cues to deception are unlikely to occur. DePaulo's diary study, discussed in Chapter 1, showed that most lies in everyday life fall into this category (DePaulo, Kashy, Kirkendol, Wyer & Epstein, 1996). Participants indicated that their lies were generally not serious, that they put little effort into planning them and did not worry much about the possibility of being caught, that they experienced little regret about their lies and would tell them again if given a second chance. They also indicated that most of their lies remained undetected. This is not surprising. It is unlikely that liars would show any clear behavioural signs of deception when telling these types of lie.

For the same reasons, false accounts—which the speaker does not know to be inaccurate—are often impossible to detect when paying attention to someone's behaviour. The woman who falsely believes that she was abused in her childhood and who goes to the police to report her alleged abuse will not show any behavioural signs of deception during her interview, as she will not experience any of the underlying processes. For example, she has no reason to feel guilty or to be afraid of being caught, because she thinks she is telling the truth, nor will she experience any duping delight.

However, in many cases when people lie they experience emotions or have to think about their answer. Which behaviours are most likely to occur in these situations?

THE BEHAVIOUR OF A LIAR

In studies of actual indicators of deception, participants are usually instructed to give either true or deceptive reports on certain issues. Their non-verbal behaviours are then analysed with particular coding systems, and the average frequencies of occurrence of certain behaviours during truthful and deceptive messages are compared. For instance, Bella DePaulo, a distinguished and leading researcher in this field, asked participants to describe in an honest way people they liked and people they disliked, and also to describe the same people dishonestly—that is, to pretend that they liked the people they really disliked and to pretend to dislike the people they really liked (DePaulo & Rosenthal, 1979; DePaulo, Lassiter & Stone, 1982). Paul Ekman, another distinguished and leading researcher in this field, showed his participants (student nurses) a pleasant film with colourful ocean scenes and asked them to describe their feelings frankly to an interviewer who could not see which film they were watching. Then he showed them a gruesome medical training film (including severe burns and an amputation), and asked them to conceal their feelings so that the interviewer would think they were seeing another pleasant film—for instance, about pretty flowers (Ekman & Friesen, 1974; Ekman, Friesen & Scherer, 1976).

Because signs of deception are only likely to occur when emotions are involved or when the lies require some thought, researchers put effort into introducing stakes or content complexity in their studies. Liars are usually asked to lie spontaneously about certain topics, which requires more effort than telling the truth. In order to raise the stakes in these experiments, participants are usually offered some money if they successfully get away with their lies. Sometimes researchers tell participants that being a good liar is an important indicator of being successful in a future career. This, by the way, is true. For example, good nurses are good liars. Their ability to conceal negative emotions (when they interact with patients who are terminally ill, or with patients with severe burns, and so on) is very useful in their jobs (Ekman, 1992). Whatever researchers try, however, the situation a liar is confronted with in these experimental studies is probably different to the real-life situations which some liars have to face (e.g. a suspect in a police interview, a smuggler at an airport or a corrupt politician in conversation with a suspicious journalist). I will come back to this issue later.

There have been numerous experiments conducted so far. A summary of the experiments that are being reviewed is given in Table 2.1, while Box 2.1 provides an overview and descriptions of the behaviours discussed.

A distinction can be made between vocal and non-vocal non-verbal behaviours. Vocal behaviours are related to voice and speech, while the other behaviours are called non-vocal behaviours. The first part of Table 2.1 (vocal characteristics) reveals two clear actual indicators of deception. First, that liars tend to have a higher-pitched voice than truth-tellers. As mentioned before, this is probably caused by stress (Ekman, Friesen & Scherer, 1976). However, these differences in pitch

Box 2.1. Overview and descriptions of the non-verbal behaviours

Vocal Characteristics

1 *Speech hesitations*: use of the words 'ah', 'um', 'er' and so on
2 *Speech errors*: word and/or sentence repetition, sentence change, sentence incompletions, slips of the tongue, and so on
3 *Pitch of voice*: changes in pitch of voice, such as a rise or fall in pitch
4 *Speech rate*: number of spoken words in a certain period of time
5 *Latency period*: period of silence between question and answer
6 *Frequency of pauses*: frequency of silent periods during speech
7 *Pause durations*: length of silent periods during speech

Facial Characteristics

8 *Gaze*: looking at the face of the conversation partner
9 *Smile*: smiling and laughing
10 *Blinking*: blinking of the eyes

Movements

11 *Self-manipulations*: scratching the head, wrists, and so on
12 *Illustrators*: functional hand and arm movements designed to modify and/or supplement what is being said verbally
13 *Hand and finger movements*: non-functional movements of hands or fingers without moving the arms
14 *Leg and foot movements*: movements of feet and legs
15 *Head movements*: head nods and head shakes
16 *Trunk movements*: movements of the trunk (usually accompanied by head movements)
17 *Shifting position*: movements made to change the sitting position (usually accompanied by trunk and foot/leg movements)

between liars and truth-tellers are usually very small (only a few hertz), and therefore only detectable with sophisticated equipment.

Second, liars seem to pause for longer when they speak than do truth-tellers. This is probably caused by having to think harder.

The data concerning errors, hesitations and speech rate show a conflicting pattern. In most studies an increase in errors and hesitations and a slower speech rate during deception has been found, but some studies have revealed the opposite pattern—that is, a decrease in errors and hesitations and a faster speech rate. It might be that variations in lie complexity are responsible for these conflicting findings, as will be shown below.

The results concerning latency period and frequency of pauses show a confused pattern as well. Unlike the conflicting findings concerning errors, hesitations and speech rate, these conflicting findings cannot be explained by lie complexity. We therefore have to conclude that a clear relationship between latency period, frequency of pauses and deception does not exist.

Table 2.1. Actual non-verbal indicators of deception

			Vocal characteristics				
	Hesitations	Errors	High-pitched voice	Speech rate	Latency period	Pauses durations	Frequency of pauses
Anolli & Cicery (1997)		∧	∧	—		—	∧
Bond et al. (1985)	—	—					
Bond et al. (1990)	∧	—	—				—
Buller & Aune (1987)			—	—			
Buller et al. (1989)		∨		—	—		∨
Buller et al. (1994a)	∧	—			∨		
Cody & O'Hair (1983)					∨		
Cody et al. (immediate response) (1984)	—	—		—	∧	∧	—
Cody et al. (delayed response) (1984)	—	∧		—	—	∧	—
Cody et al. (1989)	—	∧		—	—		—
DePaulo, Rosenthal et al. (1982)	—	∧		—			—
P.J. DePaulo & DePaulo (1989)	—	—		—			
deTurck & Miller (1985)	—	∧			∧	∧	
Ebesu & Miller (1994)	—			∨	∨		—
Ekman (1988)			∧				
Ekman et al. (1976)			∧				
Ekman et al. (1991)			∧				
Feeley & deTurck (1998)	∧	∧	—	—	—		—
Fiedler & Walka (1993)	∧			∨			
Greene et al. (1985)					∨		

Study	1	2	3	4	5	6	7
Hocking & Leathers (1980)	—	∧		—	—		—
Höfer et al. (1993)	—	∨		—	∨		∨
Kalma et al. (1996)	—				∨		∨
Knapp et al. (1974)	—			—	—		
Köhnken (1985)	—			—			
Kraut (experiment 1) (1978)	—			∨	—		
Kraut (experiment 2) (1978)					∧		∧
Kraut & Poe (1980)	∨	∧		∧	∨		
Mann et al. (1998)	∨	∧		—			—
Mehrabian (1972)		—			∧		∧
Miller et al. (1983)	—		∧		—		
O'Hair et al. (1981)		—		—			—
Riggio & Friedman (1983)	—	∨¹			∨		
Rockwell et al. (1997)	—		∧	∧			
Stiff & Miller (1986)	∧	∧	∧		∧		∧
Stiff et al. (1994)		∧		—	—		—
Streeter et al. (1977)					—	—	
Vrij (1995)	∨			∧			
Vrij & Winkel (1991)	∨						
Vrij & Heaven (difficult response) (1999)	∧	—		—			∨
Vrij (easy response) (1999)	∨	∧		∧			
Vrij et al. (1999)	∧	—		∧	∧	∧	∧
Vrij & Mann (in press)	∧	∧		∧	∧		—
Young & deTurck (1996)	—	—		—	—		

(continued overleaf)

Table 2.1. (*continued*)

	Non-vocal characteristics									
	Gaze	Smile	Self-manipulations	Illustrators	Hand/finger	Leg/foot	Trunk	Head	Shifting position	Eye blinking
Akehurst & Vrij (1999)					∨	—	—			
Bond et al. (1985)	∧	—	—	—						
Bond et al. (1990)	—	—	—	∧				—		—
Buller & Aune (1987)	∨	—	∨	—				—		—
Buller et al. (1989)	∨	—	—	—				—		—
Buller et al. (1994a)		—						—		
Buller et al. (1994b)								∨	∧	
Cody & O'Hair (1983)	—	—	—	∨		∨		—		
Cody et al. (1989)	—	—	—	—	—			—		
Davis & Hadiks (1995)			—	∨						
P.J. DePaulo & DePaulo (1989)	—		—	∧		—	—		—	
deTurck & Miller (1985)	—		∧	∧		∨		—	∧	
Ebesu & Miller (1994)			∨	∨						—
Ekman (1988)		—	∧	∨						
Ekman & Friesen (1972)			∧	∨						
Ekman et al. (1976)		—		∨						
Ekman et al. (1988)		—		—						
Ekman et al. (1990)		—								
Ekman et al. (1991)		—		—		—				
Feeley & deTurck (1998)	—	—	—	∨					—	
Fiedler & Walka (1993)	—	∧	—					∨		

Greene et al. (1985)
Hocking & Leathers (1980)
Höfer et al. (1993)
Kalma et al. (1996)
Knapp et al. (1974)
Kraut (experiment a) (1978)
Kraut & Poe (1980)
Mann et al. (1998)
McClintock & Hunt (1975)
Mehrabian (1972)
Miller et al. (1983)
O'Hair et al. (1981)
Riggio & Friedman (1983)
Schneider & Kintz (1977)
Stiff & Miller (1986)
Vrij (1995)
Vrij & Winkel (1991)
Vrij, Semin et al. (1996)
Vrij, Akehurst et al. (1997)
Vrij et al. (1999)
Vrij & Mann (in press)
Young & deTurck (1996)
Zuckerman et al. (1979)

The signs refer to the actual behaviour/deception relationship: >, increase during deception; <, decrease during deception; —, no relationship with deception; blank, relationship was not investigated.

[1] Perceptually coded pitch level. Pitch level measured with acoustic equipment did not reveal a difference in pitch level between liars and truth-tellers.

The second part of Table 2.1 (non-vocal characteristics) shows a very confusing pattern. A detailed look only reveals three actual indicators of deception, suggesting that liars tend to move their arms, hands, fingers, feet and legs less than do truth-tellers. The decrease in these movements might be the result of lie complexity. Perhaps liars have to think hard, resulting in neglect of body language. Another explanation is that liars, in an effort to make an honest impression, move very deliberately and try to avoid those movements which are not strictly essential, resulting in an unusual degree of rigidity and inhibition.

As I mentioned before, these findings do not suggest that all people raise their voice or show fewer movements when lying than when telling the truth. It only suggests that the majority of liars do this. For example, an overview of my own experiments revealed that 64% of our 181 participants showed a decrease in hand, finger and arm movements during deception, whereas 35% showed an increase in these movements during deception (Vrij & Akehurst, 1996a; Vrij, Winkel & Akehurst, 1997).

All other non-vocal characteristics (e.g. gaze aversion, smiling, self-manipulations, shifting position and eye blinks) do not consistently seem to be reliable indicators of deception. This is a striking finding, as it contradicts the stereotypical beliefs that many people hold about non-verbal indicators of deception, as will be discussed in Chapter 3. Generally, observers expect liars to show nervous behaviour and behaviours which indicate intense thinking. However, liars often do not display such behaviours. For example, people expect liars to look away. It is perhaps reasonable to expect liars to show gaze aversion, as they might be nervous or have to think hard, and gaze aversion is an indicator of both nervousness and cognitive load. It is therefore possible that liars are at least inclined to look away. However, gaze aversion is not a reliable indicator of deception. The reason for this is that it is so easy to control. It does not involve much effort for liars to look their conversation partner straight in the eyes if they wish to. Obviously, behaviours which are easy to control can never be reliable indicators of deception. Also, the belief that liars keep their hands in front of their mouth, often mentioned in the police literature (see Chapter 1), is inaccurate.

It is sometimes mentioned in police literature that eye movements provide information about whether a person is lying. In particular, the belief that liars look to the left seems to be popular. This idea is derived from the neurolinguistic programming model, although those who developed this model never referred to the relationship between eye movements and deception. To date, evidence that eye movements indicate deception is lacking. Even those authors who suggested that this relationship exists never presented any data supporting their view.

This issue will therefore not be further discussed (see Vrij and Lochun (1997) for a critical review of this police literature).

One possible reason why liars in experimental studies do not show clear patterns of nervous behaviour is that they are simply not nervous enough during these experiments. It may be the case that behavioural clues to deceit differ in low- and high-stakes situations—that is, it may be the case that liars will show the nervous behaviours which observers expect them to show when the stakes are high, but not when the stakes are low. I shall return to this issue later.

Alternatively, it might be that some indicators of deception are over-looked by researchers due to the fact that the scoring systems they use to measure the occurrence of behaviours are not detailed enough, or because they do not know where to look. For example, some researchers do not measure the *frequency of occurrence* of behaviours during lying and truth-telling, but instead measure the *duration* of these behaviours. Measuring duration is in my view not detailed enough, and might explain why some researchers have not found differences between truth-tellers and liars, whereas others did find differences. For example, Feeley and deTurck (1998), Knapp, Hart and Dennis (1974), Kraut and Poe (1980), Miller, deTurck and Kalbfleisch (1983), Riggio and Friedman (1983) and Stiff and Miller (1986) all measured the duration of behaviours and did not find significant differences between liars and truth-tellers. To date, no researcher has presented an alternative scoring method which revealed more actual indicators of deception than those already mentioned, with the exception of Ekman in his research concerning smiles. Table 2.1 shows that smiles are not related to deception. However, Ekman and his colleagues discovered that smiles are related to deception when a distinction is made between felt and false smiles (Ekman, 1988; Ekman, Davidson & Friesen, 1990; Ekman & Friesen, 1982; Ekman, Friesen & O'Sullivan, 1988). Felt smiles include all smiles in which the person actually experiences a positive emotion and presumably would report that emotion. Felt smiles are accompanied by the action of two muscles, the *zygomatic major*, which pulls the lip corners upwards towards the cheekbone, and the *orbicularis oculi*, which raises the cheek and gathers skin inwards from around the eye socket, producing a bagged skin below the eyes and crow's-feet wrinkles beyond the eye corners. False smiles are deliberately made to convince another person that a positive emotion is felt, whereas in fact it is not. The action of the orbicularis oculi is absent in a false smile. Thus a smile without the action of this muscle is a false one. However, a smile with the action of this muscle is not always a felt one. Actions of this muscle may occur during false smiles, as the muscle is involved in other felt emotions as well, such as distress, sadness or pain. When someone tries to hide those feelings with a false smile, actions of the orbicularis oculi might occur. Moreover, good facial performers may successfully manage to produce false smiles which look like felt smiles. Ekman and his colleagues found that truth-tellers make more felt smiles than liars, whereas liars make more false smiles than truth-tellers. When the distinction between felt and false smiles is not made, truth-tellers seem to smile as frequently as liars (Ekman, Friesen & O'Sullivan, 1988). Other differences between felt and false smiles are that false smiles are more asymmetrical, appear too early or too late, and often last longer (Ekman, Davidson & Friesen, 1990; Ekman & Friesen, 1982).

Paul Ekman's work has also shown that observing emotional micro-expressions in the face reveals valuable information about deception (Ekman, 1992). Emotions almost automatically activate muscle actions in the face. For example, anger results in a narrowing of the lips and lowering of the eyebrows. Eyebrows which are raised and pulled together and a raised upper eyelid and tensed lower eyelid typically denote fear, and joy, as mentioned above, activates muscles which pull the lip corners up, bag the skin below the eyes, and produce crow's-feet wrinkles beyond the eye corners. If a person denies an emotional state which is actually being felt, this person will have to suppress these facial expressions. Thus if a scared person claims not to be afraid, that person has to suppress the facial micro-expressions which typically indicate fear. This is difficult, especially because these emotions can arise unexpectedly. For instance, people do not usually deliberately choose to become frightened—this happens automatically as a result of a particular event that took place, or as a result of a particular thought. It is possible that a suspect will become frightened during a police interview at the moment when she finds out that the police know more about her involvement in the crime than she thought they would know. The moment fright occurs, a fearful facial expression may be shown which may give the lie away. It is therefore likely that the suspect would try to suppress this emotional expression as soon as it appears. People are usually able to suppress these expressions within 1/25th of a second after they begin to appear (Ekman, 1992). This is fast, and they can easily be missed by an observer (in fact, observers who blink at the moment when the expression occurs will miss the expression). Detecting these micro-expressions is difficult for untrained observers, but Ekman (1992) contends that it is a skill that can be learned.

The opposite can occur as well. Someone can pretend to experience a particular emotion, whereas in fact this emotion is not felt. A mother can pretend to be angry with her child, whereas in reality she is not angry at all. In order to be convincing, a mother should produce an angry facial expression—that is, she should try to narrow her lips. However, this muscle action is very difficult for most people to make voluntarily (Ekman, 1992).

It is also difficult to fake an emotion other than the one which is actually felt. For instance, an adulterous husband may become scared during a conversation with his wife when he realizes how much she knows about his affair, but can decide to mask this emotional state by pretending to be angry with his wife because she apparently does not trust him. In order to be convincing, he therefore has to suppress his fearful facial expression and replace it with an angry facial expression. This is difficult, because he has to lower his eyebrows (sign of anger), whereas his eyebrows tend to rise (sign of fear) (Ekman, 1992). Paying attention to microfacial expressions may provide a good opportunity to detect lies. Ekman's research has shown that it is possible to detect up to 80% of truths and lies when a trained observer pays attention to these microfacial expressions (Frank & Ekman, 1997). Even better classifications of truth-tellers and liars were obtained when several behaviours (illustrators and tone of voice) were taken into account simultaneously. In that situation, 86% of the truths and lies could be detected (Ekman, O'Sullivan, Friesen & Scherer, 1991).

FACTORS THAT INFLUENCE THE BEHAVIOUR OF A LIAR

The results regarding the objective non-verbal indicators of deception are perhaps somewhat disappointing. One would have hoped that research would have demonstrated more and perhaps stronger indicators. However, the problem is that one typical pattern of deceptive behaviour does not exist. Different people show different behaviours. Some people give their lies away via voice-related cues, others via speech-related cues, a third group via movements, and so on. The findings thus only suggest that a relatively large number of people give their lies away via their pitch of voice and via their hand movements. Moreover, behaviours will differ across deceptive situations. This section discusses the influence of five factors on deceptive behaviour, namely lie complexity, the motivation of the liar, emotions when lying, the suspicion of the observer and individual characteristics.

Content Complexity of the Lie

Sometimes it is difficult to tell a lie. Suppose that an applicant did something very stupid in her previous job and that, to her own surprise, a member of the selection board refers to this stupidity during the selection interview. The applicant, who really wants the job, does not want to admit to this blunder and must therefore instantly come up with a fabricated but plausible explanation. This will not be easy. She will probably have to think hard, which may well result in an increase in speech hesitations and speech errors, and in a slower speech rate.

However, liars are not always taken by surprise. They often know what kind of questions they can expect and can therefore prepare themselves to give convincing and plausible answers. For example, many guilty suspects reckon with the possibility that the police will interview them one day about their activities at the time when the crime was committed. They therefore prepare an answer to this question well in advance which sounds reasonable and plausible. Obviously, lying is not too difficult in this situation. When the police ask him about his activities at the time of the crime, the well-prepared guilty suspect simply gives the answer which he had prepared previously. How do liars behave when they have had the opportunity to plan their lies? There is evidence to suggest that, when compared to spontaneous lies, planned lies are associated with a shorter latency period and a faster speech rate (Zuckerman & Driver, 1985). It is easier to tell a planned lie than a spontaneous lie, resulting in fewer behavioural signs of thinking hard. Höfer and his colleagues found that planned lies resulted in few speech errors—even fewer than in truth-telling (Höfer, Köhnken, Hanewinkel & Bruhn, 1993). In their study, participants had to recall a film they had just seen. In the deception condition they were requested to include details in their account which did not in fact occur in the film. However, Höfer et al. instructed and coached them in what they should say. They found that, compared to truth-tellers, liars made fewer speech errors. There are two possible explanations for this finding. First, the liars in this study were probably facing an easier task than the truth-tellers. The liars could simply repeat the answer they had just been given, whereas the truth-tellers had to think about the film and invent an answer. As mentioned above, the easier the task, the less likely it is that speech errors will occur. Secondly, the decrease in speech errors may be influenced by liars' tendency to overcontrol their behaviour. They might have thought that speech errors would give their lies away and therefore, in an effort to make an honest impression, tried to avoid making such errors. This might have resulted in a speech pattern which sounded unusually smooth.

Sometimes a liar does not have to fabricate an answer at all, but simply has to conceal some information. When a customs officer asks them what is in their suitcase, the only thing a smuggler has to do is to conceal some information—that is, not to mention the contraband. Some of my own studies examined how liars behave in such a situation (Akehurst & Vrij, 1999; Vrij, 1995; Vrij, Akehurst & Morris, 1997; Vrij,

Semin, & Bull, 1996; Vrij & Winkel, 1991). In these studies, participants in the deception condition had to deny possession of a set of headphones which they actually possessed. In other words, their task was to conceal some information. Their answers were compared with the answers given by participants who did not possess a set of headphones and were therefore honest when they denied the possession of these headphones. In these studies, the liars made fewer speech hesitations and spoke faster than the truth-tellers. The attempted control approach offers a plausible explanation. As mentioned previously, liars want to make an honest impression, and therefore try to avoid making speech hesitations and speaking too slowly. This may result in an unusually fast speech rate and an unusually smooth speech pattern.

In summary, research findings have indicated that more complicated lies result in an increase in speech hesitations, speech errors and a slower speech rate. Easier lies, such as well-prepared lies and concealments, do not result in such a behavioural pattern and may even result in the opposite pattern—that is, in a decrease in speech hesitations and speech errors and in slower speech. Recently, we further examined the moderating impact of lie complexity on the occurrence of speech hesitations (Vrij & Heaven, 1999). In line with the attempted behavioural control approach, we hypothesized that liars will try to avoid making speech hesitations while lying. We expected that they would only achieve this when the lie was easy. Participants were shown a video of a couple having a disagreement. First, the man appeared, maintaining that he wanted to buy satellite television so that he could watch football at home rather than having to go to the pub to watch it. The woman followed, explaining that the only reason he really wanted to buy satellite television was so that he could bring his friends home from the pub to watch the porn channels. After watching this videotape, the participants were requested to lie about some aspects of the video and tell the truth about other aspects. One lie was relatively easy to fabricate, namely giving an inaccurate description of the appearance of one of the people in the video, whereas the second lie was more difficult to fabricate, namely making up a reason why the person in the video wanted to buy satellite television. As expected, liars made more speech hesitations (compared to truth-tellers) when the lie was cognitively difficult, and made fewer speech hesitations (compared to truth-tellers) when the lie was easy.

The Motivated Liar

Liars are not always equally motivated. A murderer in a police interview is probably more motivated to hide the truth than a boy who makes his mum believe that he does not want to eat his cauliflower because he ate a sandwich an hour ago. People who are highly motivated to get away with their lies may behave differently to people who care less about the outcome. In their meta-analysis, Zuckerman and Driver (1985) compared studies in which the motivation was high with those in which the motivation was lower. Motivation was considered to be high if participants were promised some monetary reward for performing well on the deception task, or if the deception was described as a test of some skill. The analysis revealed that highly motivated liars made fewer head movements and fewer shifts in position, spoke more slowly and with a higher-pitched voice, and made more speech disturbances than less motivated liars. In short, the more motivated liars are to avoid getting caught, the more likely it is that their behaviour will give their lies away. This finding might sound surprising, but it is easy to explain. Highly motivated liars probably experience stronger emotions (e.g. stronger fear of getting caught), which might result in a higher-pitched voice and more speech hesitations and errors. In addition, they probably think harder than less motivated liars (again to avoid getting caught), which might result in slower speech, more speech hesitations and more speech errors and fewer movements. Finally, they probably try harder to control their behaviour, resulting in less movement and more behavioural rigidity. The finding that highly motivated liars show more rigidity is called the *motivational impairment effect* (DePaulo & Kirkendol, 1989).

Lying While the Stakes Are High

The stakes do differ for liars as well. As previously discussed, in order to raise the stakes in laboratory experiments, lying is often introduced as an important skill, and successful liars are promised money or some other reward. Although this results in raising the stakes to some extent—and makes them more comparable to the stakes in most daily life situations—the stakes for liars in laboratory experiments are obviously not as high as the stakes for smugglers, guilty suspects, adulterous spouses, fraudulent businessmen and corrupt politicians. Unfortunately, laboratory experiments will never tell us how liars behave when the stakes are really high, as it is not ethically permissible to raise the stakes too high in such experiments. Lies in real-life high-stake situations need to be examined in order to find this out. However, observing someone's behaviour in real-life situations raises another problem. In these real-life cases it is usually difficult to determine the so-called *ground truth*—that is, to establish certainty as to whether or not someone is lying.

As far as I know, two cases of high-stake lies have been examined to date. One case concerns a televised interview with Saddam Hussein, the

President of Iraq, and the other case concerns a videotaped interview with a man who was later convicted for murder.

Saddam Hussein

Iraq's President Saddam Hussein was interviewed by the journalist Peter Arnett from Cable News Network (CNN) during the Gulf War (1991). The interview lasted 94 minutes and was broadcast on CNN. Davis and Hadiks (1995) observed and scored Hussein's behaviour during this interview. They used a very detailed scoring system to measure every single movement of his hands, arms and trunk. The scoring method was much more detailed than those usually used in experiments. Several issues were discussed during the interview, such as loyalty among Islamic countries, Israel, President Bush, Western hostages who were used as human shields, and Iraqi planes landing in Iran. Davis and Hadiks' observations revealed that Hussein used a variety of hand and arm movements, and that he made specific illustrators when discussing specific issues. When discussing Israel, Hussein made a string of short, vertical, intense jabs of the left forearm, some with a fist and some not. This behavioural pattern only emerged when he was discussing Israel and Zionism. Hussein showed the least restrained behaviour when he spoke about Bush. Verbally, he gave the impression that he did not care much about Bush when he said: 'I talk to people . . . genuine dialogue with people, not with Mr Bush.' However, speaking about President Bush was associated with clear movements of the trunk and a burst of gesture intensity. Davis and Hadiks interpreted this as strong non-verbal evidence of Hussein's intense personal animosity towards Bush. Arnett also discussed the Iraqi planes landing in Iran. Hussein told Arnett: 'There isn't one single Islamic country that is not on our side in this battle.' He then went on to describe how Iraqi planes may at times need to land in neighbouring countries. As to whether the planes will return to use, he replied: 'We respect the decisions and the regulations of Iran.' Throughout this part of the interview, Hussein's behaviour was restricted and controlled. He slowly sat up, and markedly restricted and even stopped his gesticulations. Davis and Hadiks believe that at that moment Hussein was fabricating an answer or, in their own words: 'When we found out what he was saying, it appeared to stretch credulity so far that we could not help feeling we were on the right track to interpret his narrow upright position/restricted gesture state as a constraint sign accompanying fabrication of an answer' (Davis & Hadiks, 1995, pp.37–38). However, as mentioned above, in these real-life cases it is usually difficult to determine the ground truth. In this case, it is not certain whether

Hussein was definitely lying. However, 100% certainty was obtained in the case of the murderer described below, and examined by us (Vrij & Mann, in press).

The Murderer[1]

A person went missing and was found dead a couple of days later. It was clear that the victim had been murdered. Several witnesses told the police independently from each other that they had seen a man speaking to the victim a couple of days before the body was found. On the basis of their descriptions, the police were able to create an artist's impression of the man. After a couple of months, a man was arrested and brought to a police station for interviewing. He was a Western European Caucasian man in his forties. He had little education and a blue-collar occupation in which he was employed at the time. He had a girlfriend but lived alone. Apart from the fact that he showed a clear resemblance to the face in the sketch, there were other reasons that led the police to believe that he was involved in the crime. For example, the man already had a criminal record and had previously been interviewed by the police on several other occasions.

The police interviewed this man extensively. During the first interview, he was asked to describe what he had done during the day when the victim went missing. Although the interview took place several months after the victim went missing, the man was capable of giving a very detailed description of his activities during that day. He told the police that he had thought they would interview him about this case, and that he had therefore checked his diary to find out what he had been doing on that day (even an innocent suspect could have known what day the person went missing, as the media reported extensively on the missing person both during that day and over the days immediately following it). The police checked every single detail that the man had provided. Several independent witnesses (including his employer) could confirm his story about his activities during the morning, but no confirmation could be obtained about his alleged activities during the rest of the day. This made the man even more suspect, and an intensive investigation started. Meanwhile, the man consistently denied having killed the victim, and even claimed that he had never met the victim. After a couple of weeks, substantial evidence was found which made it clear that he was the murderer. A hair found in the man's car was confirmed to have come from the victim. In addition, fibres of the cloth in which the

---

[1] The description of the case is deliberately vague in order to guarantee the man's right to be anonymous.

dead body was wrapped were found in his car. On the basis of this substantial evidence, the man admitted to having killed the victim, and gave a detailed description of what had happened. He was later convicted of murder by a criminal court and sentenced to imprisonment for the remainder of his natural life.

However, during his confession the murderer did not tell the whole truth. He told the truth about how he drove from his house to the location where he met the victim, and independent witnesses could confirm this part of the story. It is evident, however, that he lied about how he met the victim. Several independent witnesses claimed to have seen him at a particular location. In addition, an object which belonged to the man (ownership of which he admitted) was found at that particular location. Despite this substantial evidence, the man continued to deny ever having visited the location. He admitted that he had been near that location, but denied ever having actually entered it.

All the parts of the interview about which we were certain that he was lying or telling the truth were analysed. Two fragments—one lie and one truth—were derived from the interview before the confession took place. The truth consists of a description of his activities during the morning when the victim went missing. As stated previously, witnesses could confirm this part of the story. This description lasted 61 seconds. The lie, which lasted 67 seconds, consists of a description of his activities during the afternoon and evening of the same day. He told the police about several things he had done in his home town. In reality, he took his car and drove to another city where he met the victim. He killed the victim later on that day.

Four other fragments—two lies and two truths—were derived from his confession. In the first truthful fragment, which lasted 26 seconds, the man gave a detailed description of how he drove from the exit of the motorway to the place where he met the victim. Witnesses could verify this part of the story. The second truthful fragment, which lasted 27 seconds, was a repetition of the same story. His first lie during his confession was about the time he left a friend's house at his home town on the day when he killed the victim. In reality, he left the friend's house a couple of hours earlier than he claimed. Witnesses saw him with the victim at the time when he claimed to have been at his friend's house. This is an important lie because he had to account for a couple of hours (namely the hours when he visited the location which he denied ever visiting). This lie lasted 16 seconds. The second lie during the confession concerned where he met the victim. This lie lasted 32 seconds. As described above, there is compelling evidence that he met the victim at a location which he denied having visited. Although we have several hours of videotapes, only a few minutes could be used in this study. For the other parts of the interview the ground truth could not be established. For instance, the murderer gave a detailed description of the talks he had with the victim, and how he killed the victim. However, there is no possibility of verifying the truthfulness of this part of his story.

Obviously it is very difficult to predict how this man would behave during his police interview. However, despite the fact that the stakes were high, we did not expect him to behave nervously (by 'nervous behaviour' I mean gaze aversion, smiling, fidgeting movements, and so on, and not micro-expressions of emotions), for the following three reasons. First, because of his experience in police interviewing (as stated previously, he had already been interviewed by the police on several other occasions) he had probably realized that showing stereotypical deceptive behaviour (e.g. fidgeting and gaze aversion) would make the police suspicious, and so he would probably try to control his behaviour in order to make an honest impression. (Being interviewed by the police previously may also result in not being nervous during police interviews. However, we thought this was unlikely, as the consequences of the lie being detected were so great in this particular case.) Secondly, we can assume that this man was highly motivated to conceal his lie and, as mentioned before, highly motivated liars often tend to show extraordinarily rigid, rehearsed and planned behaviour. I referred to this as the motivational impairment effect. Thirdly, the circumstances under which the man had to lie were difficult. At the beginning of the interviews, he was told by the police that he was their main suspect in this murder case. Therefore he could assume that the police would pay a great deal of attention to what he was saying and would verify all of the information he provided in order to find out whether he was lying. Hence it was important for him to think carefully about what he would say, as each little mistake could have severe consequences for him. Lying under these difficult circumstances probably requires a great deal of cognitive energy. As a result, instead of deliberately trying to refrain from showing nervous behaviours, (e.g. fidgeting), an absence of nervous behaviours may automatically occur as a result of neglect of body language, due to this cognitive load. Table 2.2 shows a schematic representation of the behaviour of the man before and during his confession.

A few differences emerged between the truthful and deceptive accounts before the confession. While lying, the murderer showed more gaze aversion, made longer pauses in speech, spoke more slowly and made more speech errors than when he was telling the truth. This behavioural pattern is typical of someone who has to think hard. Apparently it was more difficult for the man to lie than for him to tell the truth. It is perhaps surprising that the man apparently had to think hard during

Table 2.2. The behaviour of a murderer during his police interview

	1 Before confession	2 During confession
Vocal characteristics		
High-pitched voice	*	*
Hesitations	—	—
Errors	>	>
Slow speech	>	>
Latency period	*	*
Pause durations	>	>
Frequency of pauses	—	>
Non-vocal characteristics		
Gaze aversion	>	<
Smiling	—	—
Eye blinks	*	*
Illustrators	—	<
Self-manipulations	—	—
Hand/finger	—	<
Leg/foot	*	*
Head	—	—
Trunk	—	—
Shifting positions	—	*

>, increase during deception;
<, decrease during deception;
—, no relationship with deception;
*, relationship was not investigated.

deception. He knew that he was a suspect, and there was enough time for him to prepare a lie. There was also evidence that he had prepared himself, as he had made false notes in his diary in an effort to dupe the police. Despite this preparation, a possible reason why the man's behaviour still showed some evidence that he had to think hard is that he is not very bright (this is the opinion of the police detectives who interviewed him). There is evidence which suggests that preparation probably does not benefit liars who are not so clever (Ekman & Frank, 1993).

Several differences between truth-telling and lying also emerged in the confession interview. While lying, the murderer showed less gaze aversion, made fewer illustrators and hand and finger movements, made more and longer pauses in speech, spoke more slowly, and made slightly more speech errors. Again, the slow speech, longer pauses, greater number of pauses and increase in speech errors can be interpreted as a sign that he had to think very hard while lying. Also the decrease in movements may be the result of lie complexity. Looking at the policeman when he was lying may be interpreted as an effort to convince the policeman that he was telling the truth. As will be discussed in Chapter 3, police officers (and people in general) often think that gaze aversion is an indicator of deception. The man may have realized this and, in order to avoid making a dishonest impression, he looked the police detective straight in the eyes. It is difficult to explain why his gaze behaviour was so different before compared to during the confession. If he tried to convince the police officer during the confession, why didn't he do that in the interview before the confession? I can only speculate about the answer to this question. There was a difference between the two interviews which may have influenced his behaviour. In the second interview, the man was probed by the officer. Earlier in the interview, the officer had told him that he did not believe his story about how he met the victim. Probing did not take place in the interview prior to the confession interview. The officer asked him an open question ('What did you do on that particular day?') and the man answered that question. It might be that he tried harder to make an honest impression after being probed. Whether or not probing generally results in displaying 'honest behaviour' is open to debate, as will be discussed in the next section.

In summary, the behavioural pattern showed by the murderer provides evidence that he had to think hard and that he tried to control his behaviour. As we expected, he did not seem to behave nervously. Our interpretation of his behaviour was supported by police officers who have seen the videotape. We showed police officers who did not know the man, and who knew nothing about the case, those fragments of the interview which we had analysed and asked them to indicate to what extent they perceived the man to be tense, controlling his behaviour and having to think hard. We did not tell them when he was lying and when he was telling the truth. The results indicated that the man particularly strongly gave the impression that he had to think hard when he was lying (Vrij & Mann, in press).

Table 2.3 shows a schematic representation of both the literature review concerning actual non-verbal indicators of deception (column 1) and the behaviour of the convicted murderer (column 2). As can be seen from this table, there is quite an overlap between the two columns. Apparently the behaviour shown by the murderer during his high-stake lie corresponds to the behaviour of liars in laboratory experiments. On the one hand, this is perhaps surprising, as there are obvious differences between police interviews and laboratory experiments. On the other hand, there are similarities as well. Both the murderer and the liars in laboratory experiments were probably afraid of getting caught (the murderer probably more so than the participants in experiments), had to think harder when lying than when telling the truth, and might have

Table 2.3. Actual non-verbal indicators of deception and the behaviour of a murderer during his police interview

	1 Actual indicators	2 Behaviour of a murderer
Vocal characteristics		
High-pitched voice	>	*
Speech hesitations	>[1]	—
Speech errors	>[1]	>
Slow speech	>[1]	>
Latency period	—	*
Pause durations	>	>
Frequency of pauses	—	>
Non-vocal characteristics		
Gaze aversion	—	—
Smiling	—	—
Eye blinks	—	*
Illustrators	<	<
Self-manipulations	—	—
Hand/finger	<	<
Leg/foot	<	*
Head	—	—
Trunk	—	—
Shifting positions	—	*

>, increase during deception;
<, decrease during deception;
—, no relationship with deception;
*, relationship was not investigated.
[1] when telling a lie involves hard thinking.

tried to make an honest impression. The overlap shown in Table 2.3 suggests that these similarities may be more important in explaining deceptive behaviour than the apparent differences.

Despite the fact that the stakes were high for both Saddam Hussein and the murderer, neither of them showed nervous behaviour when lying. This is an important finding, as it contradicts the view of police officers and many others that liars show nervous behaviour (see Chapter 3). Obviously this does not mean that liars never show nervous behaviour. There are probably liars who do so, as will be discussed in the 'Individual differences' section below. However, the findings presented here suggest that experienced criminals (such as the murderer) or people in the public eye for whom it is important to make a good impression on others (such as Saddam Hussein) are unlikely to show nervous behaviour when they are lying.

It is important to note (again) that when I speak of nervous behaviour, I refer to behaviours such as gaze aversion, smiling, fidgeting movements, and so on, and not to the micro-expressions of emotions I discussed earlier. Ekman found that such micro-expressions frequently occur in high-stake situations (Ekman, 1992; Frank & Ekman, 1997).

The Suspicion of the Observer

Sometimes liars' statements are received with scepticism. For example, the journalist does not believe the police chief when she says that she is not aware of any unlawful practices in her force, and the judge distrusts the hooligan when he claims that he used his knife only to threaten the fellow supporter and not to stab him. Buller and his colleagues and Stiff and Miller have argued that liars show 'honest behaviour' (looking someone straight into the eyes, avoiding fidgeting and so on) as soon as they realize that they are mistrusted by the people they are trying to dupe (Buller, Comstock, Aune & Strzyzewski, 1989; Buller, Strzyzewski & Comstock, 1991; Stiff & Miller, 1986). The researchers claim that their findings support this idea, but a more detailed examination of these findings reveals that it is still open to doubt. In one study, probing resulted in an increase in speech disturbances and longer pauses (Buller, Comstock, Aune & Strzyzewski, 1989). However, these behaviours lead to a dishonest demeanour, as will be shown in Chapter 3. In a second study (Buller, Strzyzewski & Comstock, 1991), probing resulted in an increase in self-manipulations, which do not create an honest impression either. It seems reasonable that liars try to show honest behaviour when they are being probed, but apparently they sometimes fail to do so. It might well be the case that liars will become nervous (e.g. as a result of being afraid of getting caught) and have to think harder (to get out of the problematic situation) after being probed. Nervousness may result in an increase in self-manipulations and an increase in speech disturbances, whereas an increase in speech disturbances may also be caused by thinking hard. In summary, although some researchers want us to believe that suspicion results in 'honest behaviour', empirical findings reveal that the impact of suspicion on behaviour is still unclear. Buller, Stiff and Burgoon (1996) and Levine and McCornack (1996a,b) had a lively exchange about the impact of suspicion on behaviour.

Individual Differences

Personality Traits

As mentioned in Chapter 1, manipulators (Machiavellians) consider lying to be a legitimate way of achieving their goals. One might therefore expect that they would feel less guilty during deception, which might influence their behaviour. However, there is hardly any evidence to support the idea that high-scoring Machiavellians show different behaviour to their low-scoring counterparts. Exline and colleagues (Exline, Thibaut, Hickey & Gumbert, 1970) did find that people who scored high in Machiavellianism maintained more eye contact than those who scored low in Machiavellianism (which might well have been caused by feeling less guilty). However, other studies did not reveal behavioural differences between people who scored high and low in Machiavellianism (Knapp, Hart & Dennis, 1974; O'Hair, Cody & McLaughlin, 1981).

There is stronger empirical support for the assumption that extraverts show different behaviour when lying compared to introverts (Riggio & Friedman, 1983; Siegman & Reynolds, 1983). Extraverted people show fewer movements during deception than during truth-telling, whereas introverts make more movements when they lie than when they are honest. Introverts also have more disturbances in their speech during deception than extraverts. Introverted people usually feel more uncomfortable in social interactions than extraverts. The fact that they have to lie perhaps makes them even more nervous, resulting in an increase in movements and non-fluencies. The findings can also be explained by cognitive demand. Extraverts are usually eloquent and therefore able to fabricate stories rather easily. Introverts, who are generally quieter and stiffer in social interactions, might find this more difficult. Lying is therefore a more complicated task for introverts than for extraverts, resulting in an increase in speech disturbances.

The ability to act also influences people's behaviour when lying (Riggio & Friedman, 1983; Vrij, Akehurst & Morris, 1997). Some people are better actors than others. For example, some people are better than others at pretending that they are enjoying themselves when they are bored. Compared to bad actors, good actors more often show a decrease in movements when they are lying, due to the fact that they are probably better at suppressing signs of nervousness.

People differ in how motivated they are to make a good impression on others. People high in public self-consciousness (adaptors; see also Chapter 1) are particularly keen to make a positive impression on others. They try to achieve this by adapting themselves to their environment. These people generally show fewer movements when they are lying than when they are telling the truth (Vrij, Akehurst & Morris, 1997). There are two ways to explain this behaviour. It may be that they realize that observers will pay attention to their movements in order to catch their lie. By refraining from making movements they try to make the lie detection task more difficult for observers. An alternative explanation is that they experience a high cognitive load during deception due to the fact that they not only have to deceive the other but also have to think how to make a positive impression. An increase in cognitive load usually leads to making fewer movements.

Intelligence

Telling a lie which sounds convincing and plausible and which does not contradict the facts which are already known by the observer can be a difficult task, especially when liars have not had the opportunity to prepare themselves. Ekman and Frank (1993) suggest that intelligent people are better at solving such a difficult task than people who are less clever. As mentioned before, lack of intelligence might also have been the reason why the murderer was unable to talk as smoothly when he was lying as when he was telling the truth, although he had the opportunity to prepare his lies carefully.

CONCLUSION

How do people behave when they lie? Unfortunately, it is not possible to provide a simple answer. The main problem is that there is no typical non-verbal behaviour which is associated with deception. That is, not all liars show the same behaviour in the same situation, and behaviours will differ across deceptive situations. In this respect the results which are presented in this chapter might be disappointing. It would be very helpful for lie-catchers if liars showed typical behaviour, such as gaze aversion or putting one of their hands in front of their mouth, but they do not.

However, some behaviours are more likely to occur when people are lying than others. For example, it is very unlikely that a smuggler will pass a customs officer without looking at him, as liars generally do not show gaze aversion. Nor is it likely that suspects will start to fidget as soon as they present their alibi, as liars generally do not show fidgeting behaviour. It is more likely that liars will show a decrease in illustrators, movements of legs and feet and subtle hand and finger movements (as Saddam Hussein and the murderer did), differences in speech fluency and speech rate or microfacial expressions of emotions. These cues are more likely to occur when the liar experiences emotions of fear, guilt or delight, and when telling the lie requires a lot of mental effort.

The complicated relationship between non-verbal behaviour and deception makes it very difficult or even impossible to draw firm conclusions about deception solely on the basis of someone's behaviour. It is therefore undesirable for an analysis of someone's non-verbal behaviour to be used as evidence in court. However, a systematic and detailed observation of behaviour may be useful for determining whether something is going on, which may result in further investigations. Consider as an example the murderer. Why did he change his behaviour all of a sudden as soon as he described his activities during the afternoon? The change in behaviour does not confirm that he was lying, but indicates that something was going on. This may result in an increased effort on the part of the observer to establish the truth, (e.g. by searching for evidence to verify the interviewee's statements and by intensifying interviewing of him). This strategy worked. Intensive investigations resulted in finding a hair of the victim in the murderer's car and a piece of the cloth in which the victim's body was wrapped, which subsequently broke the murderer's determination to keep on denying the crime.

CHAPTER 3

Perception of Non-Verbal Behaviour During Deception

HOW DO PEOPLE THINK LIARS BEHAVE?

The previous chapter discussed objective or actual non-verbal indicators of deception—that is, how liars actually behave. The chapter revealed that typical deceptive non-verbal behaviour does not exist, although it showed that some behaviours are more likely to occur during deception than others. This chapter will address subjective indicators of deception—how people believe liars behave and which cues they use to detect deceit. I shall show that people (not only lay people but also professional lie-catchers) often have incorrect beliefs about how liars actually behave. People are usually poor at detecting lies when they pay attention to someone's behaviour.

Two different paradigms have been used in the study of subjective non-verbal indicators of deception. In the first paradigm, people are asked to indicate (usually in a questionnaire) how they think that liars behave. This gives insight into *beliefs about cues associated with deception*, but it does not necessarily mean that people actually use these cues when they try to detect deceit. For example, people may indicate that they think liars look away, but it may still be the case that they subsequently judge someone who shows gaze aversion to be truthful. A second paradigm has been designed to find out which cues people actually use to detect deception. Observers are given videotapes or audiotapes and asked to judge whether each of a number of people is lying or telling the truth. These judgements are then correlated with the actual cues that were or were not present in each video clip. The outcomes give insight into *cues to perceived deception* and tell us which cues people actually use to indicate whether someone is lying. For example, if there is a tendency among lie detectors to judge those who moved a great deal to be more deceitful than those who made few movements, it can be concluded that they used the making of movements as a cue to detect deception. However, it is unclear whether lie detectors know which cues they actually do use—that is, whether they realized that they used the making of movements as a cue to detect deceit.

Studies of subjective indicators of deception have been conducted in different Western countries, including Germany (Fiedler & Walka, 1993), the UK (Akehurst, Köhnken, Vrij & Bull, 1996; West, 1992), The Netherlands (Vrij & Semin, 1996) and the USA (DePaulo & DePaulo, 1989; Ekman, 1988; Riggio & Friedman, 1983). Mainly college students were used as observers, but in some studies the observers were police officers (Vrij, 1993a; Vrij, Akehurst, Van Dalen, Van Wijngaarden & Foppes, 1996; Vrij, Foppes, Volger & Winkel, 1992; Vrij & Semin, 1996) or customs officers (Kraut & Poe, 1980). Despite this variety of research paradigms, research locations and observers, the findings are highly similar. It appears that there are clear and unanimous beliefs among observers (both lay people and professional lie-catchers) in different cultures about the relationship between non-verbal behaviour and deception. Table 3.1 gives an overview of these beliefs.

Observers associate deception with a high-pitched voice, many speech disturbances (speech hesitations and speech errors), a slow speech rate, a long latency period, longer pauses, more pauses, gaze aversion, smiling, eye blinking and many movements (illustrators, self-manipulations, movements of the hands, fingers, feet, legs and trunk, and shifting positions). Applied to daily life situations, these findings suggest that customs officers think that smugglers avert their gaze, police officers believe that guilty suspects fidget, parents believe that their children are lying when they pause before giving an answer, and journalists become suspicious when a politician starts to stutter. Many of these behaviours are signs of nervousness or content complexity, and that is probably the reason why people associate these behaviours with deception. They probably think that liars will be nervous or have to think hard, and therefore look at cues indicating nervousness and content complexity. The tendency to look for cues of nervousness and content complexity is referred to as the *representativeness heuristic* (Stiff, Miller, Sleight, Mongeau, Garlick & Rogan, 1989).

My own research (Vrij & Semin, 1996) suggests that, out of all these indicators, gaze aversion is probably the one that people rely upon most (followed by self-manipulations and foot and leg movements). Why do people have strong expectations that liars will look away? First, because it is reasonable to expect gaze aversion during deception. Observers believe that liars are nervous and have to think hard, and gaze aversion is an indicator of both nervousness and cognitive load. However, those who rely on gaze aversion do not realize how easy it is to control this behaviour. Secondly, our own ongoing research involving suspects in

Table 3.1. Subjective indicators of deception

				Vocal characteristics			
	Hesitations	Errors	High-pitched voice	Speech rate	Latency period	Duration of pauses	Frequency of pauses
Akehurst et al. (1996)	∧	∧	∧	∨	∧		∧
Apple et al. (1979)			∧	∨			
Baskett & Freedle (1974)		∧			∧,∨		
Bond et al. (1985)							
Bond et al. (1990)							∧
DePaulo, Rosenthal et al. (1982)	∧	∧		∨			
DePaulo & DePaulo (1989)	∧			∨			
Ekman (1988)							
Fiedler & Walka (1993)		∧	∧				
Gordon et al. (1987)	∧		∧	∧			
Kraut (experiment 1) (1978)					∧		
Kraut & Poe (1980)					∧		
McCroskey et al. (1969)	∧	∧					
Nigro et al. (1989)	∧	∧		∨			
Riggio & Friedman (1983)							
Ruva & Bryant (1998)	∧						
Stiff & Miller (1986)	∧		∧			∧	
Streeter et al. (1977)	∧	∧	∧	∧			
Taylor & Vrij (1999)	∧	∧		∧	∧	∧	
Vrij & Bull (1992)	∧	∧		∧	∧		∧

(continued overleaf)

Table 3.1. (*continued*)

Vocal characteristics

	Hesitations	Errors	High-pitched voice	Speech rate	Latency period	Duration of pauses	Frequency of pauses
Vrij, Foppes et al. (1992)	∧	∧					
Vrij & Winkel (1994)	∧	∧					
Vrij & Semin (1996)	∧	∧					
West (1992)			—	∧			
Westcott et al. (1991)	∧	∧			∧		
Woodall & Burgoon (1983)				∨	∧		
Zuckerman, Koestner et al. (1981)	∧	∧	∧	∧	∧		
Total	∧	∧	∧	—	∧	∧	∧

Non-Vocal characteristics

	Gaze	Smile	Self-manipulations	Illustrators	Hand/finger	Leg/foot	Trunk	Head	Shifting position	Eye blinking
Akehurst et al. (1996)	∨	∧	∧	∧		∧	∧	∧	∧	∧
Bond et al. (1985)	∨	∧	—	—				—	—	
Bond et al. (1990)	∨	—	∧	∨				∨		—
Bond et al. (1992)	∨,∧									
Brooks et al. (1986)	—									
Burgoon et al. (1985)	∨									
P.J. DePaulo & DePaulo(1989)	—		—					—	∧	

Study										
Desforges & Lee (1995)	<,>									
Ekman & Friesen (1972)								^		
Ekman (1988)			—			—				—
Fiedler & Walka (1993)			—							
Gordon et al. (1987)	∨	^	^			^				^
Hemsley & Doob (1978)	∨									
Koppelaar et al. (1986)		^	∨	^		^	^ ^			
Kraut (experiment 1) (1978)	∨		—			^		^ ^		
Kraut & Poe (1980)										
O'Sullivan et al. (1988)		^	^	^	^		—			
Riggio & Friedman (1983)	—	∨			^		^			
Rozelle & Baxter (1978)	∨		—							
Stiff & Miller (1986)	^	—	^	^			—		^ ^	
Taylor & Vrij (1999)	∨			^		^	^	^	^ ^	
Vrij, Winkel et al. (1991)	∨		^	^	^	^	^	^		
Vrij & Bull (1992)	∨		—			^	∨	^	^	
Vrij, Foppes et al. (1992)	∨	^	^		—	—			—	
Vrij & Winkel (1992a)		^	^		^	^				
Vrij, Akehurst et al. (1996)	∨	^	^	^	^	^	^			
Vrij & Semin (1996)	∨		^		^	^		—	^ ^	
West (1992)	∨									
Westcott et al. (1991)	^	^	^	^			^			
Zuckerman, Koestner et al. (1981)	∨	^	—		^	^	^		^	^
Total	∨	^	^	^	^	^	^	^	^	^

Signs refer to people's beliefs about behavioural clues to deception: >, observers associate an increase in the behaviour with deception; <, observers associate a decrease in the behaviour with deception; —, observers do not associate the behaviour with deception; blank, relationship was not investigated.

police interviews (Mann, Vrij & Bull, 1998) shows that many suspects do exhibit large differences in gaze aversion between truth-telling and lying. That makes gaze aversion a noticeable indicator. Unfortunately, the pattern is erratic. Some suspects look away more when they are lying, whereas others look away more when they are telling the truth. Different patterns of gaze aversion during lying and truth-telling also emerge within individuals. A clear example of the latter was the pattern of gaze aversion displayed by the convicted murderer (see Chapter 2). He looked away *while lying before* his confession, and also showed gaze aversion *while telling the truth during* his confession. Erratic patterns of behaviour can indeed be expected when the behaviour is so easy to control.

Bond and his colleagues give a different explanation for subjective indicators of deception (Bond, Omar, Pitre, Lashley, Skaggs & Kirk, 1992). They claim that it is not nervous behaviours or behaviours indicating increased cognitive load which create suspiciousness, but 'odd behaviour'—that is, non-verbal behaviour which violates normative expectations (the so-called *infrequency heuristic*) (Fiedler & Walka, 1993). This odd behaviour might be nervous behaviour, but not necessarily. People usually look at each other during conversations. How frequently and for how long they look at each other depends on the situation. For example, a passionate couple stare at each other more frequently and for longer than do strangers (Kleinke, 1986). Research has shown that, under normal circumstances, both excessive gaze aversion and excessive staring make a suspicious impression (Bond, Omar, Pitre, Lashley, Skaggs & Kirk, 1992; Desforges & Lee, 1995). Both total gaze aversion and staring deviate from the norm, are considered odd, and therefore evoke suspicion. Hence both the suspect who maintains continuous eye contact and the suspect who shows complete gaze aversion probably make a more suspicious impression on police officers than the suspect who shows intermediate levels of gaze aversion.

Baskett and Freedle (1974) varied response latency in their experiment. They found that responses were judged to be deceptive if they occurred too slowly or too quickly. The only responses judged to be truthful were those that followed an intermediate delay. Thus a husband will become suspicious if his wife answers the question of whether she is having an affair either too quickly or too slowly. People expect that formulating an answer will take a certain amount of time. If the response latency is shorter or longer than expected, this will be judged as odd and therefore elicit suspicion.

Although people sometimes associate staring and short latency periods with deception, these are not the types of behaviour that they expect liars to display when they are asked how they think liars behave. Vrij and Semin (1996) asked participants to indicate in a questionnaire whether, compared to truth-tellers, liars show 'an increase in gaze behaviour towards the conversation partner', 'a decrease in gaze behaviour' or 'similar levels of gaze behaviour'. Most participants filled in 'decrease in gaze behaviour'. A possible reason why people expect liars to show gaze aversion (and not eye contact) is that it is easier for them to explain gaze aversion than to explain eye contact. Gaze aversion may be the result of nervousness or content complexity, whereas eye contact can only be explained by overcontrol of behaviour (see Chapter 2). Observers probably think more about nervousness and content complexity than about overcontrol when they think of deceptive behaviour.

The differing findings of Bond and Vrij are probably related to the different research paradigms used in the two studies. We investigated beliefs about cues associated with deception, whereas Bond investigated perceived cues to deception. As mentioned above, people sometimes do not realize which cues they actually use to detect deception. Generally, however, a high correlation is found between beliefs about cues associated with deception and perceived cues to deception—that is, people actually use the cues that they think they use (Zuckerman, Koestner & Driver, 1981). Bonds research is important because it demonstrates the limitations of the findings presented in Table 3.1., which gives an overview of how observers generally believe that liars behave and which cues they generally attend to when trying to detect deception. However, it does not imply that people who exhibit behaviour that differs from this pattern necessarily make an honest impression.

To make the issue of perceptions of behaviour even more complicated, Aune, Levine, Ching and Yoshimoto (1993) found that the same behaviour can be assessed in different ways, depending on the circumstances under which the behaviours take place. Judges saw one of two simulated video-dating-service interviews with a woman. In the video the general appearance of the woman was manipulated to either emphasize or minimize her desirability as a partner. Her appearance was either typical of a young, fashion-conscious woman on a dinner date, or atypical for a dating situation. In both videos, the woman displayed cues stereotypically associated with deception, such as looking away from the interviewer and shifting her posture (the same behaviour was shown in both interviews). In both interviews the woman said, among other things, that she was an adventurous person who really enjoyed blind dating. Judges rated her as less deceptive when her appearance was typical for a dinner-date situation.

DO LIARS BEHAVE AS OBSERVERS EXPECT THEM TO BEHAVE?

Since people have their own beliefs about behaviours which indicate that a person is lying, it is worth asking how accurate these beliefs are in reality. Table 3.2 gives a schematic comparison of the research findings about subjective indicators of deception (column 1) and objective indicators of deception (column 2).

With regard to vocal characteristics, Table 3.2 reveals quite an overlap between the two columns, indicating that observers are reasonably aware of the vocal characteristics of deception. However, some of the objective indicators mentioned in Table 3.2 (increase in speech hesitations, increase in speech errors and slower speech rate) only seem to occur when the lie is difficult to fabricate (see Chapter 2).

Table 3.2. Objective and subjective non-verbal indicators of deception

	1 Subjective indicators[1]	2 Objective (actual) indicators[2]
Vocal characteristics		
High-pitched voice	>	>
Speech hesitations	>	>[3]
Speech errors	>	>[3]
Slow speech rate	>	>[3]
Latency period	>	—
Pause durations	>	>
Frequency of pauses	>	—
Non-vocal characteristics		
Gaze aversion	>	—
Smiling	>	—
Eye blinks	>	—
Illustrators	>	<
Self-manipulations	>	—
Hand and finger	>	<
Leg and foot	>	<
Head	—	—
Trunk	>	—
Position shifts	>	—

[1] >, observers associate an increase in the behaviour with deception;
  <, observers associate a decrease in the behaviour with deception;
  —, observers do not associate the behaviour with deception.
[2] >, increases during deception;
  <, decreases during deception;
  —, no relationship with deception.
[3] when the lie is difficult to fabricate.

Easy lies (concealments or well-planned lies) are not associated with this behavioural pattern, and may even be associated with the opposite pattern. However, there is no evidence that observers are aware of this.

Table 3.2 further shows that most beliefs about non-vocal indicators of deception are inaccurate. Observers associate more non-verbal behaviours with deception than actually indicate deceit. For example, subjective indicators such as gaze aversion, trunk movements, self-manipulations and shifting positions are not actual indicators of deception. Finally, observers believe that deception is associated with an *increase* in hand, arm, foot and leg movements, whereas in fact deception is associated with a *decrease* in hand and arm movements (particularly non-functional subtle hand and finger movements) and in foot and leg movements. As mentioned previously, observers seem to expect nervous behaviours and behaviours that indicate the person is thinking hard, whereas liars often do not show such behaviours.

WHY ARE THERE DIFFERENCES BETWEEN OBJECTIVE AND SUBJECTIVE INDICATORS OF DECEPTION?

There are at least three possible reasons why people have wrong assumptions about the behaviours that liars show.

- It might be a matter of experience (Köhnken, 1990, 1996). Almost everyone can think of somebody at some time who acted nervously during deception, and who was subsequently caught out because of this nervousness. Lie-catchers may then wrongly assume that all liars behave in this way. I came across a good example a couple of years ago when I spoke with a member of the Dutch military police. The Dutch military police are, among others, responsible for checking passports at airports. The military police officer told me that he thought that his organization was good at detecting lies. To support this view he showed me a videotape on which passengers were visible who were showing their passports to an officer in the military police. One woman was clearly nervous, which raised the officer's suspicion. He carefully checked her passport and discovered that it was a false document. I asked whether one or more of the other passengers on the tape who did not show nervous behaviour were in possession of a false document as well. This was not known because the passports of these passengers were not thoroughly examined. This is unfortunate, because it is possible that some other passengers who did not show nervous behaviour were in possession of a false passport as well, as not all people with false passports will exhibit nervous behaviour.

- It is remarkable that differences between objective and subjective indicators of deception exist, as this gives the impression that the behaviour we show when we are lying differs from the behaviour which other people show when they are lying! For example, if we lie we tend to decrease our movements, whereas we think that other people increase their movements during deception. Why do we think that we are an exception? Research has shown that we do not think of ourselves as exceptional, but instead that we do not know how we behave when we are lying. Vrij, Semin and Bull (1996) interviewed their participants twice. In one interview they were lying and in the other interview they were telling the truth. After the second interview, they asked their participants to indicate in a questionnaire how they thought they had behaved during the two interviews. These answers were compared with the actual behaviour the participants showed during both interviews. The results showed that the participants were not aware of the behaviour they had shown during the interviews. Although they actually showed fewer movements when they were lying compared to when they were telling the truth, they thought that they had made more movements during deception! Thus while detecting lies in others, people are looking for cues which they think (incorrectly) reveal their own lies.
- When expressing their ideas about how deceivers behave, people may tend to think of settings in which nervous behaviours might well occur, such as situations in which the stakes are apparently high or in which liars are taken by surprise. Their beliefs may be different when they are asked about other, less exceptional situations. Recently, we investigated this in a series of experiments (Taylor & Vrij, 1999; Vrij, 1998b; Vrij & Taylor, 1999) in which we asked observers to indicate their beliefs about deceptive behaviour in several specific situations. For example, in one study (Vrij, 1998b) I introduced four different scenarios in which the stakes and content complexity were systematically manipulated. The scenarios describe a driver who was interviewed by a police officer about a car accident which was caused by the driver. However, the driver did not want to admit this and told the police officer that she was innocent. In half of the scenarios the consequences of the accident were serious because someone was killed (high stakes), and in the remaining half of the scenarios it was only a minor accident (low stakes). In half of the scenarios there was a witness who implicated the driver (high cognitive demand), and in the remaining half of the scenarios there was no further evidence to help the police officer to determine the facts (low cognitive demand). The participants realized that the consequences were

more serious in the serious car accident than in the minor car accident scenario, but they expected the same nervous behaviours in all of the scenarios. Apparently observers are not fully aware that the behaviour displayed by liars depends on the situation.

Box 3.1. Creating suspects in police interviews

It is possible that the interaction with suspects in police interviews results in subtle changes in the behaviour displayed by police officers during these interviews. For example, police officers may become irritated by the information a suspect gives or refuses to give, which may result in subtle movements made by the police officer. Our recent study showed that this eventually leads to a more suspicious impression made by the suspect (Akehurst & Vrij, 1999). A police officer interviewed a number of interviewees (college students) in simulated police interviews. The movements made by the police officer in these interviews were manipulated so that he made more subtle hand and finger movements in the experimental condition than in the control condition. The results showed that this manipulation affected the movements made by the interviewees. They 'imitated' the behaviour displayed by the police officer—that is, interviewees in the experimental condition made more subtle hand and finger movements than interviewees in the control condition, a phenomenon called *interactional synchrony*. In a follow-up experiment, police detectives were shown a sample of these interviews (five interviews from the experimental condition and five interviews from the control condition) and were asked to judge the suspiciousness of the interviewees. The results showed that the interviewees in the experimental condition made a more suspicious impression than the interviewees in the control condition, due to the fact that the interviewees in the experimental condition made more hand and finger movements. None of the judges had noticed that the police officer made more hand and finger movements in these interviews as well.

THE ABILITY OF PEOPLE TO DETECT LIES

Obviously, people's ability to detect lies depends on the circumstances. In cases where the negative consequences of being caught are minor and the lie does not require much mental effort, it will often be impossible to detect deception by observing someone's behaviour. The girl who tells her friend that she likes her friend's new dress, but who in fact does not like it, will probably not show any behaviour that will betray her lie. It is more difficult to lie when the stakes are raised and the lie becomes cognitively more difficult. It might therefore be possible to detect lies in such cases. In the scientific studies concerning the detection of deception, observers (mostly college students) are typically given videotapes or audiotapes and asked to judge whether each of a number of people is lying or telling the truth. The alternatives to choose from in these studies are 'the person is lying' or 'the person is not lying', resulting in a 50% chance of giving the correct answer just by guessing. In most studies liars immediately have to fabricate an answer, which makes these lies cognitively rather complicated. Moreover, there are usually some negative consequences involved for those who are not successful in lying, and hence the stakes are moderately high (although of course, never as high as in some real-life situations). In most studies on detection of deception, videotapes of the deception studies which were described in Chapter 2 were used as material to show to the lie detectors.

Kraut (1980) published a review of studies concerning the detection of deception. The percentages of lie detection (or the accuracy rate) in most of these studies ranged from 45% to 60%, when 50% accuracy was expected by chance alone. The mean (average) accuracy rate was 57%. Apparently people are not very good at detecting lies (although detection accuracy slightly but significantly exceeds that expected by chance in many published studies).

Theoretically, accuracy in detecting deception should vary with the ability to control the channels of communication. Liars should be most successful in deceiving others when using facial expressions (because this is the easiest channel to control; see Chapter 2) and least successful when using body movements and tone of voice cues (because these channels are less controllable). The combined results of more than 30 studies support this hypothesis (DePaulo, Stone & Lassiter, 1985). Observers are able to detect deception at a rate slightly above the level expected by chance when they only hear the voice, or only see the trunk and arms, but they score no better than would be expected by chance in detecting deceit if they only have access to facial cues (by which I mean hearing the voice literally; in these studies filtered speech is usually used so that the lie detector does not understand what the speaker is saying). Furthermore, observers perform less well if facial cues are available in combination with other channels than if they only have access to these other channels. That is, lie detectors who just see body movements are more accurate in detecting lies than those who see both body movements and facial expressions. The explanation is obvious. People rely strongly on facial information to detect deceit, but most facial sources of information are not reliable indicators of deception. These data suggest that, when trying to detect lies, the best strategy may be not to pay attention to the face at all, and to focus on body movements and vocal characteristics alone! However, this strategy may be too rigid because, as mentioned in Chapter 2, facial micro-expressions of emotions may also reveal lies (Ekman, 1992).

Kraut published his review in 1980, and many studies have been published since then. Appendix 3.1 provides an overview of studies conducted from 1980 onward. Included are studies in which the observers were lay people (not professional lie-catchers) who were asked to detect lies in people with whom they were not familiar (not friends or lovers). Studies involving professional lie-catchers, friends and lovers will be discussed separately.

Appendix 3.1 gives an overview of 39 studies. The majority of the accuracy rates fall in the range 45–60%, and the mean accuracy rate is 56.6%. This is almost identical to the 57% accuracy rate found by Kraut (1980).

If accuracy in detecting lies is computed separately from accuracy in detecting truth, the results usually show a *truth bias* (Köhnken, 1989; Zuckerman, DePaulo & Rosenthal, 1981). That is, judges are more likely to consider that messages are truthful than that they are deceptive and, as a result, truthful messages are identified with more accuracy than are deceptive ones. In fact, my own review (see Appendix 3.1) shows that observers are reasonably good at detecting truths (67% accuracy rate) but particularly poor at detecting lies (44% accuracy rate). There are four possible explanations for the truth bias. First, in daily life people are more often confronted with truthful state-ments than with deceptive ones, so they are therefore more inclined to assume that the behaviour they observe is honest (the so-called *avail-ability heuristic*; O'Sullivan, Ekman & Friesen, 1988). Secondly, the rules of social conversation prevent people from being suspicious. A person will very quickly become irritated if their conversation partner questions everything that is being said. Imagine a conversation in which someone interrupts you all the time by saying things like 'I don't believe you', 'That cannot be true', or 'Could you prove that?' The conversation would probably not last very long. Unfortunately, it is often necessary to challenge what the other person is saying and ask for more information in order to find out why people are behaving in the way they are at a particular time, and to find out whether someone is lying (see Chapter 2). Thirdly, people have stereotypical views about how liars and truth-tellers behave. For example, most people expect liars to behave nervously and truth-tellers to behave normally, and they are often guided by these beliefs when trying to detect deceit. This results in truths being more often accurately detected than lies, as their stereotypical views about truth-tellers are more accurate than their views about liars. Fourthly, people may be unsure as to whether deception is in fact occurring. Given this uncertainty, the safest and most polite strategy may be to believe what is overtly expressed (DePaulo, Jordan, Irvine & Laser, 1982).

FACTORS THAT INFLUENCE THE ABILITY TO DETECT DECEIT

There are numerous factors that influence a person's ability to detect deceit. Some of these factors are related to the lie detector, while others are related to the liar or to the interaction between liar and lie detector. A third group of factors is related to the lie-detection task, particularly the possible disadvantages for lie-detectors attempting to detect lies in a laboratory setting compared to catching liars in real-life situations. I shall discuss the former setting first.

Lack of Reality in the Laboratory

Catching a liar in a laboratory experiment differs from detecting deceit in a real-life situation. However, this does not imply that a lie-detection task is easier outside the laboratory than inside it. Some differences make the task easier, and others make it more difficult (see also Zuckerman, DePaulo & Rosenthal, 1981). Compared to real-life situations, lie detectors in the laboratory have the following constraints.

- They have to make their decision quickly as to whether or not someone is lying (usually within 10 seconds), and do not have time to think about their decisions.
- They can only observe the supposed liar for a short time (usually for less than 1 minute), and would probably wish to observe the person they are exposed to for a longer time. However, the question is how realistic this would be. At present, we are analysing videotaped police interviews with suspects (Mann, Vrij & Bull, as part of a research project funded by the Economic and Social Research Council). One preliminary finding is that the lies which suspects tell tend to be short. One reason for this is that lies are often incorporated in truthful stories. Suspects tell stories which are largely accurate but lie only about certain (crucial) details, such as the time when the event took place or their particular role in the event (e.g. 'I was there, but I was not the one who stole the money'). Another reason is that lies sometimes consist of concise, total denials (e.g. 'I have nothing to do with it, I was at home, I was tired and went to bed early'). In other words, lengthy lies are rare, which makes the laboratory studies more realistic than one might think.
- They are passive observers. They are watching a video and therefore do not have the opportunity actually to interview the potential liars. However, it is doubtful, whether this is a limitation. In a study conducted by Stiff, Kim and Ramesh (1992), observers actually interviewed the potential deceiver. The detection rates were not higher than the accuracy rates in studies involving passive

observers. In their studies, Buller and his colleagues compared the accuracy scores of observers who actually interviewed potential liars with those who observed the interviews but did not interview the potential liars themselves (Buller, Strzyzewski & Hunsaker, 1991). The results revealed that the observers were more accurate in detecting lies (49% accuracy score) than the interviewers (29% accuracy score). More recently, Feeley and deTurck (1997) also found that observers were more accurate in lie detection (50%) than interviewers (43%). These findings suggest that actually interviewing someone is a disadvantage and not an advantage in detecting deceit. This is perhaps unsurprising. First, interviewers need to concentrate on the interview itself. For instance, they have to decide what to ask, how to phrase these questions, and at what moment in the interview they are going to ask these questions. In addition, they must put effort into their self-presentation, must listen to the interviewees and must reply to what they say. This requires cognitive resources which cannot be devoted to the lie-detection task. Observers, on the other hand, do not have to bother about the flow of the conversation and can concentrate fully, if they wish, on the lie-detection task. Secondly, the lower accuracy rates for interviewers may be the result of a truth bias among interviewers. Interviewers tend to believe a potential liar more often than observers do (Feeley & deTurck, 1997; Granhag & Strömwall, 1998). The reason for this truth bias among interviewers is unclear (see Burgoon and Newton (1991) and Feeley and deTurck (1997) for some suggestions).

An additional advantage for observers is that they can thoroughly observe the potential liar—literally from head to foot. Active interviewers cannot do this, as it will make an odd impression. Conversation rules prescribe that conversation partners look each other in the eyes. However, eye movements do not give reliable information about deception. An observer does not have to concentrate on someone's face, and thus can pay attention to other more useful pieces of information. It may therefore be a good idea to introduce observers in police interviews, who sit in a different room and watch the interview via a video-link system. They will then have the opportunity to observe more of the suspect without being disturbed.

A liar's statement or action may result in a reaction of the interviewer—for example, in asking for a further explanation. There are different ways of doing this, namely in a neutral way (e.g. 'I don't understand this, could you please explain this to me?'), in a positive way (e.g. 'I do believe you, but I don't understand this. How is it possible that...?') or in a negative way (e.g. 'I don't believe you, you are trying to fool me'). At first sight, you might think that further questioning facilitates the task of the lie detector. The liar is forced to continue to speak and is compelled to give more information. Obviously the more liars speak and the more information they give, the greater the likelihood that they will make a mistake and will give the lie away, either via verbal cues (by contradicting themselves or by saying something which the observer knows is incorrect) or via non-verbal cues. This reasoning is probably true when probing continues, but not in the initial stage of further questioning. Several studies have shown that liars, at least initially, make a more honest impression as a result of further questioning (Buller, Comstock, Aune & Strzyzewski, 1989; Buller, Strzyzewski & Comstock, 1991; Levine, McCornack & Aleman, 1997; Stiff & Miller, 1986). The type of probing (neutral, negative or positive) does not have an impact on this. Thus initially liars make a more honest impression even when they are accused of lying. In other words, probing initially benefits the liar.

It is not entirely clear why this is so. Stiff and his colleagues argue that as soon as liars realize that the observer is becoming suspicious, they will respond by showing more 'honest behaviour' (Buller, Stiff & Burgoon, 1996; Stiff & Miller, 1986). Levine and colleagues (Levine & McCornack, 1996a; Levine, McCornack & Aleman, 1997) dispute this view, and I agree with them. As was mentioned in Chapter 2, probing does not result in more honest behaviour. It results, among other behaviours, in more stutters and self-manipulations. Recently, Levine, McCornack and Aleman (1997) offered an alternative explanation. They suggested that many observers will believe that it is too difficult for liars to continue lying when they are challenged, and that people are probably speaking the truth when they do not change their original story, or when they continue denying. However, there is another possible explanation. It might be that lie detectors think that it will be difficult for liars to persist in lying when they are challenged, and that they therefore expect liars to show nervous behaviour or to display behaviour which indicates that they have to think hard when challenged. A liar will therefore make an honest impression as long as such behaviours do not occur.

- The stakes are not usually very high for the liar in the laboratory. It is therefore possible that their lies are associated with relatively few non-verbal cues (see Chapter 2). Obviously, the fewer deception cues that are present in the non-verbal behaviour of the liar, the more difficult it will be for the lie detector to detect a lie.
- The observers are asked to detect lies told by people they do not know, and they are therefore not familiar with their natural behaviour.

Familiarity with the potential liar does indeed increase the ability to detect lies, as will be discussed further later in this chapter.

However, there are several advantages for the lie detector in the laboratory.

- In laboratory experiments, a random sample of people is usually taken and they are all 'forced' to lie. These samples will include people who consider themselves to be bad liars and therefore hardly ever lie in daily life. These inexperienced liars might be easy to detect.
- Liars in the laboratory are told about the topic on which they have to lie. This might well be a topic with which they are not familiar. In daily life, people can restrict themselves to lies concerning topics they know about.
- Lie detectors in the laboratory are aware that someone will try to dupe them. They will therefore be alert and will observe the supposed liar carefully. In daily life, people do not usually know when someone is going to lie to them, and they are therefore less attentive most of the time. In fact, people will often be unattentive because they generally have too much good faith—that is, they assume too often that others speak the truth. Obviously people will never become good lie detectors if they take too much of the information they receive for granted. One way to decrease credulity is to point out to lie detectors that people try to dupe them more often than they might think. Research has indicated that such an intervention does decrease a person's good faith, but does not increase their accuracy in detecting deception (Stiff, Kim & Ramesh, 1992; Toris & DePaulo, 1985). In other words, as a result of such information lie detectors tend to believe fewer statements, including those which are truthful. It is not difficult to explain these findings. People are told that they have too much good faith, but do not know where to look to detect a lie. Feeley and Young (1997) therefore correctly pointed out that merely diminishing people's good faith is not sufficient to make them better lie detectors. They should also be told where to look in order to detect lies.
- Lie detectors in the laboratory have the opportunity to observe the supposed liar carefully, often literally from head to foot. This may be very useful for detecting deceit, as the absence of subtle movements may give away the lie. As mentioned above, in real life it appears odd if someone observes the other person from head to foot.

In summary, the laboratory provides a lie detector with both advantages and disadvantages. It is therefore difficult to say whether it is easier or more difficult to detect lies in the laboratory than in the outside world.

However, either way, due to these many differences between real life and the laboratory, it is probably better to be somewhat cautious in drawing conclusions about the ability to detect lies in real life on the basis of performance in the laboratory.

Characteristics of the Lie Detector

Professional Lie-catchers

Most studies related to the detection of deception have used college students as lie detectors. They are probably less experienced in detecting lies than professional lie-catchers such as police officers, police detectives or customs officers. It might be the case that these professional lie-catchers make better lie detectors than college students, due to their experience in this area. To my knowledge, eight studies have been conducted to date using professional lie-catchers as observers. These studies are listed in Table 3.3.

DePaulo and Pfeifer (1986) asked their participants—258 federal law enforcement officers, both experienced ($n = 114$) and new recruits ($n = 144$)—to detect deception when listening to audiotapes of target individuals who were answering questions about their attitudes and opinions in front of a panel. In Ekman and O'Sullivan's deception task, observers (including 34 members of the Secret Service, 60 federal polygraphers and

Table 3.3. Accuracy scores of professional lie-catchers

	Accuracy rates (%)		
	Truth	Lie	Total
DePaulo & Pfeifer (1986) (federal law enforcement personnel, experienced)	64[1]	42[1]	52
DePaulo & Pfeifer (1986) (federal law enforcement personnel, new recruits)			53
Ekman & O'Sullivan (1991) (Secret Service)			64
Ekman & O'Sullivan (1991) (Federal polygraphers)			56
Ekman & O'Sullivan (1991) (police officers)			56
Garrido, Masip, Herrero, Tabernero & Vega (1998) (police officers)	26	69	49
Köhnken (1987) (police officers)	58	31	45
Vrij (1993a) (police detectives)	51	46	49
Vrij & Graham (1997) (police officers)			54
Vrij & Mann (in press) (police officers)	70	57	64
Vrij & Mann (1999) (police officers)		50	

[1] Accuracy rates for experienced officers and new recruits together.

126 police officers) were asked to detect deception on the basis of video-tapes of nurses who described how they felt about a film they were watching. In the study by Garrido, Masip, Herrero, Tabernero and Vega (1998), 121 police students from a Spanish police academy watched a female sender who gave truthful and deceptive statements about a film she had watched previously. Köhnken showed 80 police officers videotapes of people who recalled a film (about a theft and a fight) they had just seen. Vrij showed 91 police detectives videotapes of people who denied the possession of a set of headphones. A similar procedure was used by Vrij and Graham (1997). In their study, 29 police officers participated. Vrij and Mann (in press) showed 65 police officers videotaped fragments of the police interview with the convicted murderer (this case was discussed in Chapter 2). Vrij and Mann (1999) showed 52 uniformed police officers videotaped real-life press conferences of people who were asking the general public for help in finding their relatives or the murderers of their relatives when, in fact, they were eventually deemed to be the murderers themselves. Table 3.3 shows the accuracy rates obtained in these studies.

Table 3.3 shows that the professional lie-catchers' accuracy rates mostly fall in the range 45–60%, when an accuracy rate of 50% is expected by chance alone. The mean (average) accuracy rate is 54%, which was similar to the accuracy rate (56.6%) found in studies with college students as observers. Hence we may conclude that professional lie-catchers are no better at detecting deception than are college students. The three studies conducted by DePaulo and Pfeifer (1986), Ekman and O'Sullivan (1991), and Garrido and colleagues actually support this conclusion. In these studies, college students were included as observers as well. DePaulo and Pfeifer (1986) found that law-enforcement personnel (both new recruits and experienced officers) were as good as (or perhaps it is better to say as bad as) college students in detecting deception. Ekman and O'Sullivan found that only members of the Secret Service were better at detecting lies than college students. I shall return to this issue later on in this chapter. Garrido's findings showed that university students were better at lie detection than police students. It is interesting to see that even in Ekman and O'Sullivan's study the accuracy rates were rather low. These observers were exposed to video clips of people who were facing a difficult task. First, they had to say that they were amused while they were watching burns and amputa-tions, and secondly the stakes were high because they were led to believe that being successful in the deception task was associated with being successful in their career. The results thus show that even in such a difficult situation many people can successfully get away with their lies.

The studies conducted by Vrij and Mann are interesting because these are the only studies so far where observers were exposed to realistic and high-stake lies, namely the videotape of a convicted murderer (Vrij & Mann, in press) or videotaped footage of press conferences with people who have been deemed to have killed their own relatives (Vrij & Mann, 1999), (none of the observers in either study knew about the cases which were shown). The fact that the accuracy rate obtained in the convicted murderer study was slightly higher than the accuracy rates obtained in most of the other studies may support the view that detecting real-life lies is easier than detecting lies told in the laboratory. A more detailed look at the findings of this study indicates that this is not entirely true, as the high accuracy score (64%) was caused by the fact that the observers were much better at detecting the murderer's truths (70%) than they were at detecting his lies (57%). The press conference study also found a low accuracy rate for detecting lies (50%). Hence, even in these realistic situations, police officers' skills in detecting lies were rather modest. The average accuracy rate for detecting lies in the studies listed in Table 3.3 was slightly lower (49%) than the accuracy rate for detecting truths (54%).

An interesting finding in the studies conducted by DePaulo and Pfeifer and by Garrido and colleagues was that police officers were more confident than students in their decision-making, suggesting that professional lie-catchers are more confident, not more accurate, than lay people in detecting lies.

Confidence. The strong confidence that professional lie-catchers have in their ability to catch a liar can be harmful in their deception-detection task, as it is likely that when individuals are highly confident in their ability to detect deception, they are less likely to scrutinize a person's behaviour actively (Levine & McCornack, 1992; Lord, Ross & Lepper, 1979). High levels of confidence often result in quick decisions being made on the basis of limited information. Imagine the following situation. Someone is ready to go on holiday by car. Unfortunately, the weather is particularly bad at the time when the person wants to leave. In such a situation, an insecure driver would probably obtain more information about the circumstances on the road than an experienced driver, and would therefore make a more well-considered decision as to whether or not to drive. For example, the insecure driver will listen to the weather forecast to find out how the situation will develop. The experienced driver will probably rely on inadequate heuristics such as 'The weather cannot stay that bad for a very long time' or 'The weather is notoriously bad here, but it will probably improve when I get nearer to my holiday destination', and so on. Similarly, high confidence in deception detection may also lead to the use of inadequate heuristics, such as 'liars look away', 'liars stutter', and so on. The use of heuristics in detecting deception is fundamentally wrong. As mentioned in

Chapter 2, the relationship between deception and non-verbal behaviour is too complicated to translate into simple heuristics.

Lack of feedback. The fact that professional lie-catchers seem to be as inaccurate as lay people in detecting lies indicates that professional lie-catchers do not appear to learn how to interpret non-verbal behaviour validly from their daily work experience. One explanation concerns the feedback they usually receive about the accuracy of the decisions that they make. It may be that real-life experience in detecting lies results in better insight among professional lie-catchers only when they receive adequate outcome feedback—that is, adequate information as to whether their truth/lie judgements are either right or wrong. In real life such outcome feedback is usually lacking (DePaulo & Pfeifer, 1986). Consider, for example, customs officers. Good feedback in their occupation means that they gain insight into how many of the travellers they stopped and searched did actually try to smuggle, but also how many of the travellers they did *not* stop tried to smuggle. The latter form of feedback is usually lacking. They will almost never find out whether or not the travellers they did not search were smuggling goods, and they therefore cannot learn from these cases.[1]

It may well be the case that a customs officer who has caught many smugglers in his career, and therefore believes himself to be good at detecting lies, turns out to be less successful when the number of smugglers who managed to dupe this particular officer is taken into account.

A study conducted by Vrij and Semin (1996) supported the feedback argument. They investigated, via a questionnaire, beliefs about non-verbal indicators of deception of various groups, namely college students, customs officers, prison guards, uniformed police officers, police detectives and prisoners. Several differences emerged between these groups, including the following differences in beliefs concerning gaze aversion and hand and finger movements.

Gaze aversion (Figure 3.1) is not a reliable indicator of deception—that is, liars and truth-tellers usually show similar patterns of gaze aversion. However, many students, customs officers, uniformed police officers and detectives, indicated that they considered that gaze aversion is associated with deception. The actual relationship (there is none) was mentioned most frequently by prisoners.

Many people show a decrease in hand and finger movements when they are lying. A relatively large number of prisoners marked this relationship

---

[1] There is a very easy way to investigate how good customs officers are at catching smugglers. Ask them to stop 100 people randomly and let them indicate for each person whether they think that that person tried to smuggle. Then search all 100 people in order to find out to what extent the officer's intuitions were correct.

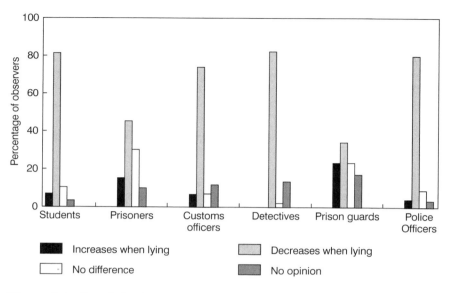

Figure 3.1. Gaze behaviour.

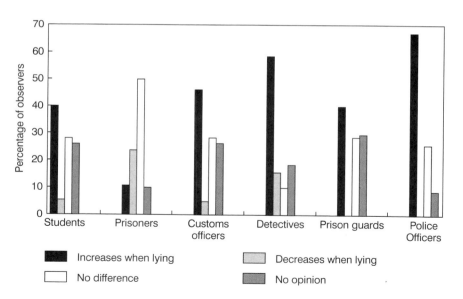

Figure 3.2. Hand and finger movements.

(Figure 3.2). On the other hand, students, customs officers, uniformed police officers and police detectives mainly associated an increase in such movements with deception.

These two examples reveal that prisoners had more accurate beliefs about the actual relationship between non-verbal behaviour and deception than did both professional lie-catchers and lay people. This suggestion was further supported by the other outcomes of the study. Prisoners had more accurate beliefs about the relationship between non-verbal behaviour and deception than any of the other groups. The beliefs of the other groups did not differ significantly from each other. We explained this by suggesting that prisoners are likely to have the most adequate feedback. We stated that:

> 'Criminals live in a culture that is much more deceptive than the world that "normal" people live in. Associating with other criminals as well as generally unsavoury people in the underworld may expose any sample of prisoners to a great deal of posing, bluffing, threats, promises, "cons", and so forth, many of which may be false or dishonest. Being successful in, and adapting to, such a world depends in part on the ability to tell when you are being lied to' (Vrij & Semin, 1996, p.67).

A second study that I conducted provided further evidence that professional lie catchers are not fully aware which non-verbal behavioural cues indicate deception (Vrij, 1993a). In this study, 91 police detectives were exposed to short videotaped interviews with 20 students who were or were not lying about the possession of a set of headphones. The detectives were requested to indicate whether each person was lying or not. Some information was known to me about these 20 people—for example, how they behaved during the interviews, as their gaze aversion, smiling, speech hesitations, speech errors, pitch of voice, and movements of the trunk, head, hands, fingers, arms, feet and legs had been scored. In addition, physical characteristics (gender and style of dress) and personality traits (social anxiety and public self-consciousness) were measured (these traits were investigated via a questionnaire which was completed prior to the interviews). First of all, the results showed that the police detectives were not good at detecting the students' lies. Their accuracy rate was 49%, which is close to the level expected by chance (50%). Secondly, and interestingly, even though the detectives did not successfully identify the liars, the level of agreement among them about who was lying and who was telling the truth was high. Because many detectives made similar decisions, their judgements must have been based on the same cues, or they must have processed the cues in a similar manner. Therefore it seemed reasonable to examine the way in which the detectives processed the cues. In order to determine this, I conducted a statistical test called regression analysis, which gives insight into the cues the detectives actually used to make their decisions (so-called cues to perceived deception; see the beginning of this chapter). The results are shown in Figure 3.3.

The analysis of the behaviour displayed by the 20 students in the videotape revealed one noteworthy difference between liars and truth-tellers. Liars actually made fewer hand and finger movements than those who were telling the truth. The detectives could therefore have caught many liars by paying attention to their hands and fingers. Figure 3.3 shows that the detectives did examine hand and finger movements, but that they made the wrong decision, as they thought that those who made *more* hand and finger movements were lying. They were further influenced by the smiles the students produced, although smiling was not a reliable indicator of deception. Students' personality traits also had an impact on the decisions made by the police detectives. Socially anxious students made a more dishonest impression than those who were not socially anxious, and those who scored high in public self-consciousness were believed more than those who scored low in public self-consciousness. Apparently the detectives interpreted the behaviour displayed by the people who had less public self-consciousness and more social anxiety not as a form of natural behaviour, but as deceptive behaviour. Even the style of clothing had an impact on the detectives' decisions. Those students who were smartly dressed made a more honest impression than those who were not so well dressed. Obviously it is dubious to base the decision as to whether people are lying or not on the style of their clothing. Finally, the police detectives took the speech

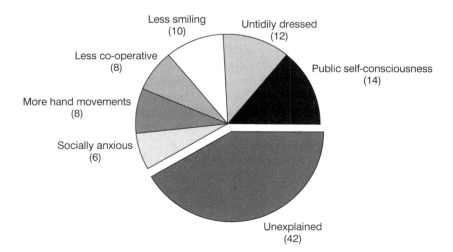

Figure 3.3. Cues used by the detectives

content into account as well. The students who were more co-operative throughout the interview made a more honest impression than those who were less co-operative. None of the indicators that the police detectives were using were reliable indicators of deception. It is therefore not surprising that they were duped by the students.

Gender of the Observer

Women express themselves non-verbally more clearly and more dynamically than do men. They smile and gaze at others more than men do, approach others more closely, and are more tactile (DePaulo, Epstein & Wyer, 1993). The result is that women elicit more warmth than men. Women are also better than men at expressing their thoughts and feelings with facial expressions. They are also better at reading other people's non-verbal behaviour—that is, they are better than men at understanding the messages that others want them to convey (Hall, 1979, 1984; Rosenthal & DePaulo, 1979). They have the greatest advantage over men in reading facial expressions, which are the ones that are easiest for people to control (see also Chapter 2) (DePaulo, Epstein & Wyer, 1993). Women take more time when observing and interpreting non-verbal cues, and they use more cues in their decision-making process (Hurd & Noller, 1988).

Hall (1979, cited in DePaulo, Epstein & Wyer, 1993) examined women's superiority over men in understanding non-verbal messages in 11 different countries. She found that women were most skilled at this in those countries in which they seemed to be most oppressed (e.g. in countries in which there were proportionately fewer women in higher education). A tendency to accommodate might be the explanation for this. Women's gender role in many societies implies that they have to accommodate themselves to others more than men do. Knowing how to interpret people's non-verbal behaviour accurately may be very valuable in helping them to achieve this.

Although women are superior to men in interpreting non-verbal messages, they are not better than men at detecting lies (DePaulo, Epstein & Wyer, 1993; Hurd & Noller, 1988; Manstead, Wagner & MacDonald, 1986). However, McCornack and Parks (1990) found that women were better than men at detecting lies told by their partner. Women are less suspicious than men, and more often think that someone is telling the truth (DePaulo, Epstein & Wyer, 1993). The following explanation sounds reasonable. Women are better than men in decoding the information that a person wants to convey. However, during deception, liars try to *hide* their true feelings and thoughts. When detecting lies, observers should not look at what people *want to convey* but at what they *are trying to conceal*. However, women are not better trained than men at doing this. When they try to detect lies they are probably too much affected by what someone is trying to convey, which makes them more credulous than men.

Characteristics of the liar

Familiarity with the Liar

In most studies of the detection of deception, observers are asked to detect lies told by people they do not know. Although this does often happen in real-life situations (e.g. when judging salespeople or politicians), many situations will involve detecting lies told by people with whom we are familiar. It seems reasonable to suggest that it should be easier to detect lies in people we know than in strangers. For example, we are more familiar with the natural behaviour of people we know, and are therefore able to detect even minor changes in their behaviour. Research has consistently indicated that people become better at detecting truths and lies when they are familiar with the truthful behaviour of the person they have to judge (Brandt, Miller & Hocking, 1980a, b, 1982; Feeley, deTurck & Young, 1995). For example, Feeley and his colleagues exposed some observers to baseline interviews of the people they had to assess in the lie-detection task. Their accuracy rates were significantly higher (72%) than the accuracy rates of observers (56%) who were not exposed to baseline interviews prior to the lie-detection task. However, O'Sullivan, Ekman and Friesen (1988) found that baseline messages only benefited observers when these messages were truthful. They argued that, since observers are inclined to assume that the behaviour they observe is honest (availability heuristic), they are more likely to assume that the first behaviour (i.e. baseline behaviour) they see is honest rather than dishonest. If the first behaviour is honest, then it becomes easier to identify subsequent different behaviour as dishonest. However, if the first behaviour is actually deceptive but mislabelled as honest, then errors may occur when subsequent behaviours are assessed.

There is no support for the assumption that it is easier to detect lies in friends or lovers than in strangers (see Table 3.4). The average accuracy rate in the studies listed in Table 3.4 is 58%, which is slightly higher than the average accuracy rate found with strangers (56.6%; see Appendix 3.1). Miller, Mongeau and Sleight (1986) mentioned a study conducted by Bauchner which indicated that friends detected 74% of each other's lies. This is a high accuracy rate, which as far as I know has never been found in research with strangers. However, this finding has not been replicated in other studies. Buller and his colleagues (Buller,

Table 3.4. Accuracy rates of lay observers judging friends or lovers

	Accuracy rates (%)		
	Truth	Lie	Total
Bauchner (friends) (cited in Miller, Mongeau & Sleight, 1986)			74
Levine, McCornack & Park (1998) (not married couples)	82	34	58
McCornack & Levine (1990) (not married couples)			58[1]
McCornack & Parks (1986) (not married couples)			59
Millar & Millar (1995) (study 1: friends and relatives)			46[2]
Millar & Millar (1995) (study 2: friends and relatives)			51[2]

[1] All conditions combined.
[2] Voice and video information condition.

Strzyzewski & Comstock, 1991a) found no differences in accuracy rates when observers judged truths and lies told by friends or strangers. Millar and Millar (1995) found that observers were less accurate when they judged friends (46% hit rate) than when they assessed strangers (54% hit rate). Comadena (1982) found no differences in accuracy rates when judging friends or intimates.

In a series of studies, McCornack and Levine have shown that even lies told by intimates are difficult to detect (see also Table 3.4). They argue that this is due to the fact that, as relationships become more intimate, partners develop a strong tendency to judge the other as truthful, the so-called *relational truth-bias heuristic* (Levine, McCornack & Park, 1999). McCornack and Parks have developed and tested a model to explain this (described in Levine & McCornack, 1992). As soon as the relationship between two people intensifies, they will become more confident that they can detect each other's lies ('I know the other person very well, I am able to tell whether he or she is lying'). High levels of confidence will then result in the belief that the other person probably would not dare to lie ('The other had better watch out, I will detect every lie that person tells me'). This will result in putting less and less effort into trying to discover whether the person is lying ('I don't have to worry that much, the other does not lie to me anyway') (Stiff, Kim & Ramesh, 1992). Obviously, the less effort someone puts into trying to detect deceit, the easier it will be to dupe that person.

However, these findings seem to contradict the results of DePaulo and Kashy's (1998) diary study. They found in their study (already described in Chapter 1) that lies told to people to whom individuals felt close were more often discovered than lies told to people to whom they did not feel close. A possible explanation for this is that in McCornack and Levine's experimental studies the observers had to focus on their partner's non-verbal behaviour in order to detect lies, and their findings showed that observers are not particularly good at this. In real life, however, people are not restricted to observing a person's behaviour, and they often have the opportunity to check whether what the person actually says is true. It may well be that the participants in DePaulo's study discovered the lies told by people to whom they felt close by checking the information actually given by these liars.

Chahal and Cassidy (1995) exposed social workers, schoolteachers and students to videotapes of children (aged 8 years) who were either lying or telling the truth. For each child, the judges had to decide whether he or she was lying or not. They hypothesized that social workers and teachers would be better at this lie-detection task than students, because they are more experienced with children. Their hypothesis was not supported, but they did find, that those judges who had children of their own were better lie detectors (they detected 82% of the lies) than judges without children (they detected 52% of the lies), suggesting that having children of one's own facilitates detection of children's lies.

Familiarity with the Topic

It is easier to catch a liar when the lie detector is familiar with the topic that is being discussed by the liar (Levine, McCornack & Aleman, 1997). However, a lie detector is not any better at interpreting non-verbal behaviour when the liar is discussing a familiar topic compared to an unfamiliar one, but in the case of familiar topics has the additional benefit of being able to check the speech content to find out whether the person is lying. A mother will have to make little effort to detect her son's lie when he tells her that the library was closed, if she knows that the library was open.

Liars do realize this. They tend to tell different lies to their partners than to people they know less well (Metts, 1989). The majority of lies that people tell are outright lies (see Chapter 1). However, people are much less likely to tell outright lies to their partners, as they believe that the risks are too high and that the partner will eventually find out that they are lying. Moreover, they can expect problems as soon as the lie is detected, because how do you explain to your partner that you lied to them? Lies told to spouses are therefore usually subtle lies such as concealments. This type of lie is usually difficult to detect, because the liar does not reveal information that can be checked. The lie is also easier to justify if it emerges. It is always possible for liars to say that they simply forgot to tell the other the information, or to say that they did not mention the information before because they did not realize that the other was interested in this information, and so on.

Familiarity with the style of communication

It facilitates detection of deceit if the lie detector is familiar with the communicating style of the liar. For example, people have a more open communication style when they are speaking to attractive people than when they are speaking to unattractive people. This means that attractive and unattractive people are used to different communication styles (DePaulo, 1994). DePaulo, Tang and Stone (1987) examined whether this has an impact on detection of lies. People were asked to tell truths and lies to attractive and unattractive conversation partners. These statements were videotaped and presented to attractive and unattractive observers. On the videotape, only the potential liars were visible, not the attractive and unattractive people to whom the lies were told. The findings revealed that attractive observers were better at detecting truths and lies which were told to attractive people, whereas unattractive observers were more accurate in detecting lies and truths when they were told to unattractive people. Hence attractive or unattractive people are better at detecting lies when they are approached in a style with which they are familiar.

A similar pattern emerges when lie detectors try to detect lies that are told by people who belong to their own culture or to another culture (Bond, Omar, Mahmoud & Bonser, 1990). Observers have been found to be able to some extent to distinguish lies from truths when they were told by people of their own ethnic origin, whereas they failed to do so when the people had a different ethnic origin. For example, American observers managed to detect lies and truths at a rate above the level expected by chance when they were told by fellow Americans, but failed to do so when the people they had to judge were Jordanians. Jordanian judges showed the reverse pattern. They were able to detect lies and truths at a rate above the level of chance when they were told by other Jordanians, but not when they had to detect truths and lies which were told by Americans (observers had to assess videotaped truthful and deceptive statements which were presented without sound).

The Liar's Age

Lying is a skill which must be learned. For example, it is easier to detect lies in younger children than in older children (DePaulo, 1991; Feldman,

Jenkins & Popoola, 1979). The process of becoming more skilful in telling lies does not end at the outset of adulthood. Lie detectors have more difficulty in detecting lies told by 79-year-olds than in detecting those told by 19-year-olds (Parham, Feldman, Oster & Popoola, 1981). However, this does not mean that young children are not good at telling lies. On the contrary, some of them are surprisingly good at it. In our research (Vrij & Van Wijngaarden, 1994), for example, 5- and 6-year-olds tasted two drinks, namely grapefruit juice and orange juice. After each drink they were requested to convince the interviewer that each drink tasted good, regardless of how the drinks actually tasted. A camera recorded the children. After both interviews had been completed, each child was asked about his or her true opinions of the two drinks. Nearly all of them actually liked the orange juice but disliked the grapefruit juice. A random selection of recordings of those children who lied in one interview and told the truth in the other interview was shown to adults. After each fragment they were asked to indicate whether the child really liked the drink or not (we changed the colour of the recordings somewhat, so that the observers were unable to identify the drink on the basis of the colour in the clear glass). Only 56% of the truths and lies were detected.

In another study (Westcott, Davies & Clifford, 1991), children aged 7 to 11 years were asked to describe a visit to a museum. Some children had actually been there and could therefore truthfully describe this visit. However, other children had never been to the museum, but saw a movie about it. They were asked to pretend that they had actually been to the museum. The judges had to indicate for each child whether he or she was telling the truth or not. They were only able to detect 59% of the truths and lies.

Jackson's (1996) research clearly shows how skilled children can be in telling lies. Some children aged 11 and 12 years were shown a film about a chimpanzee, and were interviewed about this film afterwards. Another group of children of the same age did not see the film but had to pretend in the interview that they had seen it. The videotaped interviews with the children were shown to barristers and students. The results indicated that the children who did not see the videotape were very successful in duping the barristers and students. Only 31% of the barristers and 25% of the students realized that the statements of these children were false. This is a remarkable percentage, because the task the children were facing was not easy. However, most of the children in the lying condition had previously seen a film about chimpanzees, and had talked about these experiences.

Some of the children who lied were using an ingenious strategy (although they might have done this unconsciously). All of the children were asked whether they liked the film they had just seen about the chimpanzees. Those who actually saw the film said that they had liked the film more than did those who had not actually seen the film. Those liars who said that they did not like the film used this in the subsequent interview. When they were asked to describe some of the details in the film, they replied that they could not remember these details because they did not like the film and therefore did not watch it carefully. In summary, they provided a plausible reason why they could no longer remember the details.

The Personality of the Liar

One of the factors that hamper lie detection is that some individuals' non-verbal behaviour gives the impression that they are telling the truth (honest demeanour bias), whereas others' natural behaviour leaves the impression that they are lying (dishonest demeanour bias) (Riggio, Tucker & Throckmorton, 1988; Vrij, 1993a; Vrij & Van Wijngaarden, 1994; Vrij & Winkel, 1992b; Zuckerman, DeFrank, Hall, Larrance & Rosenthal, 1979). This is related to personality traits.

Expressive people, for example, exude credibility regardless of the truth of their assertions. It is not that they are particularly skilled at lying, but that their spontaneity tends to disarm suspicion, which makes it easier for them to get away with their lies (Riggio, 1986).

People with a strong sense of *public self-consciousness* also tend to make a credible impression on others, regardless of whether they are telling the truth. This is because they seem to know how to act so as to make a credible impression. For example, as was shown in Chapter 2, these are the people who tend to restrict their movements when lying, which is a behavioural pattern that observers associate with truth-fulness. These are also the people who lie frequently (see Chapter 1).

On the other hand, *introverts* and *socially anxious* people, impress others as being less credible. The social clumsiness of introverts and the impression of tension, nervousness or fear that is natural to socially anxious individuals are interpreted by observers as indicators of deception. If these results also apply to professional lie-catchers such as customs officers, and there is no reason why they should not, they then imply that introverted and socially anxious people run a higher risk of their luggage being searched than their counterparts. However, it is doubtful whether these are the types of people who smuggle much. Introverts do not lie very often (see Chapter 1), and they commit fewer crimes than extraverts (Eysenck, 1984). Furthermore, socially anxious people are the type of people who are less likely to persist in lying as soon as they are challenged (see Chapter 1).

It was also revealed in Chapter 1 that people who score high in Machiavellianism often lie. One might think that they are very good at it, because they do not experience much guilt when they lie. However, it is neither easier nor more difficult to detect lies told by people who score high in Machiavellianism than to detect lies told by people who score low in Machiavellianism (Manstead, Wagner & MacDonald, 1986).

Box 3.2. A test to examine what kind of impression you make on others

---

There may be an easy way to find out whether or not you make a credible impression on others. Riggio and Friedman (1983) found that people who are good at expressing basic emotions via facial expressions (happiness, anger, fear, surprise, sadness and disgust) make a more credible impression on observers than those who are not so good at this. Therefore try to express basic emotions with your face and ask others to determine which emotions you are trying to express. The percentage of correct answers given by the observers might be an indication of the credibility of the impression that you make on others.

Ethnic Origin of the Liar

I have already mentioned that it is more difficult to detect lies when the liar and lie detector do not share the same ethnic background. Research has indicated that black suspects make a more suspicious impression on white police officers than do white suspects, regardless of whether they speak the truth or not. This is due to the fact that the behaviour shown by black suspects differs from the behaviour shown by white suspects (Vrij, 1991; Vrij & Winkel, 1990, 1991).

Several researchers have pointed out that non-verbal behaviour is culturally mediated and must therefore be interpreted with a background knowledge of the culture (Ruby & Brigham, 1997; Vrij, 1991). For example, looking into the eyes of the conversation partner is polite in Western cultures, but is considered to be rude in many other cultures especially towards authorative people such as police officers (Ickes, 1984; Vrij, 1991). This may well be the reason why Afro-American people display more gaze aversion than white American people do (Fugita, Wexley & Hillery, 1974; Ickes, 1984), and why people from Turkey and Morocco who are living in The Netherlands show more gaze aversion than native Dutch people (Van Rossum, 1998; Vrij, Dragt & Koppelaar, 1992). Other researchers have found that Afro-American people make more move-ments than white people (Garratt, Baxter & Rozelle, 1981; Smith, 1983).

Together with several colleagues, I investigated the non-verbal behavioural patterns of white native Dutch and black Surinam citizens

(citizens originating from Surinam but now living in The Netherlands) during simulated police interviews in The Netherlands (Vrij, 1991; Vrij & Winkel, 1990, 1991; Vrij, Winkel & Koppelaar, 1988). Dutch and Surinam shoppers were approached in a shopping centre and were asked to participate in a study to determine how good police officers are at interviewing people. The shoppers who agreed to participate in the study were then interviewed by a uniformed police officer in a mobile laboratory about the possession of a set of headphones. (We used two interviewers, a Surinam police officer and a native Dutch police officer. We actually gave half of the shoppers a set of headphones and asked them to hide the headphones and to deny possession of them during the

Table 3.5. Objective and subjective non-verbal indicators of deception and non-verbal differences between white and black people

	1 Subjective indicators[1]	2 Objective (actual) indicators[2]	Differences between black and white people[3]
Vocal characteristics			
High-pitched voice	>	>	*
Speech hesitations	>	>	—
Speech errors	>	>	>
Slow speech rate	>	>	>
Latency period	>	—	*
Pause durations	>	>	*
Frequency of pauses	>	—	*
Non-vocal characteristics			
Gaze aversion	>	—	>
Smiling	>	—	>
Eye blinks	>	—	
Illustrators	>	<	>
Self-manipulations	>	—	>
Hand and finger	>	<	*
Leg and foot	>	<	*
Head	—	—	—
Trunk	>	—	>
Position shifts	>	—	—

[1] >, observers associate an increase in the behaviour with deception;
 <, observers associate a decrease in the behaviour with deception;
 —, observers do not associate the behaviour with deception.
[2] >, increase in behaviour during deception;
 <, decrease in behaviour during deception;
 —, no relationship with deception.
[3] >, behaviour occurs more frequently in black people than in white people;
 —, no difference in behaviour between white and black people;
 *, not investigated.

interview). All of the interviews were videotaped with a hidden camera and the shoppers' behaviour was scored afterwards (after the interviews were finished we informed the interviewees about the videotapes and obtained their permission to use the tapes for our research). The outcomes revealed many behavioural differences between Dutch and Surinam 'suspects'. The differences between Dutch and Surinam people are schematically represented in the third column of Table 3.5.

Surinam people made more speech errors, spoke more slowly, spoke with a higher-pitched voice, exhibited more gaze aversion, smiled more often and made more self-manipulations, illustrators and trunk movements, regardless of whether they were lying or not.

The findings presented in the third column of Table 3.5 show a large overlap with the findings concerning subjective indicators of deception (column 1), indicating that typical black behaviour corresponds to behaviour that makes a suspicious impression on white observers. This gives rise to possible *cross-cultural non-verbal communication errors* during cross-cultural police interviews. That is, non-verbal behavioural patterns that are typical of black people may be interpreted by white observers as being betrayed attempts to hide the truth. This idea was tested in a series of experiments (Vrij & Winkel (1992a, 1994; Vrij, Winkel & Koppelaar, 1991). Videotapes were made of simulated police interviews in which white (native Dutch) and black (Surinam) actors showed either typical white or typical black non-verbal behaviour. For example, the actors showed gaze behaviour typical of black people in one version (they looked away for 35 seconds per minute of the interview), and gaze behaviour typical of white people (they looked away for 26 seconds per minute of the interview) in the other version. They showed movements typical of black people in one version (they made 7.5 self-manipulations and hand and finger movements per minute of the interview) and movements typical of white people in the other version (they made 4 self manipulations and hand and finger movements per minute of the interview), and so on. The norm data for typical 'white' and 'black' behaviour were derived from the study just described. The video began with shots of a street and a living-room. A voice commented on the scenes, saying that a young woman had been assaulted and raped and that the police assumed that the offender lived on that street. Accordingly, the police were making door-to-door calls to have brief interviews with all of the men. Subsequently, a man appeared in view, evidently talking with a police officer (who remained invisible). Dutch white police officers were exposed to one interview and were asked to indicate to what extent the man made a suspicious impression. The outcomes are presented in Figure 3.4.

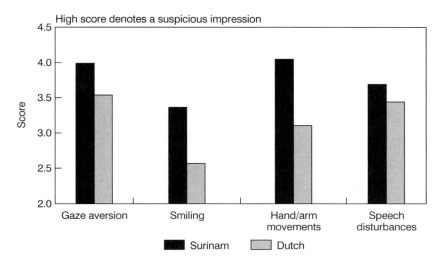

Figure 3.4. The cross-cultural non-verbal communication error.

Figure 3.4 shows a consistent pattern. In all of the studies, the actors made a more suspicious impression when they showed black non-verbal behaviour than when they displayed white non-verbal behaviour. For example, the experiment concerning movements revealed that 72% found the suspect they were confronted with suspicious when he showed black non-verbal behaviour (relatively many movements), whereas only 41% found the same suspect suspicious when he showed white non-verbal behaviour (fewer movements). Interestingly, ethnic background did not have an impact on police officers' impressions—that is, they found white suspects as suspicious as black suspects. However, both white and black suspects made a more suspicious impression when they showed black non-verbal behaviour than when they exhibited white non-verbal behaviour. These findings support the assumption that cross-cultural non-verbal communication errors do occur during cross-cultural police interviews, and that non-verbal behavioural patterns that are typical of black people are interpreted by white observers as signs of deception.

WHY ARE PEOPLE SO UNSKILLED IN DETECTING LIES?

This chapter and the previous one provide several explanations as to why people are so poor at detecting lies. In this section I shall briefly summarize these. Some of them suggest that observers make unnecessary mistakes. Therefore their skills in detecting deceit might improve when they are told which mistakes they usually make. Whether or not training makes people better lie detectors will be discussed in the following section.

- People are poor at detecting lies because they do not want to know the truth (Ekman, 1993). For example, as stated in Chapter 1, people often do not want to know whether the host really likes the present they just gave him or her, as there is no benefit for them in knowing this. They are therefore keen to believe the host when they tell the guest that they really like the present. Moreover, people are often pleased when others pay them compliments about what they do or how they look. Therefore they would not make efforts to discover whether the person who pays the compliment actually means it. However, in many circumstances people do want to find out whether someone is lying, but even lie detectors who are highly motivated to find out whether someone is lying to them are quite easily duped. The remaining points make clear why this is so.
- There is no such thing as typical deceptive behaviour—that is, there is no behaviour or set of behaviours that all liars exhibit. Deceptive behaviour depends on someone's personality and on the circumstances under which the lie is told. Obviously, the fact that generic deceptive behaviour does not exist makes it difficult for observers to decide what to look for.
- Differences between liars and truth-tellers are usually very small. Freud's view that 'betrayal oozes out of liars at every pore' (see Chapter 2) is often incorrect. Obviously, the smaller the differences, the more difficult it will be to detect them.
- Conversation rules prevent lie detectors from analysing an accused liar properly. To keep on lying will become increasingly difficult for the liar when the observer persists in asking questions. As already mentioned in Chapter 2, the liar must avoid self-contradiction, should not say things which the observer already knows to be untrue, and must remember the things that have already been said in case someone asks for a repetition or clarification. Moreover, liars have to control their behaviour all the time in order to avoid possibly giving these lies away via obvious signs of nervousness or content complexity. These difficulties will increase when the observer continues asking questions and therefore forces the liar to keep on lying. However, as pointed out earlier in this chapter, a person will become very quickly irritated if their conversation partner questions everything they say. It will also benefit the lie detector when they have the opportunity to observe the potential liar literally from head to foot, as (the absence of) body movements may give away a lie. Such head-to-foot observation is very unusual in conversations

and makes an odd impression. We usually restrict ourselves to looking into the eyes of the conversation partner. However, eye movements do not give reliable information about deception.

- Observers' judgements are often affected by a variety of systematic errors and biases. Instead of actively scrutinizing the behaviour of others, observers may instead rely on relatively mindless decision rules, often labelled cognitive heuristics (Levine, McCornack & Park, 1999). One example is the availability heuristic. In real life, people are more often confronted with truthful statements than with deceptive ones, and they therefore assume that the behaviour they observe is usually honest (this behaviour leads to a truth bias). The infrequency heuristic occurs because people tend to judge behaviours which are odd or infrequent as deceptive, regardless of whether they are actually deceptive. The relational truth-bias heuristic occurs because, as relationships become more intimate, partners develop a stronger tendency to judge the other as truthful. Finally, there is the representativeness heuristic, in which people believe that nervous behaviours and behaviours showing content complexity indicate deception. As a result, they often use the wrong cues to detect deception, as liars often do not actually show such behaviour.

- Even when people show nervous behaviour or behaviour indicating content complexity, this does not necessarily mean that they are lying (Bond & Fahey, 1987). A truthful, innocent suspect who is worried that he will not be believed by the police officer may, because of that fear, show the same nervous behaviour that a guilty liar who is afraid of being caught may manifest.

- Observers often fail to take individual differences in behaviour into account. For example, introverts and socially anxious people often make a dishonest impression on observers, as do black people (at least on white observers). The behaviour that these groups of people naturally show is often incorrectly interpreted by observers as indicative of lying.

TRAINING PEOPLE TO DETECT DECEIT

Bull (1989) expressed a pessimistic view of the prospects of training people to detect lies. He noticed that a number of police recruitment advertisements and police training books seem to imply that the detection of deception from behavioural cues is a simple affair and that training with regard to these cues can enhance the detection of deception. Bull reviewed the published literature on the effects of training and found no evidence of a training effect. He concluded that 'until a number of publications in refereed journals appear demonstrating that training enhances the detection of deception, it appears that some police recruitment advertisements and police training books are deceiving their readers' Bull (1989, p.83).

To challenge Bull's request, to my knowledge 11 studies have been published in refereed journals examining the influence of training on detecting lies. Most of them are listed in Appendix 3.2.

In all of the studies, observers were exposed to videotaped or audiotaped short interviews with a number of people who were telling either truths or lies. Generally, three different procedures have been used in these training sessions. Some used a 'focusing procedure' and asked their judges to pay attention to specific cues and to ignore others (namely those which do not seem to indicate deception). For example, DePaulo, Lassiter and Stone (1982) asked their participants in their 'tone of voice' condition to pay attention to how the speakers were saying what they said, rather than to pay attention to the content of what they were saying or to how they looked when they were saying it. (This study is not mentioned in Appendix 3.2, as the authors did not provide accuracy rates.) deTurck and his colleagues used a similar procedure. Others used an 'informational procedure' and gave their judges information about the actual relationship between certain behaviours and deception. For example, Fiedler and Walka (1993) told their judges that lying is often accompanied by a higher voice pitch. Vrij (1994) and Vrij and Graham (1997) used a similar procedure. Finally, in some studies (Fiedler & Walka 1993; Vrij, 1994; Zuckerman, Koestner & Colella, 1984, 1985) observers were provided with outcome feedback— that is, observers in the learning sessions were told after each clip that they watched whether the decision they had just made about the veracity of the statement was actually correct.

In some studies more than one type of information was given. For example, Fiedler and Walka (1993) gave information about the actual relationship between deception and some behaviours to one group of observers, and gave outcome feedback in addition to this information to another group of observers. In some studies, different observers were exposed to different videotapes. For example, in Zuckerman, Koestner and Colella's (1985) experiment, one group of observers only saw the face of the accused liars, while some only heard their voice, and others were exposed to both face and voice. In all of the studies the observers were college students, except for the studies conducted by Köhnken (1987), Vrij (1994) and Vrij and Graham (1997), in which police officers were used.

As can be seen from Appendix 3.2, most of the studies revealed an improvement in lie detectors' skills in detecting deceit, regardless of the training method to which they were exposed. Hence it is possible to improve people's ability to detect lies. In three studies (Köhnken, 1987; Vrij, 1994; Vrij & Graham, 1997) the information impaired the judges' ability to detect deceit. Interestingly, these are the three studies in which the observers were police officers and not students, which suggests that students benefit more from these information sessions than do police officers. This idea is supported by the fact that, in Vrij and Graham's (1997) study, students did become better lie detectors as a result of the information they received, whereas the police officers performed less well after having received information. I can only speculate as to why police officers do not appear to benefit from the information they are given. One possible explanation is that the information given is too complicated and makes them confused. This might have been the case in the study by Vrij and Graham (1997), as the information they were given about the relationship between personality traits and deceptive behaviour was perhaps too complicated for people who are not familiar with personality theories. The student observers in this experiment (who did benefit from the information) were psychology students and were already familiar with personality theories (but not, however, with the relationship between personality traits and deception). Moreover, Köhnken (1987) cites complexity of the information as an explanation for the fact that in his study training did not result in the desired effects.

A possible reason why information resulted in a lower accuracy score in Vrij's (1994) study is that police officers refused to use the information provided because they did not believe it. The information provided was that liars show a decrease in hand and finger movements. This contradicts police officers' beliefs, as they believe that an increase in hand and finger movements indicates deception (Vrij & Semin, 1996).

All of the studies showed only limited effects. The average accuracy rate for the trained observers was 57%, whereas the untrained observers achieved an accuracy rate of 54%. In most studies the accuracy rates of trained observers did not exceed 65%. However, when interpreting these results one should take into account the fact that all training sessions in these experiments were brief, not extensive, and therefore probably insufficient given the highly complex characteristics of lie detection. A more extensive and sophisticated training programme might possibly yield better results. In my view, such a training programme should use a different design to those employed in previous studies. For example, it is not particularly useful to inform observers about actual indicators of deception, as not every liar will show these behaviours. In my view, to develop a better programme one should consult good lie detectors.

Research has indicated that these do exist. As mentioned earlier, Secret Service agents are better at detecting deception than others (see Table 3.3). For instance, 53% of these agents achieved an accuracy rate of at least 70%, and 29% obtained an accuracy rate of 80% or more (Ekman & O'Sullivan, 1991). In Vrij and Mann's (in press) study of the convicted murderer, 29% of the lie detectors (police officers) obtained an accuracy rate of at least 80%, and 9% achieved a 100% accuracy rate. Thus some people seem to be able to detect deception rather accurately.

Obviously it is only possible to learn from good lie detectors when it is clear which cues they use when they detect lies. Unfortunately, this is still unknown, as hardly any research has been conducted to find out what makes a person a good lie detector. The ability to detect lies is not correlated with gender, age or experience in interviewing suspects (Ekman & O'Sullivan, 1991; Vrij & Mann, in press). Men are as skilled as women, older lie detectors are not superior to younger ones, and those who are experienced in interviewing suspects are not better than those who lack such experience. Nor is the ability to detect deceit correlated with being confident (see DePaulo, Charlton, Cooper, Lindsay & Muhlenbruck, 1997 for a meta-analysis of the relationship between accuracy and confidence). Inaccurate lie detectors are as confident as accurate lie detectors. It perhaps seems reasonable that good lie detectors will be good liars as well, but it is not clear whether this is true, as research has provided conflicting findings. DePaulo and Rosenthal (1979) have suggested that there is no connection between being a good liar and being a good lie detector, whereas Manstead, Wagner and MacDonald (1986) challenged this view.

Ekman and O'Sullivan's (1991) preliminary results showed that good lie detectors use different cues when observing different people (e.g. they mention speech-related cues when detecting a lie in one person, voice-related cues for a second person, and body movement-related cues for a third person), whereas inaccurate lie detectors seem to adopt a 'rule of thumb' strategy using the same cues in order to detect lies in different people. Vrij and Mann (in press) also found that good lie detectors rely less on stereotypical beliefs such as 'liars look away' and 'liars fidget' than poor lie detectors. As mentioned before, a stereotypical rule of thumb strategy is doomed to fail because different people show different behaviours when lying.

Ekman and his colleagues found that observers' ability to detect facial micro-expressions of emotions (as measured with a special micro-expression test) was positively correlated with their ability to detect deceit in the lie-detection task (Ekman & O'Sullivan, 1991; Frank & Ekman, 1997). In other words, good lie detectors are skilled at noticing facial micro-expressions of emotions.

Alternatively, it may be a good idea to make more of the skills already possessed by lie detectors. There is some evidence that people have implicit knowledge about deception which they do not quite know how to access (DePaulo, 1994). For example, when people talk out loud as they try to decide whether someone is lying or not, they sound less confident if the message they are considering is a lie than if it is a truth, and they are more likely to mention the possibility that the message is fabricated if it really is (DePaulo, 1994; Hurd & Noller, 1988).

RECOMMENDATIONS

Observers—not only lay people but even professional lie-catchers—very often have incorrect beliefs about cues to deception, and are not very successful at detecting deception on the basis of non-verbal behaviour displayed by deceivers. This lack of ability to detect deception is perhaps not surprising, bearing in mind that non-verbal behaviour displayed during deception depends on the characteristics of the individual, the type of lie and the circumstances under which the lie is told, and that the differences between truth-tellers and liars are usually very small.

Despite these apparent difficulties, it would be wrong to conclude that it is impossible to detect deception by paying attention to a person's non-verbal behaviour. As mentioned in Chapter 2, Frank and Ekman (1997) could detect 80% of the truths and lies by observing emotional expressions. In one of our recent studies (Vrij, Edward, Roberts & Bull (1999)), 81% of truths and lies were correctly classified by paying attention to behaviours which are influenced by content complexity (latency period, speech errors, speech hesitations, hand, arm, foot and leg movements).

It might be possible for many people to improve their skills in detecting a liar, as many lie detectors make mistakes which could easily be avoided. Moreover, some people are rather accurate in detecting lies by observing non-verbal behaviour. This implies that non-verbal lie detection is an art—that is, a skill that can perhaps be learned. More research is needed to find out which cues such individuals use and how difficult it is to instruct other people to use these cues. For the time being, it may be useful to instruct professional lie-catchers to get rid of their incorrect, stereotyped beliefs about cues to deception, because these lead to undesirable effects, such as cross-cultural non-verbal communication errors.

Some conclusions that can be drawn from research for those who want to detect lies via behavioural cues are listed in Box 3.3.

Box 3.3. Guidelines for the detection of deception via behavioural cues

1   Lies may only be detectable via non-verbal cues if the liar experiences fear, guilt or excitement (or any other emotion), or if the lie is difficult to fabricate.
2   It is important to pay attention to mismatches between speech content and non-verbal behaviour, and to try to explain these mismatches. Keep in mind the possibility that the person is lying, but consider this as only one of the possible reasons for this mismatch.
3   Attention should be directed towards deviations from a person's 'normal' or usual patterns of behaviour, if these are known. The explanation for such deviations should be established. Each deviation may indicate that the person is lying, but do not disregard other explanations for these deviations.
4   The judgement of untruthfulness should only be made when all other possible explanations have been negated.
5   A person suspected of deception should be encouraged to talk. This is necessary to negate the alternative options regarding a person's behaviour. Moreover, the more a liar talks, the more likely it is that they will finally give their lies away via verbal and/or non-verbal cues (as they continuously have to pay attention to both speech content and non-verbal behaviour). Bear in mind that probing in itself might elicit behavioural changes.
6   There are stereotyped ideas about cues to deception (such as gaze aversion, fidgeting, and so on), which research has shown to be unreliable indicators of deception. The actual indicators are listed in Chapter 2. These can be a guide, but bear in mind that not everyone will exhibit these cues during deception, and the presence of such cues *may* indicate deception, but does not do so in every case.

Appendix 3.1. Accuracy rates of lay observers judging strangers[1]

	Accuracy rate (%)		
	Truth	Lie	Total
Bond, Kahler & Paolicelli (1985)			63
Bond, Omar, Mahmoud & Bonser (1990)			56[2]
Bond *et al.* (1992) (experiment 1)			50
Bond *et al.* (1992) (experiment 2)			55
Bond *et al.* (1992) (experiment 3)			52
Brandt, Miller & Hocking (1980a)			38
Brandt, Miller & Hocking (1980b)			42
Brandt, Miller & Hocking (1982)			31
DePaulo & Pfeifer (1986)			54
deTurck (1991)			54
deTurck, Feeley & Roman (1997)			57
deTurck, Harszlak, Bodhorn & Texter (1990)			64
deTurck & Miller (1990)			53
Ekman & O'Sullivan (1991)			53

Feeley & deTurck (1995)	72	54	63
Feeley & deTurck (1997)			49
Feeley, deTurck & Young (1995)			56
Fiedler & Walka (1993)	55	51	53
Frank & Ekman (1997) (experiment 1)			58[3]
Frank & Ekman (1997) (experiment 2)			60
Garrido, Masip, Herrero, Tabernero & Vega (1998)	51	66	59
Granhag & Strömwall (1998)	69	44	57
Lane & DePaulo (1999)			59
Levine, McCornack & Park (1999) (study 2)	70	38	54
Levine, McCornack & Park (1999) (study 3)	69	27	48
Littlepage & Pineault (1985)	82	30	56[4]
Mei-tai Fan, Wagner & Manstead (1995)			58
Millar & Millar (1995) (study 1)			54[5]
Millar & Millar (1995) (study 2)			61[5]
Millar & Millar (1997)			49
Miller et al. (1981) (study 1)			55[6]
Miller et al. (1981) (study 2)			56[7]
Miller, deTurck & Kalbfleisch (1983)			51[8]
O'Sullivan, Ekman & Friesen (1988)	69	48	54
Smith, Archer & Costanzo (1991)			60
Stiff & Miller (1986)	67	41	54
Vrij & Graham (1997)			42
Zuckerman, Koestner & Alton (1984)			62
Zuckerman, Koestner & Colella (1985)			58[9]

[1] Only control conditions are used.
[2] Jordanian and American judges together.
[3] Scores of crime video and opinion video combined.
[4] Spontaneous and planned conversations combined.
[5] Voice and video information condition.
[6] Audio and visual condition, factual and emotional statements combined.
[7] Live condition.
[8] All conditions combined.
[9] Face only, speech only and face plus speech conditions combined.

Appendix 3.2. The impact of training observers on lie detection accuracy scores

	Training			
	None (%)	1 (%)	2 (%)	3 (%)
deTurck (1991) (183 students)	54	69[1]		
deTurck, Feeley & Roman (1997) (165 students)	57	55[2]	62[3]	64[4]
deTurck, Harszlak, Bodhorn & Texter (1990) (188 students)	55	64[1]		
deTurck & Miller (1990) (390 students)	53	61[1]		
Fiedler & Walka (1993) (72 students)	53	65[5]	65[6]	

(continued overleaf)

Appendix 3.2. (*continued*)

	Training			
	None (%)	1 (%)	2 (%)	3 (%)
Köhnken (1987) (80 police detectives)	47	42[7]	48[8]	40[9]
Vrij (1994) (360 police detectives)				
One interview	49	52[10]	54[11]	
Two interviews spontaneously, total image[12]	51	47[10]	47[11]	
Two interviews spontaneously, hands only[12]	44	56[10]	60[11]	
Vrij & Graham (1997) (40 students)	42	55[13]		
Vrij & Graham (1997) (29 police officers)	54	48[13]		
Zuckerman, Koestner & Alton (1984)				
(132 students)	62	70[14]		
Zuckerman, Koestner & Colella (1985) (117				
students)				
Face only[15]	53	59[16]		
Speech only[15]	61	63[16]		
Face plus speech[15]	59	65[16]		

[1] Observers were asked to pay attention to message duration, response latency, pauses, non-fluencies, self-manipulations and hand gestures.

[2] Observers were asked to pay attention to speech errors, pauses, response latency and message duration.

[3] Observers were asked to pay attention to self-manipulations, hand gestures, head movements and hand shrugs.

[4] Observers were asked to pay attention to speech errors, pauses, self-manipulations and hand gestures.

[5] Information about the relationship between deception and smiles, head movements, self-manipulations, pitch of voice, speech rate, pauses and channel discrepancies was given.

[6] Information described in footnote [5] plus outcome feedback.

[7] Observers were asked to pay attention to changes in head movements, eyeblinks, gaze, illustrators, self-manipulations, body movements and foot and leg movements.

[8] Observers were asked to pay attention to changes in speech rate, pauses, speech errors and speech hesitations.

[9] Observers were trained in Criteria-Based Content Analysis (see Chapter 5), and particular emphasis was placed on logical consistency, amount of detail, unusual details and spontaneous corrections.

[10] Information about the relationship between deception and hand and finger movements was given.

[11] Information described in footnote [10] plus outcome feedback.

[12] Observers were exposed to a truthful and deceptive account simultaneously (i.e. they saw the two clips at the same time). In the total image condition the whole subject was visible; in the hands only condition only their hands were visible.

[13] Information about the relationship between deception and hand and finger movements for people high or low in public self-consciousness and for good and poor actors was given.

[14] Outcome feedback was given. Only the 'feedback after 8 senders' condition is reported.

[15] Observers only saw the face of the accused liars (face only), or could only hear them (speech only), or were exposed to both face and speech (face plus speech).

[16] Outcome feedback was given.

PART II

VERBAL CHARACTERISTICS OF DECEPTION

CHAPTER 4

Initial Research Concerning Verbal Characteristics

Sometimes a liar says something which the observer knows is not true. For example, a boy tells his mother that he stayed at home all afternoon, while she knows that this is untrue because she noticed that he was not there when she herself unexpectedly had to go home for a short time that afternoon. The boy told a transparent lie which was discovered because his story contradicted the facts. This example shows that speech content may be a useful tool for detecting deceit. The listener compares the story of the alleged liar with the facts that he or she knows and checks whether the statement conflicts with these details.

In many cases, however, the listener does not know the facts, or the liar tells a story which fits in with the facts that the listener does know. In these cases, lies cannot be discovered in the way just described. The question arises whether other aspects of the speech content reveal deception. For example, do liars tend to say certain things, or do they tend to avoid saying certain things, and are lie detectors able to catch liars when they pay attention to speech content? These questions will be discussed in this and the following two chapters. As with the relationship between non-verbal behaviour and deception, there is no typical verbal deceptive behaviour. That is, not all liars say certain things or avoid saying specific things. However, some verbal criteria appear to discriminate between deceptive and truthful statements.

The empirical development of verbal techniques to measure the veracity of statements started in the late 1980s. To date, Statement Validity Assessment (SVA) is the most popular technique, and this will be discussed in Chapter 5. Recently, an increasing number of scholars have investigated Reality Monitoring as an alternative verbal technique for lie detection. Their findings will be discussed in Chapter 6. Research into verbal characteristics of deception had started before the introduction of Statement Validity Assessment. In particular, the relationship between deception and negative statements, plausible answers, irrelevant information, overgeneralized statements, self-references, direct responses and response length have been investigated. (Plausible answers are one of the criteria of Statement Validity Assessment, and will therefore also be discussed in Chapter 5). I shall now describe research concerning these seven characteristics. Some of these characteristics provide information about deception—perhaps more than observers tend to believe. Descriptions of the seven characteristics are given in Box 4.1.

Box 4.1. Overview and description of the verbal characteristics

Verbal characteristic	Description
1　*Negative statements*	Statements indicating aversion towards an object, person or opinion, such as denials and disparaging statements, and statements indicating a negative mood
2　*Plausible answers*	Statements which make sense and which sound credible and reasonable
3　*Irrelevant information*	Information which is irrelevant to the context, and which has not been asked for
4　*Overgeneralized statement*	The use of words such as 'always', never', 'nobody', 'everybody', and so on
5　*Self-references*	The use of words referring to the speaker himself or herself, such as 'I', 'me' or 'mine'
6　*Direct answers*	To-the-point and straightforward statements (for example, 'I like John' is more direct than 'I like John's company')
7　*Response length*	Length of the answer or number of spoken words

---

It is assumed that the same three aspects which may affect non-verbal behaviour during deception (i.e. emotions, content complexity and attempted control) will also influence these seven verbal criteria.

EMOTIONS

Sometimes liars feel guilty, either because they are lying, or due to the topic they are lying about. For example, children may feel guilty when they lie to their parents because they may think that is wrong to do this. An adulterous husband may feel guilty when he denies having an affair, because he feels guilty about having this romance. Liars may also be afraid of getting caught. The result of this guilt and fear could be that deceivers do not want to associate themselves with their lies, and they therefore give answers which are *indirect*, or which are *overgeneralized* or which do *not explicitly refer to themselves*. A possible answer to the question 'Do you smoke?' could be 'Nobody smokes in this house'. When President Clinton was asked in the Paula Jones case whether Monica Lewinsky was lying when she told someone that she had had a sexual affair with him that started in November 1995, Clinton answered: 'It's certainly not the truth. It will not be the truth' (*The Independent*, 30 July 1998, p.14).

Guilt and anxiety are both negative emotions which may result in the liar being irritable or not co-operative. One indicator of irritation might be giving *negative statements*. For instance, President Nixon said 'I am not a crook' instead of 'I am an honest man' in the Watergate scandal (DePaulo, 1998, cited in *The Sunday Times*, 24 May 1998, p.14). An adulterous wife who is asked about her alleged affair may become angry when the topic arises and may show this irritation (for example, by shouting at her husband that he dares to distrust her). A boy who secretly stole some sweets may show his irritation by falsely claiming that he does not even like those sweets. Not being co-operative may result in giving *short answers*. There are more reasons why one might expect liars to give shorter answers than truth-tellers. These will be discussed in Chapters 5 and 6.

CONTENT COMPLEXITY

It is sometimes more difficult to lie than to tell the truth (for example, when a liar instantly has to invent an answer). Not everybody will be good at this. As a result, deceptive statements might be *short* and might sound unconvincing and *implausible*. It might also be the case that liars will *not refer to themselves*, due to the lack of personal experience. Suppose that a boy did not go to the zoo (as he has told his parents), but went to the cinema instead. When he is asked about his experiences in the zoo, he might give a concise and objective report of a visit to a zoo, whereas children who really went to the zoo will lard their stories with personal experiences, such as 'It was hot in the reptile house', 'The monkeys smelled awful', 'The tiger made me scared', and so on.

ATTEMPTED CONTROL

Liars often try hard to make an honest impression on observers. They might assume that it will appear suspicious if they do not provide enough information. They are therefore keen to give some information, which is difficult when they do not know the information required. One possibility is to give *irrelevant information* as a substitute for information that the deceiver cannot supply. The boy who wants to conceal that he went to the cinema with his friend could tell his parents what he discussed with his friend when they ask him to describe his visit to the zoo.

REVIEW OF OBJECTIVE AND SUBJECTIVE VERBAL CRITERIA FOR DECEPTION

Research findings concerning speech content are rather consistent, and support most of the expected differences between liars and truth-tellers. As can be seen in Table 4.1, liars tend to make more negative statements and fewer self-references, and their answers are shorter, more indirect and sound less plausible. There is no strong evidence to suggest that liars provide more irrelevant information or make overgeneralized statements.

Some of the answers that President Clinton gave in his testimony in the Kenneth Starr investigation on 17 August 1998 were implausible, and others were indirect. For example, Clinton was asked in the Paula Jones case whether anyone else other than his attorneys told him that Monica Lewinsky had been served with a subpoena in that case. His answer under oath was 'I don't think so'. This answer is in conflict with the testimony of Vernon Jordan (Clinton's friend) in the Starr investigation, as Jordan had said that he discussed Lewinsky's subpoena with the President. When they confronted President Clinton with this contradiction, he gave what was in my view an implausible answer by saying that he was trying to remember who was the *first* person who told him about Lewinsky's subpoena. This answer is unconvincing because, in that case, one would expect him to give the name of a person and not to say 'I don't think so'.

In his testimony, Clinton read a statement in which he admitted that there had been encounters with Monica Lewinsky which did involve inappropriate contact, but he denied that several specific sexual acts ever took place which were described by Monica Lewinsky in her testimony. Starr's team cited several statements made by Monica Lewinsky about specific sexual acts, and asked President Clinton whether Monica Lewinsky was lying when she said that these acts did take place. Clinton's answers were indirect. He did not answer 'yes' or 'no', but instead he said 'I refer to my former statement'.

These answers perhaps make President Clinton's testimony suspicious, but it would be incorrect to conclude that he was lying. As I said

Table 4.1. Objective verbal indicators of deception

	Negative statements	Plausible answers	Irrelevant information	Overgeneralized statements	Self-references	Direct answers	Response length
Anolli & Ciceri (1997)							∧
Bond et al. (1985)	—				—		
Burgoon et al. (1996, study 1)					∨	∨	
Burgoon et al. (1996, study 2)					∨	∨	
Cody & O'Hair (1983)							∨
Cody et al. (1989)				∧			
DePaulo, Rosenthal et al. (1982)	∧			—			
DePaulo et al. (1984)[a]					∨	∨	
DePaulo & DePaulo (1989)	—		—	—			
deTurck & Miller (1985)					∨		∨
Dulaney (1982)							
Ebesu & Miller (1994)				—	∨	∨	∨
Feeley & deTurck (1998)					—		∨
Greene et al. (1985)							
Knapp et al. (1974)	∧			∧	∨		

(continued overleaf)

Table 4.1. (*continued*)

	Negative statements	Plausible answers	Irrelevant information	Overgeneralized statements	Self-references	Direct answers	Response length
Kraut (1978)		<					<
Kraut & Poe (1980)							
Miller *et al.* (1983)			—			—	—
O'Hair *et al.* (1981)		<					<
Riggio & Friedman (1983)							
Roberts *et al.* (1998)					<		
Rockwell *et al.* (1997)							<
Sporer (1997)							—
Stiff & Miller (1986)		<			—		—
Vrij *et al.* (1999)							<
Young & deTurck (1996)					<		—
Zuckerman *et al.* (1979)							
Zuckerman, DePaulo *et al.* (1981)[b]	>		>				<

>, verbal characteristic occurs more often during deception than during truth-telling;
<, verbal characteristic occurs less often during deception than during truth-telling;
—, no relationship between verbal characteristic and deception.
[a] Described in DePaulo, Stone and Lassiter (1985).
[b] Summary of unpublished studies.

earlier, there is no typical verbal deceptive behaviour, and the presence of certain verbal criteria does not indicate that someone is lying. There might be alternative reasons why Clinton gave such answers. For example, suppose that he is telling the truth about the affair and that Monica Lewinsky is lying. Even in this situation, answering 'yes' to the question about whether Monica Lewinsky is lying might be difficult for him to do because that would imply that he is openly accusing her of lying under oath, which he perhaps would not want to do.

To date, not much research has been conducted into subjective verbal indicators of deception. Therefore we have to be cautious when drawing conclusions. Table 4.2 suggests that particularly short statements, indirect responses and answers which sound implausible raise suspicion. I asked students, prisoners and professional lie-catchers such as police officers, police detectives, prison guards and customs officers about their beliefs concerning verbal characteristics of deception. As can be seen in Table 4.2, prisoners and professional lie-catchers do not associate any of the investigated verbal criteria with deception, whereas students believe that liars make more overgeneralized statements and give more indirect responses. As mentioned above, liars do indeed have a tendency to give indirect responses.

CONCLUSION

Some verbal criteria are more likely to occur in false than in truthful statements. Liars make more negative statements, give more implausible answers, give shorter responses, make fewer self-references and give more indirect replies. Although the amount of research that has been conducted to date is somewhat limited, it is remarkable that the findings are relatively consistent. This is in contrast to research into non-verbal indicators of deception, where much more conflicting findings have been reported. It suggests that the relationship between deception and these verbal criteria is somewhat clearer than the relationship between deception and most non-verbal behaviours. It might therefore be useful for lie detectors to take these verbal criteria into account when they try to detect deceit. While observers do not associate some of the verbal criteria (such as negative statements and self-references) with deception, these criteria do actually appear to be related to deception. This pattern is the opposite of what we saw in Chapters 2 and 3—observers associate more non-verbal behaviours with deception than they in fact should. In other words, there seems to be a tendency for observers to *overestimate* the likelihood of being able to detect deceit by paying attention to someone's behaviour, and to *underestimate* the

Table 4.2. Subjective verbal indicators of deception

	Negative statements	Plausible answers	Irrelevant information	Overgeneralized statements	Self-references	Direct answers	Response length
Akehurst et al. (1996)		—				<	<
Bond et al. (1985)	—				<		
Bond et al. (1990)	<						—
DePaulo, Rosenthal et al. (1982)	>			>	<		
DePaulo et al. (1984)[a]						<	
DePaulo & DePaulo (1989)	—		—	—			
Kraut (1978)		<		—			
Kraut & Poe (1980)			>				
Stiff & Miller (1986)		<				<	<
Stiff et al. (1989)		<			—		
Taylor & Vrij (1999)							>
Vrij & Bull (1992)	>		>	>	—		
Vrij (1993b) (students)	—		—	>	—	<	
Vrij (1993b) (prisoners)	—		—	—	—	—	
Vrij (1993b) (professionals)	—		—	—	—	—	
Westcott et al. (1991)		<					
Zuckerman, DePaulo et al. (1981)[b]					—		—
Zuckerman, Koestner et al. (1981)	—		>				<

>, observers believe that the verbal characteristic occurs more often during deception than during truth-telling;
<, observers believe that the verbal characteristic occurs less often during deception than during truth-telling;
—, observers do not associate the verbal characteristic with deception.
[a] Described in DePaulo, Stone and Lassiter (1985).
[b] Summary of unpublished studies.

possibility of catching liars by paying attention to their speech content. Observers might improve their lie detection skills by paying more attention to what someone is saying. However, there is one problem. It is possible that as soon as liars obtain insight into the verbal criteria for deception, they will try to change their speech content in such a way that these verbal indicators will become less obvious. The possibility cannot be ruled out that liars will actually achieve this, because people are usually good at controlling their speech content, as was discussed in Chapter 2. I shall return to this issue in Chapter 5.

It might be that personal characteristics have an impact on the verbal indicators which are discussed in this chapter. For example, eloquent or intelligent people may perhaps show fewer verbal indicators of deception than people who are less eloquent or less intelligent. There is some evidence to suggest that this is the case. DePaulo and DePaulo (1989) compared truthful and deceptive statements made by sales people. Not a single verbal difference between their truthful and deceptive statements was found (see also Table 4.1). One might assume that sales people are eloquent individuals. Therefore these findings suggest that eloquent people may show fewer verbal indicators of deception than people who are less eloquent.

To date, most studies have been conducted with college students, whose intelligence we might assume will be above average. As can be seen in Table 4.1, several verbal differences did occur between students who were telling the truth and those who were lying. Apparently, a higher IQ does not guarantee that verbal indicators of deception will not occur.

Chapter 1 revealed that people who score high in Machiavellianism lie frequently in order to achieve their goals. One might therefore expect people who score high in Machiavellianism to have superior verbal lying skills. However, there is no evidence for this. For example, Knapp and colleagues and O'Hair and colleagues have not found differences in verbal behaviour between people who had low or high levels of Machiavellianism (Knapp, Hart & Dennis, 1974; O'Hair, Cody & McLaughlin, 1981). Riggio and Friedman (1983) did not find differences in providing plausible answers between introverts and extraverts, or between people who are good actors and those who are not.

Finally, it is also possible that the circumstances under which the lie is told influence verbal deceptive behaviour. For example, it might be that spontaneous lies contain more verbal indicators of deception than planned lies. I am not aware of research investigating this issue to date.

CHAPTER 5

Statement Validity Assessment

Statement Validity Assessment (also referred to as SVA) is the most popular technique to date for measuring the veracity of verbal statements. The technique has been developed in Germany to determine the credibility of *child* witnesses' testimonies in trials for *sexual offences*.[1] It is not surprising that the technique is aimed at sexual abuse and children. It is often difficult to determine the facts of a sexual abuse case. Often there is no medical or physical evidence. Frequently the alleged victim and the defendant give contradictory testimonies and there are often no other witnesses to say what has happened. This means that the perceived credibility of the defendant and alleged victim are important. The alleged victims are in a disadvantageous position if they are children, as adults have a tendency to mistrust statements made by children (Ceci & Bruck, 1995). Recently, research has addressed the question of whether SVA might be useful to assess testimonies given by adults and defendants who talk about issues other than sexual abuse. This chapter gives a detailed description of SVA and provides an overview of research that has been conducted to test its accuracy. The findings reveal that people are able to detect deception above the level that would be expected by chance by utilizing SVA. However, the technique has several problems, which mean that SVA is not as indisputable as German practice in particular would like us to believe. I shall start with a brief historical background of the development of SVA.

THE HISTORY OF STATEMENT VALIDITY ASSESSMENT

In 1954 the Supreme Court of West Germany summoned a small number of experts to a hearing. The Court wanted to assess to what

---

[1] It is unclear how many child witness statements about sexual abuse are (partially) inaccurate. American estimates of the proportion of invalid sexual abuse reports range from 6% to 60% (Craig, 1995). The reported cases of invalid reports of sexual abuse include pressure from adults and/or peers to give a false report, misidentification of the alleged perpetrator, and outright fabrications.

extent psychologists could help in determining the credibility of child witnesses' testimonies (particularly in trials for sexual offences). The forensic psychologist Udo Undeutsch reported the case of a 14-year-old alleged victim of rape which he had investigated. The five Justices of the Senate:

> 'were impressed by the demonstration and convinced themselves that in assessing the truthfulness of the testimony of a child or juvenile witness an expert psychologist conducting an out-of-court examination has other and better resources than the persons acting as fact-finders within the formal atmosphere of a courtroom trial' (Undeutsch, 1989, p.104).

Subsequently a ruling was made by the German Supreme Court in 1955 that required the use of psychological interviews and assessments of credibility in virtually all contested cases of child sexual abuse. This led to numerous cases in which psychologists were called on as experts. Arntzen (1982) estimated that by 1982 expert testimony had been offered in more than 40 000 cases. In West Germany and Sweden this also resulted in the development of various content criteria to assess the credibility of statements made by alleged victims of sexual abuse (Arntzen, 1983; Trankell, 1972; Undeutsch, 1967, 1982). Based on the work of these Swedish and German experts, Steller and Köhnken (1989) have compiled a list of such content criteria and have described a procedure for evaluating the veracity of a statement. This is now known as Statement Validity Assessment or SVA.

SVA is well established in German courts. Prosecutors and defence lawyers very rarely challenge the reliability or validity of the test, although they are allowed to do this (Köhnken, 1997, personal communication). Both the prosecution and the defence are also allowed to challenge or discredit SVA evidence—for instance, by finding weak points in the expert witness' reasoning, by cross-examining the expert in court, or by hiring another expert to advise them about the quality of the expertise (Köhnken, 1997, personal communication). In Germany, there does not as yet exist a formal way of becoming an expert. To date 'you become an expert when you are nominated as such by court' (Köhnken, 1997, personal communication). This situation will probably change in the future, as the German Psychology and Law Society is currently developing an official education programme to allow psychologists to become SVA experts (Köhnken, 1997, personal communication).

To date, SVA is accepted as evidence in other European courts as well, such as in The Netherlands (Vrij & Akehurst, 1998). SVA assessments are not, however, accepted in UK courts (Vrij & Akehurst, 1998). Opinion in North America (Canada and the USA) about using SVA in court is divided. For example, Honts (1994), Raskin and Esplin (1991b) and Yuille (1988b) are in favour of presenting the results of SVA in court, while others (Boychuk, 1991; Lamb, 1998; Ruby & Brigham, 1997; Wells & Loftus, 1991) are more sceptical. The results of SVA are presented as evidence through expert testimony in some North American courts (Ruby & Brigham, 1997, 1998), but this is considerably less common than in Germany. The main value of SVA in North America seems to lie in its utility for guiding police investigations and exercising prosecutorial discretion (Raskin & Esplin, 1991b). In summary, opinion about SVA is divided, and the technique is more popular in some countries than in others.

STATEMENT VALIDITY ASSESSMENT (SVA)

SVA consists of three major elements:

1   a structured interview;
2   a criteria-based content analysis (CBCA) that systematically assesses the contents and qualities of the obtained statement;
3   evaluation of the CBCA outcome via a set of questions (Validity Check-list).

The Structured Interview

The first phase consists of interviewing the child. Conducting a proper interview is never an easy task, but interviewing children is particularly difficult. Children's descriptions of past events are notably incomplete (Bull, 1998). This leads interviewers to ask specific questions to elicit further, often critical, information. A logical strategy is to ask questions which fit in with the interviewer's understanding of the event, and such questions can be leading. A leading interview style may result in inter-viewees mentioning things which never happened. Children are more vulnerable to a leading interview style than adults. The following example of a 'conversation' between an adult and a quiet child perhaps looks familiar:

> Adult: 'Where have you been today?' Child does not answer. 'Did you visit grandma perhaps, have you been to her house?' Child makes a head nod. 'OK, that is nice, did you like it at grandma's place?' Child makes another head nod. 'Yes, did you like it there?' Child nods again. In fact, the child has not visited her grandma.

Such a leading interview style, in which adults answer their own questions, will not do much harm in many situations. However, the results might be devastating if this happens in a criminal case. Special interview techniques based on psychological principles have been designed to obtain as much information as possible from interviewees in a free narrative style (Bull, 1992, 1995, 1998; Lamers-Winkelman, 1995; Soppe, 1995a, 1997).

SVA interviews are often audiotaped. The interviews will then be transcribed afterwards, and these transcriptions are used for the criteria-based content analysis. In addition, videotape recording may be useful as any possible biasing effects of the interviewer can then be identified more easily (Honts, 1994; Lamb, Sternberg & Esplin, 1994; Yuille, 1988b). However, it is preferable that the content analysis takes place on the basis of the transcription and not on the basis of the tape. Raters have to indicate the presence or absence of each of 19 different criteria, which is much easier to do on the basis of written transcripts then on the basis of taped interviews. The use of transcripts excludes the opportunity to take interviewees' non-verbal behaviour into account when judging the veracity of their statements. Some people believe that this is a disadvantage (Landry & Brigham, 1992). On the other hand, the non-verbal information available on a videotape concerning the interview may distract the SVA rater. As we saw in Chapter 3, many observers have incorrect, stereotyped beliefs about deceptive behaviour and often make incorrect judgements when they detect deceit on the basis of someone's behaviour. This perhaps makes the use of videotapes less advantageous.

The Content Analysis

The second phase of SVA is the systematic assessment of the credibility of the statement given during the interview, the so-called *criteria-based content analysis* (CBCA). Table 5.1 provides an overview of the 19 criteria used in the assessment. (Some researchers only use criteria 1 to 14, as will be discussed later.) Trained evaluators examine the statement and judge the presence or absence of each of the 19 criteria, usually on a 3-point scale where '0' is assigned if the criterion is absent, '1' if the criterion is present and '2' if the criterion is strongly present. CBCA is based on the hypothesis, originally stated by Undeutsch (1967), that a statement derived from memory of an actual experience differs in content and quality from a statement based on invention or fantasy. This is known as the *Undeutsch hypothesis* (Steller, 1989). The presence of each criterion in the statement enhances the quality of the statement and strengthens the hypothesis that the account is based on genuine personal experience. CBCA is not a 'verbal lie detector'—that is, it is not searching for 'lie symptoms'. The absence of a criterion does not necessarily mean that the statement is fabricated (Yuille, 1988b). The next section gives a description of the 19 CBCA criteria and reasons why these criteria are less likely to occur in lies or fantasies.

Table 5.1. Content criteria for statement analysis[1]

General characteristics
   1 Logical structure
   2 Unstructured production
   3 Quantity of details

Specific contents
   4 Contextual embedding
   5 Descriptions of interactions
   6 Reproduction of conversation
   7 Unexpected complications during the incident
   8 Unusual details
   9 Superfluous details
   10 Accurately reported details misunderstood
   11 Related external associations
   12 Accounts of subjective mental state
   13 Attribution of perpetrator's mental state

Motivation-related contents
   14 Spontaneous corrections
   15 Admitting lack of memory
   16 Raising doubts about one's own testimony
   17 Self-deprecation
   18 Pardoning the perpetrator

Offence-specific elements
   19 Details characteristic of the offence

[1] Adapted from Steller and Köhnken (1989).

General Characteristics

The general characteristics of the statement include criteria which refer to the statement as a whole.

1. Logical structure. Logical structure is present if the statement essentially makes sense—that is, if the statement is coherent and logical and the different segments are not inconsistent or discrepant.

2. Unstructured production. Unstructured production is present if the information is scattered throughout the statement rather than spoken in a structured, coherent and chronological order. However, the statement as a whole should not include inconsistencies (criterion 1). Unstructured reproduction occurs in particular when people are upset. For example, someone may start by explaining the core of the event ('My money has been stolen, I've been robbed'), may then go back to the beginning ('I was in the shop, and put my purse back in my bag after I had paid'), then gives information about events that happened later ('The guy ran so quickly, I could not follow him'), goes back to the beginning again ('I must have left my bag open'), and so on. Winkel, Vrij, Koppelaar and Van der Steen (1991) found that emotionally disturbed adult rape victims tend to give their account in very unstructured and incoherent ways. This criterion is less useful when someone has already told the story a couple of times, or if someone has frequently thought about the event, as this will result in telling a story in a more chrono-logical order.

3. *Quantity of details*. This criterion requires that the statement must be rich in detail—that is, specific descriptions of place, time, people, objects and events should be present. For example, 'I used the cash machine on Albert Road near the traffic lights. It was getting dark, it was drizzling and cold, too. It was quite busy near the cash machine, at least eight or nine people were standing there. And then, after I took my money, this guy came to me, put a knife in front of my face, grabbed my money and ran away around the corner. I screamed "stop him, he's got my money" but nobody did anything, unbelievable' would fulfil this criterion. Moreover, Soppe and colleagues argue that a request to elaborate on some issues is more likely to result in additional information if the story is truthful than if the statement is fabricated (Soppe, 1995b; Soppe & Hees-Stauthamer, 1993).

Specific Contents

Specific contents refer to particular passages in the statement and are meant to reveal the concreteness and vividness of the statement.

4. *Contextual embedding*. Contextual embedding is present if the events are placed in time and location, and if the actions are connected with other daily activities and/or customs. For example, a victim describes the fact that the crime occurred in a park at lunch-time when he was walking his dog.

5. *Descriptions of interactions*. This criterion is fulfilled if the statement contains information about interactions involving at least the alleged perpetrator and witness. For example, 'I said go away, but he didn't and smiled, and then I started crying' would fulfil this criterion.

6. *Reproduction of speech*. Reproduction of speech is present if speech, or part of the conversation, is reported in its original form and if the

different speakers are recognizable in the reproduced dialogues. This criterion is not satisfied by a report about the content of a dialogue; it is only satisfied if there is a virtual replication of the utterances of at least one person. Thus 'I said "please stop" to him' fulfils this criterion, but 'Then we talked about sport' does not.

7. *Unexpected complications during the incident.* This criterion is present if there are elements incorporated in the event which are somewhat unexpected. For instance, it might be mentioned that the alleged perpetrator's car alarm went off at the time of the crime, or that the alleged perpetrator had difficulty in starting the engine of his car, and so on.

8. *Unusual details.* Unusual details refer to details of people, objects or events which are unusual and/or unique but meaningful in the context, such as a witness who gives a description of a tattoo on the perpetrator's arm, or a witness who says that the perpetrator had a stutter, and so on.

9. *Superfluous details.* Superfluous details are present if the witness describes details in connection with the allegations which are not essential for the accusation, such as a child witness who says that the alleged adult perpetrator tried to get rid of the cat which entered the bedroom because he (the adult) was allergic to cats.

10. *Accurately reported details misunderstood.* This criterion is fulfilled if the witness speaks of details that are beyond the comprehension of the witness—for instance, a child who describes the adult's sexual behaviour but attributes it to a sneeze or to pain. Research has indicated that most children younger than 8 years have hardly any detailed knowledge about sexual behaviour (Gordon, Schroeder & Abrams, 1990; Volbert & Van der Zanden, 1996).

11. *Related external associations.* A related external association is present if events are reported which are not part of the alleged offences but are related to these offences—for example, if the interviewee says that the perpetrator talked about sexual affairs with other women.

12. *Accounts of subjective mental state.* This criterion is present if the witness describes feelings or thoughts experienced at the time of the incident, such as how scared she was, or how relieved she was when it was all over, and so on. This criterion also includes reports of cognitions, such as a witness who mentioned that she was thinking about how to escape while the event was in progress.

13. Attribution of perpetrator's mental state. This criterion is present if the witness describes the perpetrator's feelings, thoughts or motives during the incident ('He was nervous too, his hands were shaking', 'He actually liked it! He was smiling all the time!' or 'He thought about the possibility that I would start screaming, because he closed all the windows and played loud music before he started to touch me', and so on).

Motivation-related Contents

Motivation-related contents refer to the way in which the statement is presented by the witness. As with 'specific contents', it refers to specific passages of the statement.

14. Spontaneous corrections. This criterion is fulfilled if corrections are spontaneously offered or information is spontaneously added to material previously provided in the statement (spontaneous means without any interference by the interviewer). 'It was about 2 o'clock, or wait, it must have been later because it was already getting dark' is an example of a correction and 'We were in his car and he drove fast, by the way it was a Volvo, and he drove so fast that he almost failed to stop for a traffic light' is an example of an addition.

15. Admitting lack of memory. This criterion is present if a witness spontaneously admits lack of memory either by saying 'I don't know' or 'I don't remember', or by giving an answer such as 'I forgot all about this except for the part when we were in the car.' In response to a direct question, answers such as 'I don't know' or 'I can't remember' do not count as admitting lack of memory.

16. Raising doubts about one's own testimony. This criterion is present if the witness expresses concern that some part of the statement seems incorrect ('I think', 'Maybe', 'I am not sure', and so on) or unbelievable ('You know, this thing is so weird and he seemed to be such a nice man, the whole neighbourhood likes him, that I thought nobody would ever believe me').

17. Self-deprecation. Self-deprecation is present if the witness mentions personally unfavourable, self-incriminating details—for example, 'Obviously it was stupid of me to leave my door wide open because my purse was clearly visible on my desk.'

18. Pardoning the perpetrator. Pardoning the perpetrator is present if the witness tends to favour the alleged perpetrator in terms of making excuses for him or her or failing to blame the alleged perpetrator—for example, a girl who says she now feels sorry for the defendant possibly facing imprisonment because she does not think it was his intention to hurt her.

Offence-specific Elements

Offence-specific elements relate the statement to the particular crime. They differ from the category 'specific contents' because they are not related to the general vividness of the statement *per se*, but only in its relationship to the particular crime.

19. Details characteristic of the offence. This criterion is present if a witness describes events in a manner in which professionals know that certain crimes typically occur. For instance, the progression of events in an incestuous relationship would be expected to differ from the dynamics surrounding a single-incident assault by a stranger, in that the first type of crime usually involves less violence and less resistance by the victim than the latter type of crime (Soppe & Hees-Stauthamer, 1993). Raskin and Esplin (1991b) moved criterion 19 of the CBCA list into the validity check-list section (described later), arguing that the criterion is not related to the general vividness of the statement *per se* but to the particular crime.

There are at least seven reasons why these criteria are less likely to be present in fabricated statements.

- People who fabricate a story sometimes do not have enough imagination to invent the relevant characteristics. For example, they are not creative enough to introduce complications or to reproduce parts of the conversation, or to mention interactions, or to describe their own or someone else's mental state.
- Fabricators are sometimes creative enough to consider incorporating such characteristics into their stories, but since they do not realize that judges use such characteristics to evaluate the veracity of statements, they do not include them in their accounts.
- Fabricators sometimes lack the knowledge to incorporate certain criteria in their fabricated stories. This is especially the case for criterion 10, as it would be impossible to include details about sexual acts without having sufficient knowledge about sex.
- It is very difficult to incorporate many of the criteria in a fabricated statement. Consider, for example, unstructured production. It is much easier to tell a fabricated story in a chronological order (this happened first, and then this happened, and then he said this, and so on) than purposely in an unstructured way.

- Fabricators sometimes do not want to provide many different details, because they are afraid that they will forget what they have said. Forgetting what has already been said is problematic, because there is always the possibility that the fabricator will be asked to repeat their story, in which case liars must be able to repeat the same story without changing details and without contradicting themselves on important issues. Obviously, the less liars say initially, the easier it is to remember what they have said the first time and the less likely it is that contradictions will subsequently occur.
- Fabricators sometimes do not want to provide much detail because they are afraid that an observer will check these details and will find out that they are fabricated. Every single detail that is mentioned provides the interviewer with an opportunity to check whether the story is accurate. We saw this in Chapter 2 when describing the case of the murderer. The murderer described in detail what he had done in the afternoon and evening, providing the police with a wealth of details to check. His status as a likely suspect increased when the police could not find any evidence for the activities he described. Not mentioning details makes the task more difficult for the interviewer.
- Fabricators sometimes do not want to include certain characteristics (for example, admitting lack of memory, raising doubts about their own memory) because they believe that these characteristics will make their stories sound less credible and convincing. It is also unlikely that people who want to put the blame on someone else will admit any of their own wrongdoing or will excuse the other person, as they believe that this will decrease the likelihood of the other person being found guilty and/or convicted.

However, it is always possible that liars would try to incorporate some of these criteria into their accounts in order to make an honest impression if they knew that observers use CBCA criteria to evaluate the veracity of statements. I shall return to this issue later on.

The Validity Check-list

CBCA itself is not sufficient to allow a definite conclusion concerning the truthfulness of a statement. Even fabricated stories can be rich and might contain a lot of detailed information—for example, because the interviewer guided the interview too much and filled in too many gaps, or because the interviewee was well prepared, or because others had instructed the interviewee on what to say, and so on. The reverse may occur as well. A truthful statement may be of poor quality and may lack a lot of detail—for example, because the interviewee is very young, or verbally relatively unskilled, or too upset to say much, or because the interviewer did not give the interviewee enough opportunity to tell the whole story, and so on.

This implies that CBCA is not a standardized test. A standardized test has clear norms which give the test psychological meaning and make interpretation possible (Kline, 1993). An intelligence test is a standardized test. If a person obtains a score of 130, then we know that they are very intelligent and also that they are more intelligent than someone who obtains a score of 70. Without any norms at all the meaning of a test score is impossible to gauge. Therefore, standardization of a test is essential. In an effort to organize and standardize CBCA assessments, a Validity Check-list has been developed (Steller, 1989; Steller & Boychuk, 1992). The Validity Check-list is presented in Table 5.2. By systematically addressing each of the topics, the evaluator can explore and consider alternative interpretations of the CBCA outcomes. A negative response by the evaluator to each topic is consistent with the outcome adopted on the basis of the CBCA. Each affirmative response raises a question about the appropriateness of the CBCA outcome. The Validity Check-list consists of the following 11 topics.

Psychological Characteristics

The first category of topics deals with individual characteristics of the interviewee.

Table 5.2. Validity Check-list[1]

Psychological characteristics
   1 Inappropriateness of language and knowledge
   2 Inappropriateness of affect
   3 Susceptibility to suggestion

Interview characteristics
   4 Suggestive, leading or coercive questioning
   5 Overall inadequacy of the interview

Motivation
   6 Questionable motives to report
   7 Questionable context of the original disclosure or report
   8 Pressures to report falsely

Investigative questions
   9 Inconsistency with the laws of nature
  10 Inconsistency with other statements
  11 Inconsistency with other evidence

---

[1] Adapted from Steller (1989).

1. Inappropriateness of language and knowledge. This issue refers to whether the witness's use of language and display of knowledge was beyond the normal capacity of a person of his or her age and beyond the scope of what the witness might have learned from the incident. When this occurs, it may indicate the influence of other people in preparing the statement. For example, in order to obtain custody a woman may wish her child to falsely accuse her ex-husband of having had an incestuous relationship with the child in the past.

2. Inappropriateness of affect. This issue refers to whether the affect displayed by the witness when being interviewed (usually via non-verbal behaviour) is not commensurate with the witness's alleged experiences. For example, sexual offences are emotionally disturbing and likely to upset victims. One could therefore usually expect a clear display of emotions from a truthful victim when they are being interviewed. The absence of these emotions may indicate that the story has been fabricated.

3. Susceptibility to suggestion. This issue refers to whether the witness demonstrates any susceptibility to suggestion during the interview. Some people are more suggestible than others. Using the example above about questioning children who had not, in fact, visited their grandma, some children will actually say correctly that they did not visit their grandma. Yuille (1988b) and Landry and Brigham (1992) recommend asking the witness, at the end of the interview, a few leading questions in order to assess their susceptibility to suggestion. Obviously these leading questions should be asked about peripheral information and not about central information. For example, the interviewer might suggest to the child that the defendant has a fish tank in his living-room (which the interviewer knows is not true) and then observe how the child responds. If the child goes along with these specially devised suggestive questions, this could indicate that he or she is highly suggestible.

Interview Characteristics

Interview characteristics (items 4 and 5) refer to the interviewer's style or manner while conducting the interview.

4. Suggestive, leading or coercive interviewing. One should check how the interviewer conducted the interview, whether they put suggestions to the interviewee, whether they exerted any kind of pressure on the interviewee, and so on. Even if a child seems to go along with the suggestive questions deliberately asked at the end of the interview (see point 3) this does not mean that he or she is incapable of giving a full and correct account in a non-suggestive interview. Statements should not be analysed using SVA if the interview was suggestive, leading or oppressive.

5. Overall inadequacy of the interview. Factors other than its suggestiveness also determine the quality of an interview. For example, child interviewees often do not necessarily realize that they are allowed to say 'I don't know' when they do not know the answer to a question. Instead of admitting lack of memory or knowledge, children (and also adults) have a tendency to answer questions even if they are not sure about the answer. This may well lead to fabrications. It is therefore important that the interviewer makes clear to the interviewee at the beginning of the interview that an 'I don't know' answer is an acceptable one and that they should say 'I don't know' when it is appropriate (Milne & Bull, 1999; Mulder & Vrij, 1996) (for more on the psychology of interviewing see Memon and Bull, 1999).

Motivation

This section explores the motives of the witness in reporting the incident.

6. Questionable motives to report. This issue refers to whether the witness may have questionable motives for reporting the matter. It is always possible that someone else encouraged the witness to make a report. It is therefore important to know the relationship between the witness and the accused and to be aware of the possible consequences of the accusation for all of the individuals involved. Relevant in this context is a possible custody/access dispute or divorce procedure between the child's parents. For example, it is possible that one of the parties in a conflict or a custody dispute could coach the child to make an incriminating statement about the other party in an attempt to win the dispute.

7. Questionable context of the original disclosure or report. This issue refers to the origin and history of the statement, particularly the context of the first report. Possible questionable elements in the context of the original disclosure of the accusation are explored—for example, whether the first report was voluntary and who (if anyone) asked the witness to report it (boyfriend, girlfriend, parents, teacher, psychologist, and so on).

8. Pressures to report falsely. This issue deals with the question of whether there are indications that others suggested, coached, pressured or coerced the witness to make a false report or to exaggerate certain elements in an otherwise truthful report.

Investigative Questions
The fourth category deals with the statement in relation to the type of crime and previous statements.

9. Inconsistency with the laws of nature. This issue refers to the possibility that the events described are unrealistic. If someone says that she became pregnant during the incestuous relationship, one might check whether that could have been possible, given the age of the witness at the time of the relationship.

10. Inconsistency with other statements. There is often more than one testimony about a certain event. The witness may have been interviewed about the issue before, or other people might have been interviewed about the event as well. This issue refers to the possibility that major elements of the statement are inconsistent with or contradicted by another statement made by the witness or by another witness.

11. Inconsistency with other evidence. This issue refers to the possibility that major elements in the statement are contradicted by reliable physical evidence or other concrete evidence.

WHAT DO TRUTH-TELLERS SAY?

A Literature Review of CBCA Studies

Although, as I mentioned earlier, SVA is used as evidence in courts in several countries, only a little research has been conducted to test the accuracy of SVA to date. SVA was developed specifically for use with children, but not a single study has been published so far investigating the accuracy of SVA evaluations in very young children. Although statements of very young children were included in several studies, they did not report the accuracy of SVA evaluations for that group of children separately. An exception is Lamers-Winkelman's study (Lamers-Winkelman, 1995; Lamers-Winkelman & Buffing, 1996). However, her sample did not include statements of children who gave false reports.

The accuracy of SVA can be investigated either via laboratory research or via field research. In laboratory experiments participants are requested to lie or to tell the truth (for instance, about a film they have just seen) and their statements are assessed afterwards by raters utilizing the CBCA technique. The major advantage of this approach is that the scientist knows with certainty which participants are lying and which are telling the truth. However, the problem with laboratory experiments is that they differ from real-life situations. Recalling a film someone has just seen is different to describing a sexual abuse experience. Undeutsch (1984) therefore believes that, because of this lack of ecological validity, laboratory studies would be of little use in testing the accuracy of SVA analyses. He suggests that field studies should be conducted instead to assess the validity of the technique.

In field studies, children's statements in real sexual abuse cases are examined. The advantage of this type of research is that it is realistic, as it examines actual cases. However, the disadvantage is that in most criminal cases it is virtually impossible to check the 'basic reality'—that is, to establish some sort of so-called *ground truth* (Raskin, 1982). In other words, in real-life cases it is often impossible to know for sure which people are telling the truth and which people are not. Confessions of the alleged perpetrators are usually used to establish the ground truth. Steller and Köhnken (1989) argued that there are certain problems associated with the use of confessions as a ground-truth criterion. Steller and Köhnken wrote:

> '(In Germany) Statement analyses by psychological experts are usually obtained if no other incriminating or exonerating evidence is available. If, under such conditions, an incriminating statement is judged as truthful, the chances for the defendant to obtain an acquittal decrease dramatically … and, if there is no chance of avoiding a guilty verdict, it may be a beneficial strategy to confess to a crime that was not committed, since this is usually considered as repentance by the court and results in a reduction of the penalty. …On the other hand, there is no reason for the defendant to confess to a crime if the expert witness has judged the major witnesses' statement to be deceptive. As a result, the probability of a confession may be influenced by the diagnosis itself, and the attempt to validate this diagnosis by the confession is clearly circular.' (Steller and Köhnken, 1989, p.239).

See Gudjonsson (1992), Kassin (1997) and Vrij (1998a) for literature about false confessions.

As far as I know, 15 studies (three field studies and 12 laboratory studies) have been conducted to date in which statements were evaluated with the CBCA method, and in which it has been assessed for each individual criterion whether or not truthful statements differed from fabricated statements. The results are presented in Table 5.3. Some researchers have published results for overall CBCA scores, without presenting data for each individual criterion. Their results are presented in the text.

Table 5.3. Objective verbal characteristics of truth-telling (criteria-based content analysis)

	CBCA criteria																		
	1	2	3	4	5	6	7	8	9	10	11	12	13	14	15	16	17	18	19
Field studies																			
Boychuk (1991)	∧	∧	∧	∧	∧	∧	∧	∧	∧	—	∧	∧	—	∧	—	—	—	—	—
Esplin et al. (1988)	∧	∧	∧	∧	∧	∧	∧	∧	∧	—	∧	∧	∧	∧	∧	—	—	∧	∧
Lamb et al. (1997)	—	∧	∧	∧	∧	∧	—	∧	—	—	—	—	—	—	—	—	—	∧	
Experimental laboratory studies																			
Akehurst et al. (1995)[1,2]	∧	—	∧	—	∧	∧	—	—	—	—	∧	∧	—	—	—	—			
Höfer et al. (1996)[1]	∧	—	∧	∧	—	∧	∧	—	—	—	∧	∧	—	—	—	∧			
Köhnken et al. (1995)[1]	—	∧	∧	—	—	—	—	—	—	—					∧				
Landry & Brigham (1992)[1]	∨	—	∧	∧	∧	∧	—	∧	∧	—	—	∧	∨	∧	∧	∧	—	—	—
Porter & Yuille (1996)[1]	∧	—	∧	—	—	—	∧	—	—	—	∨	—	—	—	∧	—	—	—	—
Ruby & Brigham (1998)[1,3]	∧	∨	—	∨	∧	—	∧	∧	∧	—	∨	∨	—	—	∧	—	∨	—	
Steller et al. (1988)	∧		∧	∧	—			∧	∧	∧	∧	∧	—	∧	∧	—	∨		
Vrij & Heaven (1999)[1]	—	—	∧	∧	∧	∧	—	∧	∧	—		—	∧	∧	—	∧			
Vrij et al. (1999)[1]	—	—	∧	∧	∧		—	∧		—			∧	∧	—	∧			
Vrij et al. (in press)[1]	—	—	∧	—	∧											—			
Winkel & Vrij (1995)	∧	∧	∧	∧							∧					∧			
Zaparniuk et al. (1995)[1]																—		—	—

∧, verbal characteristic occurs more frequently in truthful than in deceptive statements;
∨, verbal characteristic occurs more frequently in deceptive than in truthful statements;
—, no relationship between the verbal characteristic and lying/truth-telling
[1] Used adults' statements.
[2] Results of adults and children are combined, as there were no differences between age groups.
[3] Results of black and white adults are combined.
Porter & Yuille (1996) used suspects' statements.

Field Studies

According to Lykken (1988), a scientifically credible field study should fulfil four criteria: (i) the cases selected in the study should be a representative sample of cases; (ii) the statements should be derived from interviews which have been conducted under real-life circumstances; (iii) the statements should be independently scored by at least two evaluators who were blind to case disposition (that is, who were unaware of the ground truth); and (iv) these scores should be compared with the ground truth established by some criterion that is independent of the CBCA findings (such as physical evidence) (see Horowitz, Lamb, Esplin, Boychuk, Reiter-Lavery and Krispin (1996) for a discussion about establishing ground truths in studies of child sexual abuse). Only the field study conducted by Lamb, Sternberg, Esplin, Hershkowitz, Orbach and Hovav (1997) fulfilled these four scientific criteria. Those researchers had access to 1187 interviews of allegedly sexually abused victims conducted by 50 youth investigators in Israel. They used all cases (98 in total) which fulfilled the following four criteria: (i) alleged assailants were known; (ii) alleged victims were between 4 and 13 years of age; (iii) the alleged incident involved physical contact; and (iv) there was sufficient independent evidence available. The statements were rated by more than one rater, and these raters only had access to these statements. Ground truth was established via medical evidence, suspect statements (confessions) and witness statements. The only possible disadvantage of this study was that the interviewers who conducted the interviews with the children on which the transcripts were based had prior knowledge about the case which might have influenced their style of interviewing. The findings of the other two field studies presented in Table 5.3 should be interpreted with caution.

The first CBCA study ever presented was a field study by Esplin, Boychuk and Raskin (1988, described in Raskin and Esplin, 1991a). The problems with this study were that only one evaluator scored the transcripts and that the ground truth was not based on independent case facts, as will be described below. They analysed the statements of 40 children (aged 3 to 15 years) concerning alleged sexual abuse. Twenty of these cases were 'confirmed', and the other 20 cases were classified as 'doubtful'. The transcribed statements were evaluated by one rater who had received training in CBCA and who was blind to the group membership (confirmed or doubtful) of the cases. If a criterion was not present in the statement it received a score of 0, if it was present it received a score of 1, and if it was strongly present it received a score of 2. Hence total possible CBCA scores were in the range 0 to 38. The results were striking. The confirmed cases received a mean CBCA score of 24.8 and the doubtful statements received a mean score of 3.6.

Moreover, the distributions of scores of the confirmed and doubtful groups did not show a single overlap. The highest score in the doubtful group was 10 (one child received that score, and three children obtained a score of 0) and the lowest score in the confirmed group was 16 (one child obtained that score, and the highest score was 34). By assessing the differences between the two groups on each criterion, differences between the doubtful and confirmed groups emerged for 16 of 19 criteria, all in the expected direction. That is, the criteria were more often present in the confirmed cases than in the doubtful cases, which provides strong support for the *Undeutsch hypothesis* (see Table 5.3).

Wells and Loftus (1991, p.139) refer to the findings of Esplin and colleagues as 'among the most impressive we have ever encountered in a psychological study'. Lamers-Winkelman (1995) describes the findings as 'too good to be true'. Wells and Loftus offer alternative explanations for the outcomes. First, the differences between the two groups could be caused by age differences between these groups. Indeed, the children in the 'confirmed' group were older (average 9.1 years) than the children in the 'doubtful' group (average 6.9 years). Moreover, the doubtful group included eight statements from children who were less than 5 years old, whereas the 'confirmed' group only contained one statement from a child under 5 years old. Secondly, the independent criteria used for the 'doubtful cases' in the study were 'judicial dismissal', 'no prosecution' 'no confessions made by the defendant' and 'persistent denial by the accused'. Wells and Loftus argue that these criteria are not independent case facts. Judicial dismissal, absence of prosecution, no confession and persistent denial by the defendant may not only have occurred because the reports were false (as suggested by the researchers), but also because the children were unconvincing even though they were telling the truth and sexual abuse did actually take place.

> 'They might have been unconvincing because these children might have deficiencies in logical reasoning, they might have been frightened to the extent that they could not process peripheral detail, they might have poor verbal skills, and so on. Because they are unconvincing witnesses, prosecutors might be unlikely to press charges (lack of prosecution), judges might feel that conviction is unlikely (judicial dismissal), and defense attorneys might be unlikely to advise their clients to admit to the charges (no confessions and persistent denial by the accused)' (Wells & Loftus, 1991, p.169).

As many CBCA criteria are related to how convincing the subjects are, the CBCA ratings of unconvincing children will probably be low and will lead the CBCA rater to believe that the report was false. Thirdly, perhaps the cases selected in this study were extreme cases, and less striking outcomes may appear when more uncertain cases are assessed.

Boychuk (1991) addressed some of these criticisms in her subsequent study. The statements of 75 children between 4 and 16 years of age were analysed by three raters who were blind to case disposition, and Boychuk included in her sample (apart from 'confirmed' and 'doubtful' groups) a third group, namely a 'likely abused' group. The 'likely abused' were those without medical evidence but with confessions by the accused or criminal sanctions from a Superior Court. Unfortunately, in all of her analyses (including the one presented in Table 5.3) she combined the confirmed group and the likely abused group. By assessing the differences between the two groups on each criterion, Boychuk found less significant differences than Esplin and colleagues (see Table 5.3), but all 13 differences found were in the expected direction. That is, the criteria were more often present in the confirmed cases than in the doubtful cases, which again supports the Undeutsch hypothesis.

Lamb and his colleagues analysed the plausibility of the statements of 98 alleged victims of child sexual abuse (aged 4 to 12 years). Based on independent evidence (such as medical evidence, confessions and polygraph examinations), the statements of 76 children were classified as plausible, the statements of 13 children were classified as implausible and the remaining 9 statements were classified as questionable (the questionable category was excluded from the analyses). They found fewer significant differences than Boychuk and Esplin and colleagues (partly because not all of the 19 criteria were included in the assessment). However, again all differences were in the expected direction, i.e. the criteria were more often present in the plausible group than in the implausible group. Like Esplin and colleagues, they also calculated the mean CBCA scores of their two groups. If a criterion was not present in the statement it received a score of 0, and if it was present it received a score of 1. Only 14 criteria were used in this study, which means that the total CBCA score could range between 0 and 14. Significantly more criteria were present in the confirmed cases (6.74) than in the doubtful cases (4.85). However, this difference is much smaller than the difference found by Esplin and colleagues.

Craig (1995) did not find large differences either. He examined 48 statements of children aged 3 to 16 years, who were alleged victims of sexual abuse. A statement was classified as 'confirmed' if the accused made a confession and/or failed a polygraph test. A statement was classified as 'highly doubtful' if the child provided a detailed and credible recantation and/or the accused passed a polygraph test. The average CBCA scores of his confirmed cases (7.2) were only slightly higher than the average scores of his doubtful cases (5.7). Only 14 criteria were used, and the possible scores could range between 0 and 14.

Lamers-Winkelman (1995) examined the statements of 97 children aged 2 to 12 years. All of these children were alleged victims of sexual abuse. Statements in the 'confirmed group' were compared with statements in a 'likely abused group'. There was no 'doubtful group'. The comparison between the two groups resulted in one difference. Compared to statements in the 'likely abused group', statements in the confirmed group contained more information about the mental state of the perpetrator (criterion 13).

In summary, all of the field studies support the Undeutsch hypothesis. However, the differences between truthful and doubtful statements are not always large.

Perhaps as important as the ability of the criteria to discriminate is the frequency of occurrence in statements. A criterion that discriminates strongly between truthful and fabricated statements is not so useful if it is hardly ever present in statements. The benefit of the first three criteria (logical structure, unstructured production and quantity of details) is that they could occur in all statements. Other criteria, such as unusual details, can only occur if something peculiar happened. The field studies which have been conducted to date show that, in particular, criterion 10 (accurately reported details misunderstood), criterion 16 (raising doubts about one's own memory) and criterion 17 (self-deprecation) seldom seem to occur in statements. The presence of criteria is also dependent on the age of the witness, as will be discussed later on.

Experimental Studies

Although SVA is specifically aimed at children, not much experimental research has been conducted with children to date. In only three studies (Akehurst, Köhnken & Höfer, 1995; Steller, Wellershaus & Wolf, 1988; Winkel & Vrij, 1995) did children actually participate. In the other studies adults were used as participants. There is disagreement as to whether or not CBCA evaluations could be used for adults' statements. Some authors still describe CBCA as a technique solely used to evaluate statements of *children who are alleged victims in sexual abuse cases* (Honts, 1994; Raskin & Esplin, 1991b). Indeed, a criterion such as criterion 10 (accurately reported details misunderstood) may only be useful for young children. A consequence of this point of view is that laboratory research with CBCA is not possible, as for ethical and legal reasons sexual crimes cannot be committed in the laboratory in order to create victims of sexual abuse.

Others have advocated the additional use of the technique to evaluate the testimonies of suspects or adult witnesses who talk about issues other than sexual abuse (Köhnken, Schimossek, Aschermann & Höfer,

1995; Ruby & Brigham, 1997; Steller & Köhnken, 1989). They pointed out that the underlying Undeutsch hypothesis is restricted neither to children, witnesses and victims nor to sexual abuse.

In 11 out of 12 laboratory studies the participants were bystander witnesses. They witnessed a particular event and were instructed either to lie or to tell the truth about the event. Only in Porter and Yuille's (1996) study were the participants guilty and innocent 'suspects'.

Compared to the field studies, the laboratory studies reveal fewer differences between liars and truth-tellers (see also Table 5.3)[2]. However, almost all of the differences were in the expected direction, with the criteria occurring more frequently in truthful reports than in deceptive reports, supporting the Undeutsch hypothesis. Almost all of the findings which deviated from the general pattern were obtained in Ruby and Brigham's study. I can only speculate as to why this might be. First, they used raters who were trained in CBCA scoring for only a very short period (45 minutes), and could therefore possibly not be classified as experienced judges or as 'CBCA experts'. Secondly, Landry and Brigham explain their unexpected findings regarding logical structure and attribution of another's mental state by saying that the participants might have tried hard to make their false story seem believable, and one fairly obvious way to do this would be to make certain that, for example, a logical structure exists. This suggests that liars can influence CBCA ratings. I shall return to the issues of training people in making CBCA assessments and fooling CBCA experts later on.

Table 5.3 further shows that the criteria emerge more frequently in truthful reports made by both children and adults. The study by Akehurst and colleagues is the most direct test of this, as they included statements from both adults and children. They found no differences between age groups, and they also found that the criteria emerged more frequently in the truthful reports of both age groups. Porter and Yuille's (1996) study revealed that some criteria occurred more frequently in the statements of innocent suspects than in the statements of guilty suspects. These findings support the idea that CBCA ratings are not restricted to statements of victims and children about sexual abuse, but could be used in different contexts and with other types of interviewee as well.

A look at the empirical support for each of the 19 criteria shows that criterion 3 received the most support. Truth-tellers include more details in their accounts than liars. Contextual embedding (criterion 4),

---

[2] In laboratory experiments the terms 'truth-teller' and 'liar' can be used. However, in field studies it is not possible to use the term 'liar' as it is not known whether someone who did not tell the truth did so on purpose.

descriptions of interactions (criterion 5), reproduction of conversation (criterion 6) and unusual details (criterion 8) are the types of detail that in particular occur more often in truthful accounts than in deceptive ones. I have already offered several explanations for this. That is, liars have a lack of fantasy to invent such details, they do not mention these details because they are unaware that such details are used to assess the veracity of their statements, they do not have enough knowledge to provide these details, or they do not want to mention many details as this will increase the likelihood that they will contradict themselves or that, when the interviewer checks what they have said, he or she will find out that they were lying.

Unstructured production (criterion 2) received considerable support as well. Compared to truth-tellers, liars tend to tell their stories in a more chronological order (first this happened, then that happened, the next thing that happened was ..., and so on). Liars' statements might be more structured because it is probably difficult to tell a fabricated story in an unstructured way, especially when someone has to make up a story spontaneously. Compared to telling a story in chronological order, telling something in bits and pieces will increase the likelihood that liars contradict themselves. In the study by Zaparniuk, Yuille and Taylor (1995), a difference in unstructured production between truth-tellers and liars was the only difference found. However, on the basis of this criterion alone they were able to classify correctly 70% of the lies and 90% of the truths!

Several criteria, such as criterion 10 and criteria 16 to 19, have received weak support to date. Criterion 17 (self-deprecation) has not received any support at all. Some researchers, such as Lamb and Craig, did not investigate criteria 15 to 18, perhaps because they believe that liars could easily incorporate these criteria into their accounts if they wished to. I shall return to this issue later.

Many other studies focus in particular on differences between truthful and fabricated accounts concerning consistency (criterion 1), quantity of details (criterion 3) and contextual embedding (criterion 4). Generally, these studies provide further evidence for the Undeutsch hypothesis. Most studies found that truth-telling is associated with consistencies (see DePaulo, Stone & Lassiter (1985) for a literature review), many details (Burgoon, Buller, Guerrero, Afifi & Feldman, 1996; Jones & McGraw, 1987; Jones & McQuinston, 1989; Köhnken & Wegener, 1982; Lindsay & Johnson, 1987) and contextual embedding (Alonso-Quecuty, 1991; Johnson & Foley, 1984; Johnson, Foley, Suengas & Raye, 1988; Johnson & Raye, 1981). However, some studies have yielded contradictory findings concerning the number of details (Neisser, 1981).

DETECTING TRUTHS WITH CBCA

To what extent are evaluators who use assessments based on the list of CBCA criteria able to classify truth-tellers and liars correctly? Research indicates that evaluators who are familiar with CBCA achieve higher accuracy rates than evaluators who are not familiar with CBCA (Landry & Brigham, 1992; Steller, Wellershaus & Wolf (1988), cited in Steller, 1989). This suggests that utilizing CBCA improves the accuracy of evaluating the truthfulness of statements. I shall return to this issue later. Table 5.4 lists the accuracy rates of all of the CBCA studies which have reported hit rates so far. A distinction is made between classifications of truths and lies. It is also indicated whether the study dealt with adults or children.

Table 5.4. Accuracy rates of classifying truths and lies when using the CBCA scoring method

	Truth (%)	Lie (%)	Total (%)
Field studies			
Esplin *et al.* (1988) (children)[1,2]	100	100	100
Experimental laboratory studies			
Akehurst *et al.* (1995) (adults and			
children)[3]	73	67	70
Akehurst *et al.* (1995) (adults)[3]			90
Akehurst *et al.* (1995) (children)[3]			71
Höfer *et al.* (1996) (adults)[3]	70	73	71
Köhnken *et al.* (1995) (adults)[3]	88	82	85
Landry & Brigham (1992) (adults)[2]	75	35	55
Porter & Yuille (1996) (adults)[3]	77	80	78
Ruby & Brigham (1998) (white adults)[3]	72	65	69
Ruby & Brigham (1998) (black adults)[3]	67	66	67
Sporer (1997) (adults)[3]	70	60	65
Steller *et al.* (1988) (children)[2]	78	62	70
Vrij (1999) (adults)[3]	77	74	75
Vrij *et al.* (in press) (adults)[2]	80	60	70
Vrij *et al.* (in press) (adults)[3]	53	80	67
Yuille (1988a) (children)[2]	91	74	83
Zaparniuk *et al.* (1995) (adults)[4]	80	77	78

[1] The term lie is inappropriate for Esplin's field study, as it is not known whether participants were actually aware that they were not telling the truth.
[2] Hit rates are calculated by CBCA raters.
[3] Hit rates are calculated by discriminant analysis.
[4] Hit rates are calculated via the decision rule 'first five criteria should be present plus two others'.

The results are mixed. The field study by Esplin and colleagues (1988) achieved the highest accuracy rate possible, namely 100% (a perfect classification of each statement). Landry and Brigham (1992), on the other hand, obtained an accuracy rate of 55%, which is only slightly above the level expected by chance (50%). Others studies obtained accuracy rates between these two extremes, ranging from 65% (Sporer's study) to 90% (the study by Akehurst and colleagues).

A distinction between 'detecting truths' and 'detecting lies' shows the existence of a *truth bias*, i.e. CBCA is more successful in detecting truths than in detecting lies. As was discussed in Chapter 3, a truth bias also emerges if people detect lies and truths by paying attention to non-verbal behaviour. The truth bias in CBCA research is perhaps not surprising, given the fact that CBCA is a truth-verifying method rather than a lie-detection technique. The lower hit rates in detecting lies imply that a relatively large number of deceptive accounts are judged by CBCA raters to be truthful. In other words, many liars are perceived as truth-tellers by CBCA raters. I shall return to this issue later.

Finally, the findings do not reveal differences in accuracy rates when assessing the statements of children and adults, which again suggests that CBCA analyses need not be restricted to children's statements.

Factors Influencing the Presence of CBCA Criteria in Statements

Numerous factors can influence the presence of CBCA criteria in statements. To date, research has focused on five factors in particular.

Age of the Child

Statements of children under 8 years old include fewer criteria than the statements of older children (Boychuk, 1991; Craig, 1995; Hershkowitz, Lamb, Sternberg & Esplin, 1997; Lamb, Hershkowitz, Sternberg, Esplin, Hovav, Manor & Yudilevitch, 1996; Lamers-Winkelman, 1995). This is not surprising. Cognitive abilities and command of language develop throughout childhood, making it gradually easier to provide detailed accounts of what has been witnessed. Boychuk compared the CBCA scores of statements from children of different age groups and found that criterion 5 (descriptions of interactions) and criterion 15 (admitting lack of memory) were more often present in the statements of older children (between 8 and 16 years of age) than in the statements of younger children (between 4 and 7 years of age). She also found that younger children were unable to manifest criterion 13 (accounts of a perpetrator's mental state). The latter finding is not surprising given the fact that children under 8 years of age can only view the world from their own perspective (Flavell, Botkin, Fry, Wright & Jarvis, 1968). Craig (1995) found that the number of criteria present in the statements was significantly greater for older children (age 10–16 years) than for younger children (age 3–9 years). However, CBCA criteria do sometimes occur in the statements of very young children. Lamers-Winkelman analysed the statements of very young children (2- and 3-year-olds) and found that most of the criteria were sometimes present even in the statements of these very young children. Only superfluous details (criterion 9), attribution of perpetrator's mental state (criterion 13), raising doubts about one's own testimony (criterion 16) and self-deprecation (criterion 17) were never present.

Interviewer Style

The style of interviewing has an impact on the number of details elicited from interviews. Open-ended invitations ('Could you please tell me what happened?', 'Is there anything else you want to tell me?', and so on) yield more information than directive utterances—that is, focusing the interviewee's attention on details that the interviewee had not previously mentioned, or refocusing the interviewee's attention on details that he or she had previously mentioned (Hershkowitz, Lamb, Sternberg & Esplin, 1997; Lamb, Esplin & Sternberg, 1995; Lamb, Hershkowitz, Sternberg, Esplin, Hovav, Manor & Yudilevitch, 1996; Sternberg, Lamb, Hershkowitz, Esplin, Redlich & Sunshine, 1996; Sternberg, Lamb, Hershkowitz, Yudilevitch, Orbach, Larson, Esplin & Hovav, in press).

Number of Interviews

The number of interviews conducted with the interviewee is related to the amount of information revealed by the interviewee. Children, for instance, may provide more details in a second interview than in the first interview (Goodman & Schwartz-Kenney, 1992; Yuille & Cutshall, 1989). A possible explanation for this is that children may feel uncomfortable during the first interview with an interviewer they don't know, and they therefore do not dare to say much. Alternatively, they may not trust the interviewer yet and therefore do not wish to say much. In a second interview they may feel more comfortable, or they may trust the interviewer more, which may result in them providing more information. However, Boychuk's field study, showed that conducting too many interviews has a negative impact on the information provided by interviewees. She compared the CBCA scores of children who were interviewed once, twice, three times or at least four times. The interviews with the children who were interviewed at least four times contained less richness than the statements of the other children. As a possible explanation for her findings, Boychuk suggests that after a couple of interviews a child may be tired of talking about the topic and recalling the whole story again. Taken together, these findings suggest that only a limited number of interviews (up to two or perhaps three interviews) is appropriate.

Cognitive Interview

Special interview techniques are designed to increase the amount of information that can be obtained from an interviewee. One of these techniques, known as the *cognitive interview*, was initially developed by the American psychologists Ron Fisher and Ed Geiselman (1992). Nowadays this technique is often used by police officers in Germany, England and the USA when interviewing witnesses. The technique is based on the fact that sometimes information is stored in people's memory but, for whatever reason, they are unable to retrieve this information spontaneously. Using special techniques which are based on psychological principles of remembering and retrieving information from memory, people may well be able to recall information which they initially could not remember. People who are interviewed with this technique have repeatedly been found to provide more information than those who are not interviewed using this method (Köhnken, Milne, Memon & Bull, in press). Furthermore, witness statements obtained with the cognitive interview have been found to receive higher CBCA scores than statements obtained using a standard interview technique (Köhnken, Schimossek, Aschermann & Höfer, 1995; Steller & Wellershaus, 1996) (see Memon (1998) for more detailed information about the cognitive interview technique).

Stressful Events

It is difficult to investigate how good people are at remembering very stressful events, as it is not ethically permissible to create stressful events for the purposes of research. In order to examine people's memory of stressful events, researchers are therefore dependent on real-life cases. However, it is often unclear what actually happened in these cases, which makes it impossible to determine whether someone's recollection of the event is complete and accurate. Peters (1991) investigated what children could report about different stressful events where he did actually know what happened. He investigated children's accounts about a visit to the dentist, an inoculation in a clinic or a staged theft.

His findings revealed that stress sometimes led to impaired recollection of the event. However, there are some striking examples documented in the literature of people who were able to give detailed information about stressful events in which they were involved. Pynoos and Eth (1984), for example, interviewed more than 40 children who witnessed the homicide of one of their parents. They found that these children correctly remembered several details of what they had witnessed. Another study revealed that some children who had witnessed the rape of their mother could still remember this event very well (Pynoos & Nader, 1988). Jones and Krugman (1986) found that a 3-year-old girl who was abducted, sexually abused and left in a pit by a stranger could give a detailed account of both the event and the stranger. People who were in the concentration camp Erika during the Second World War still had detailed memories of this period more than 40 years later (Wagenaar & Groeneweg, 1990). In this study, prisoners were interviewed twice about their stay in the concentration camp, once in the period 1943–1947 and once in the period 1984–1987. It was found that camp experiences were generally well remembered, although sometimes specific and essential details were forgotten. Among these were forgetting about being maltreated, and forgetting having been a witness to murder.

AN ASSESSMENT OF THE VALIDITY CHECK-LIST

Research into the effectiveness of the Validity Check-list (see Table 5.2) has not been carried out to date. Validity checks in experimental CBCA studies are unnecessary, as the circumstances are always standardized in these types of study. However, in the CBCA field studies which were mentioned earlier, validity checks of the CBCA ratings were also not reported (or perhaps not carried out).

On the basis of existing research, it is possible to question the justification of some of the Validity Check-list criteria, namely 'inappropriateness of affect' (criterion 2), 'susceptibility to suggestion' (criterion 3) and 'inconsistency with other statements' (criterion 10).

Criterion 2 stated that if an interviewee reports details of abuse without showing any signs of emotion, the story is less trustworthy than if clear signs of emotion are displayed. In my view, this is an incorrect conclusion, as not all people show clear emotions when they inform others about negative experiences. One of my own experimental studies (Vrij & Fischer, 1995) suggested that some 'victims' show clear signs of distress whereas others do not, and a field study by Littmann and Szewczyk (1983) found that showing distress during an interview was not a valid predictor of the validity of the statement. I therefore believe that it is inappropriate to draw conclusions on the basis of whether or not victims display emotional behaviour.

Criterion 3 deals with susceptibility to suggestion. Some witnesses are more susceptible to suggestions made by interviewers than others, and might provide information which confirms the interviewer's expectations, but which is in fact inaccurate. As mentioned earlier, Yuille (1988b) and Landry and Brigham (1992) therefore recommend asking the witness a few leading questions at the end of the interview in order to assess their susceptibility to suggestion. They recommend asking some questions about peripheral information (e.g. 'When you were with your sister, which friend was there as well, Claire or Sarah?', when the interviewer knows that there was no friend present). Obviously, it is not permissible to ask any questions about central information, as this may distort the interviewee's memory. That is, questions may influence a person's memory of an event, and people may remember events which never took place only because the interviewer suggested to them that these events did occur. A study conducted by Loftus and Palmer (1974) is a classical example of this phenomenon. Participants saw a film of a traffic accident and then answered questions about the event, including the question 'About how fast were the cars going when they *contacted* each other?' Other participants received the same information, except that the verb 'contacted' was replaced by either *hit, bumped, collided* or *smashed*. Even though all of the participants saw the same film, the wording of the questions affected their answers. The speed estimates (in miles per hour) were 31, 34, 38, 39 and 41, respectively. One week later, the participants were asked whether they had seen broken glass at the accident site. Although the correct answer was 'no', 32% of the participants who were given the 'smashed' condition said that they had. Hence the wording of the question had influenced their memory of the incident. The fact that questions can only be asked about peripheral information causes a problem, as children show more resistance to suggestibility for central parts than for peripheral parts of the event (Goodman, Rudy, Bottoms & Aman, 1990). Moreover, they are more resistant to suggestibility for stressful events (which are likely to be central events) than for events which are less stressful (and likely to be peripheral events) (Davies, 1991). Thus, if an interviewee yields to a leading question about a peripheral part of the event, this does not imply that they were not resistible to suggestion when more important aspects were discussed. This criterion also seems to assume that suggestion is more the result of individual differences than of circumstances. This may not be a valid assumption (Milne & Bull, 1999).

Criterion 10 deals with inconsistencies between different statements made by the same witness, and it suggests that one statement may in fact be fabricated if interviewees contradict themselves in two different statements. In my view, this belief is incorrect. Research has shown that contradictory statements made by one child do not always mean that one of the statements is fabricated (Moston, 1987; Poole & White, 1991). Conflicting statements may well be the result of question repetition. Young children in particular may give two different answers to the same question, because they might think 'If the same question is asked on a second occasion, the first answer I gave must have been wrong.' This reasoning of children makes sense because this often happens to them. Parents and teachers often repeat the question when the initial answer they received was wrong. For example, when parents are reading a picture-book about a zoo with their children, the following type of conversation often takes place: 'What is that? A cat? Is that a cat? No, look carefully. What is this, isn't he much bigger than a cat? That's right, it is a tiger! Well done!' In summary, inconsistent or contradictory statements made by interviewees may be the result of the interviewer repeating the questions. In judging inconsistencies or contradictions, this interviewer factor should therefore be taken into account.

PROBLEMS IN USING SVA

The problems related to SVA are caused by two shortcomings. First, SVA is not a standardized instrument, and secondly, the method lacks theoretical underpinning. The first four problems I shall now discuss are all related to the lack of standardization.

Number of Criteria

At present there are no formalized CBCA decision rules to determine whether a statement is truthful or not. Different experts use different rules, and some of these are very detailed. According to Yuille (cited in Horowitz, 1991), statements can be classified as truthful if they fulfil the first five criteria plus any two of the remaining criteria. Raskin (cited in Zaparniuk, Yuille & Taylor, 1995) considered a statement to be truthful if criteria 1 to 3, plus any four of the remaining criteria, are present. Craig (1995) argued that statements containing more than five criteria are likely to be valid. A factor that makes this 'number of criteria issue' even more complicated is that not all experts use all 19 criteria when assessing statements. However, the fact that some experts do use decision rules is remarkable. It suggests that assessments about the veracity of statements can be made on the basis of CBCA outcomes alone, whereas the same experts argue that this is impossible, as external factors may influence the richness of statements and may thus influence the CBCA scores. I therefore agree with Lamers-Winkelman (1995), a Dutch SVA expert who stated that the use of such decision rules is inappropriate. Steller (1999, personal communication) and Köhnken (1999, personal communication) are also strongly opposed to the use of decision rules.

Weight of the Criteria

Steller and Köhnken (1989) noted that some criteria may be of more value in assessing truthfulness than others. For example, the presence of accurately reported but misunderstood details in a statement (criterion 10), such as a child who describes the adult's sexual behaviour but attributes it to a sneeze or to pain, is apparently more significant than the fact that she describes where the alleged sexual encounter took place (criterion 4). (The problem with criterion 10, however, is that it is not often present in statements.)

One possible way to determine the importance of individual CBCA criteria is to conduct laboratory research and to examine those criteria on which truth-tellers and liars particularly differ. As mentioned earlier, differences emerge especially with regard to unstructured production (criterion 2), quantity of details (criterion 3), contextual embeddings (criterion 4), descriptions of interactions (criterion 5), reproduction of conversation (criterion 6) and unusual details (criterion 8).

Köhnken (1999, personal communication) pointed out that there is a fundamental problem with using the discriminative value (between truthful and fabricated stories) of individual CBCA criteria in laboratory studies as an indicator of their discriminative value in real-life assessments. According to Köhnken, the discriminative value of criteria might strongly depend on the type of event that is being assessed. Consequently, some criteria may be very important for the assessment of real-life cases, although they rarely emerge as significant in laboratory studies.

Given the above problems concerning the number of criteria and the weighting of the criteria, CBCA researchers use different methods to make their truth–lie classifications. In some studies, CBCA raters made their own overall truth–hit classifications (see Table 5.4). In most other studies, CBCA raters scored the statements, but the truth–lie classifications were made by computer utilizing a statistical analysis program. The major difference is that CBCA raters might have given individual criteria different weightings, whereas the computer analyses did not do this. One might therefore conclude that CBCA raters' classifications would be more accurate. One specific element in a statement (a misunderstood detail, an unusual detail, a detailed description of a complicated interaction, and so on) might have convinced an expert that a statement is truthful, whereas such a detail was not given particular weight in the computer analysis. However, the studies conducted so far do not support the view that experts are more effective. As can be seen in Table 5.4, the hit rates in studies based on raters' classifications are similar to the accuracy rates in studies based on computer analysis classifications. A reliable way to test the differences in decision-making by experts and by computer analysis is by comparing experts' and computers' classifications in the same study. Only Vrij, Kneller and Mann (in press) made such a comparison in their experiment. The expert was more accurate in detecting truths (hit rates were 80% and 53% for expert and computer, respectively; see Table 5.4), whereas the computer was more accurate in detecting lies (hit rates were 60% and 80% for expert and computer, respectively). The differences in hit rates between expert and computer support the idea that the expert did not make the classification solely on the basis of the CBCA scores, but also used some kind of weighting system. However, this weighting process, did not result in better hit rates overall.

Impact of External Factors

It is difficult or even impossible to determine the exact nature of the impact on witnesses' accounts of each of the factors summarized in the Validity Check-list. For example, interview style often has an impact on the amount of information that witnesses report. However, this does not mean that a witness will necessarily be affected by a particular interview style during a particular interview. And even if the witness was affected by the style of interviewing, it is impossible to determine afterwards the precise impact. In other words, the precise impact of a specific factor on an individual report can never be determined—it can only be *estimated*. Obviously, mistakes in these estimations may well occur. It is also possible that there are still unidentified factors, which are not listed in the Validity Check-list, that do affect a person's account.

SVA Assessments are Subjective

The above issues make it clear that SVA assessments are subjective. This means that they are dependent on the interpretation of the individual assessor. It is therefore important to know to what extent different evaluators obtain the same outcome when assessing the same statements. SVA decisions would be unreliable and therefore inappropriate to use when different evaluators reach different conclusions on the basis of the same material. Two different inter-rater agreements between evaluators are possible. First, different evaluators might agree concerning the total CBCA score of a given statement. That is, evaluators might agree about the number of criteria present in a statement. Secondly, there might be agreement between evaluators concerning the presence and absence of each individual criterion. Research has indicated that inter-rater agreement regarding total CBCA scores is quite high and satisfactory. However, inter rater agreement per criterion is sometimes quite low[3].

An alternative method for testing reliability involves having one evaluator rate the same statement twice at different times, and checking whether there is agreement between these two ratings. Horowitz and his colleagues asked evaluators to do this. As with inter-rater agreements, these intra-rater agreements were satisfactory with regard to total CBCA scores, but were quite low for some of the individual criteria (Horowitz, Lamb, Esplin, Boychuk, Krispin & Reiter-Lavery, 1997).

Höfer and Köhnken (1999) argued that poor inter-rater agreement in CBCA studies may have been due to poor training of raters. They developed a 3-week training programme and reported satisfactory inter-rater agreement between their raters even for the individual CBCA criteria after the 3-week training exercise.

There has not yet been any research investigating inter-rater agreement on SVA decisions—that is, CBCA scores and Validity Checklist judgements combined. Lamers-Winkelman (1995) believes that they may well not always be satisfactory. Köhnken (a German professor in forensic psychology who is frequently an expert witness in German

---

[3] Studies in which overall inter-rater agreement rates were reported obtained quite high but never perfect, inter-rater agreement rates (Anson, Golding & Gully 1993; Boychuk, 1986; Höfer, Akehurst & Metzger, 1996; Steller, Wellershaus & Wolf, 1988) (these studies report the proportion of agreement rates for the presence of criteria). More studies have reported inter-rater agreement rates per criterion, which are sometimes quite low. For instance, Höfer, Akehurst and Metzger (1996) had to exclude three criteria (out of 15 criteria used) from further analyses due to there being no significant inter-rater agreements. Akehurst, Köhnken, and Höfer (1995) had to delete three criteria for similar reasons. Anson, Golding and Gully (1993) argued that their low inter-rater agreement rates per criterion could be caused by the fact that they provided their raters with videotapes which could have affected the reliability of the recorded judgements, particularly as the CBCA system is designed for use with transcripts (see Chapter 3 concerning how videotapes can disturb judgements). We may conclude that CBCA is a satisfactorily reliable assessment technique as long as transcripts and total CBCA scores are used, although some improvements could still be made. On the basis of their literature review, Horowitz, Lamb, Esplin, Boychuk, Krispin and Reiter-Lavery (1997) concluded that in particular criterion 8 (unusual details), criterion 9 (superfluous details), criterion 11 (related external associations), criterion 14 (spontaneous corrections) and criterion 15 (admitting lack of memory) need to be defined more clearly. See Tully (1998) and Horowitz (1998) for a recent debate about the importance of high levels of inter-rater agreement.

criminal court cases) agrees with Lamers-Winkelman and believes that this is due to the Validity Check-list. If two experts disagree about the truthfulness of a statement in German criminal cases, they often disagree about the likely impact of some external factors on that statement (Köhnken, 1997, personal communication).

Unclear When the Method Can be Used

CBCA is based on the Undeutsch hypothesis which states that 'a statement derived from a memory of an actual experience differs in content and quality from a statement based on invention or fantasy'. However, this is merely a working hypothesis that postulates that certain differences should appear, but which does not specify why these differences are to be expected (Sporer, 1997). The development of CBCA is based on the experience that professionals have with interviewing sexually abused children, and is specifically designed to assess the veracity of judgements in such cases. One of the benefits of a theoretical approach is that it makes it possible to predict in which situations the method can be used. Because SVA lacks theoretical underpinning, it is difficult to say in which situations it could be applied and, as I discussed earlier in this chapter, CBCA experts do actually disagree about the circumstances in which the method can be used.

WHAT DO PEOPLE THINK TRUTH-TELLERS SAY?

CBCA Criteria

Which verbal characteristics make a story more or less credible to observers who are not familiar with the CBCA literature? Very little research has been conducted so far addressing this issue. To my knowledge, only two (very similar) studies have been conducted addressing observers' beliefs about the relationship between CBCA criteria and truthfulness. The studies are listed in Table 5.5. In these studies, participants were provided with a list of CBCA criteria and were asked whether they believed that the frequency of occurrence of these criteria increases or decreases during fabrication compared to truth-telling, or whether it does not differ between truth-telling and fabrication. Both studies were conducted in the UK and included both lay people and police officers as participants.

The findings of both studies did not reveal differences between lay people and police officers, indicating that police officers and lay people have similar beliefs about the verbal characteristics of truth-telling. The findings further indicate that the 'correct relationship'

Table 5.5. Subjective relationship between verbal characteristics and truth-telling (criteria-based content analysis)

	CBCA criteria																		
	1	2	3	4	5	6	7	8	9	10	11	12	13	14	15	16	17	18	19
Akehurst *et al.* (1996)	>	<	>	—	—	<	<	<	<			<	>	<	<	<	—		
Taylor & Vrij (1999)	—	—	—	<			<	<	<					<	<	>	>		

>, observers believe that the verbal characteristic occurs more frequently during truth-telling than when lying;
<, observers believe that the verbal characteristic occurs less frequently during truth-telling than when lying;
—, observers do not associate the verbal characteristic with lying/truth-telling.

(i.e. that these criteria occur more frequently during truth-telling) was only mentioned a few times, namely three times in the study by Akehurst and colleagues and twice in the study by Taylor and Vrij. Participants in the study conducted by Akehurst and colleagues believed that, compared to a fabricated account, a truthful account has a more logical structure (criterion 1), incorporates more details (criterion 3) and includes more attributions of the perpetrator's mental state (criterion 13). Participants in the study conducted by Taylor and Vrij believed that truthful statements include more doubts about one's own memory (criterion 16) and more self-deprecation (criterion 17).

On the other hand, an incorrect relationship (i.e. that CBCA criteria occur less frequently during truth-telling) was mentioned nine times in the study by Akehurst and colleagues and six times in the study by Taylor and Vrij. In both studies, observers believed that truthful accounts compared to fabricated accounts included fewer unexpected complications (criterion 7), fewer unusual details (criterion 8), fewer superfluous details (criterion 9), fewer spontaneous corrections (criterion 14) and fewer admissions of lack of memory (criterion 15). In addition to this, participants in the study by Akehurst and colleagues thought that, compared to fabricated accounts, truthful accounts were more structured (criterion 2) and included fewer reproductions of conversation (criterion 6), fewer accounts of the mental state of the witness (criterion 12) and fewer doubts about one's own testimony (criterion 16). Participants in Taylor and Vrij's study further believed that truthful statements contain less contextual embedding (criterion 4) than deceptive statements. I have to be careful when drawing conclusions on the basis of the studies performed so far, as only two studies have been conducted and both reveal some different findings. However, the results suggest that people are not very aware of the verbal characteristics of truth-telling. This is interesting, as it may influence what motivated liars will say when they wish to make a credible impression. For example, they will probably not purposely include unexpected complications, unusual details and superfluous details in their accounts, because they believe that truth-tellers do not mention these types of details either. The absence of these types of details may then give away their lies. Obviously, obtaining knowledge about the verbal characteristics of truth-telling (for example, by reading this book) may change a liar's strategy in order to make an honest impression on observers. I shall return to this issue later.

Further studies have not actually included the list of CBCA criteria, but focused more on the relationship between perceived credibility and number of details. Most studies found that the inclusion of many details makes an honest impression (Bell & Loftus, 1988, 1989; Conte, Sorenson, Fogarty & Rosa, 1991; Wells & Leippe, 1981). For instance, Bell and Loftus (1989) and Wells and Leippe (1981) found that mock-jurors tended to believe witnesses who recalled more trivial and irrelevant details about a crime more than they believed those who remembered only central information. However, Freedman, Adam, Davey and Koegl (1996) found that this relationship depends on the context. When observers are suspicious that someone is lying, maximum impact is incurred by an intermediate level of detail. Too many details in these circumstances could easily give observers impressions such as 'They were trying too hard to be convincing', 'They were being defensive' or 'They were making up some of the material'. Coolbear (1992) also mentioned that too much detail evokes suspicion because it suggests that the child has been given the story.

SVA Check-list

Coolbear (1992) investigated to what extent professionals (not familiar with SVA) actually use criteria similar to the Validity Check-list to assess the credibility of allegations. She held structured interviews with 51 professionals (from the legal profession and human services who had experience with child sexual abuse allegations) about the methods used to assess the credibility of such allegations. The most common response was that the use of childlike language was an indicator of truthfulness (item 1 on the check-list). Emotional congruence with the nature of the material covered by the child (item 2 of the check-list) was also mentioned as indicative of a truthful story. Finally, many participants stated that they would proceed cautiously with a sexual abuse allegation if they knew that there was a custody/access dispute or divorce process between the child's parents (items 6 to 8).

EVALUATION

SVA assessments are accepted as evidence in criminal courts in several countries world-wide. The findings presented in this chapter generally support the Undeutsch hypothesis—that is, they support the idea that 'a statement derived from memory of an actual experience differs in content and quality from a statement based on invention or fantasy'. However, in my view, there are several problems with SVA assessments which make the use of such assessments in courts as a substantial piece of evidence undesirable, at least at present. I shall discuss five of these problems.

Problems with Correctly Classifying Fabricated Stories

Unfortunately, most field studies conducted so far have not reported data on how accurate evaluators were in classifying truthful and fabricated statements. In the field study by Esplin and colleagues there was no overlap between truthful and fabricated statements, resulting in a 100% hit rate. However, this study was methodologically flawed, which makes the findings unreliable. The accuracy rates in laboratory studies revealed that evaluators do make incorrect decisions when classifying truth-tellers and liars, particularly when classifying liars. In most studies, an accuracy rate of between 65% and 75% was found (with a chance level of 50%), indicating that incorrect decisions were made in 25% to 35% of cases. In these cases, liars were incorrectly classified as truth-tellers. These percentages of incorrect classifications are shocking, assuming that they reflect how decisions in real life are made. We do not know whether the findings of laboratory research reflect findings in real life, and we do not know whether SVA evaluators in real life have a similar tendency to classify fabricated stories as truthful. However, let us assume that the laboratory findings reflect a trend which appears in real life, and that SVA experts have a tendency to believe fabricated stories. Such an incorrect decision would have serious consequences. In real life the SVA method is usually used to assess the statements of witnesses or victims. Such an error could result in someone who is actually innocent being falsely convicted of a crime because the fabricated statement of the witness was incorrectly classified as truthful. False convictions of innocent suspects are unacceptable, at least in Western legal systems which are founded on the principle that it is better to acquit 10 guilty people than to convict one person who is innocent. Thus, achieving higher accuracy rates in classifying fabricated statements is necessary before the introduction of SVA assessment as substantial evidence in court can be considered.

What is 'the Truth'?

It is perhaps not surprising that CBCA assessments have relatively low hit rates in classifying lies, given the fact that CBCA is a truth-verifying rather than a lie-detection tool. However, the question is 'What is the truth?'. Suppose that someone has been sexually abused and therefore provides a rich account of her experiences, but misidentifies the perpetrator and accuses an innocent suspect of being the culprit. It may well be the case that experts believe her story, given the quantity and richness of the details provided. If courts base their decisions on these evaluations, innocent people could well be convicted.

It is also possible that a witness believes he or she has witnessed a particular event, and has detailed memories of this type of event, although their memories are not in fact of this event. A recent and compelling example was given by Crombag, Wagenaar and Van Koppen (1996). Their study was based on a real-life event, namely the crash of a cargo El Al Boeing 747 into an 11-storey apartment building in Amsterdam (The Netherlands) on 4 October 1992. Dutch television reported extensively on this national disaster, showing the fire brigade fighting the blaze and rescuing people from the collapsing building. The disaster was the main news item for several days, and eventually everyone in the country knew—or thought they knew—in great detail what had happened. In all of these news programmes, the television could only show what had happened after the crash; the crash itself was never filmed and thus never broadcast. Nevertheless, 61 (66%) of the 93 students who participated in the study answered the question 'Did you see the television footage of the moment the plane hit the apartment building?' in the affirmative. Many 'witnesses' provided further details of this non-existent television footage of the crashing plane. For instance, 41 students remembered that they had seen that the plane hit the building horizontally, 10 students remembered that the plane hit the building vertically, and 14 students indicated that they had seen on television that the plane was already burning when it crashed. In summary, many participants had rich and vivid memories about an event they had never witnessed, but which they thought they had seen.

Johnson, Hashtroudi and Lindsay (1993) describe a CBS television programme in which the then President Reagan recounted a story to navy personnel about an act of heroism that he attributed to a real US pilot. However, no record of this real act or a similar act of heroism could be found, but the story bore an uncanny resemblance to a scene from a Dana Andrews movie released in the 1940s.

It is common knowledge that children sometimes have rich and vivid fantasies[4]. Children, more than adults, sometimes have difficulties with *reality monitoring*—that is, they may become confused about what they have *actually experienced* and what they have only *imagined* (Foley &

---

[4] One reason why children have more difficulties than adults in distinguishing between experienced and imagined events is that they do not yet use the tricks adults employ to make such distinctions. For example, suppose you were with your family at a Mediterranean beach resort during the Christmas holiday. You talked with your family about going for a swim several times, but you never went because it was winter and too cold to go for a swim in the sea. A couple of years later a friend visits your family and asks whether you went swimming in the sea during that particular Christmas holiday at that beach resort. Adults will probably be less confused than children about this issue, because they realize that they would never have gone for a swim in the sea during the winter.

Johnson, 1985; Johnson & Foley, 1984; Markham, 1991; Parker, 1995). Ceci and his colleagues asked 3- to 6-year-olds to imagine several events, including events that had never happened to them, such as falling off a tricycle and receiving stitches in the leg (negative event) and going on a hot-air balloon ride with their classmates (positive event) (Ceci, Loftus, Leichtman & Bruck, 1994). They held weekly interviews with the children about the events they had imagined. During the eleventh interview, 59% of the 3- and 4-year-olds and 51% of the 5- and 6-year olds thought that they had actually once been in a hot-air balloon and 31% of the 3- and 4-year-olds and 28% of the 5- and 6-year-olds told the interviewer that they had once actually fallen off their tricycle and received stitches in the leg. All of the interviews were videotaped, and these tapes revealed internally coherent, detailed, yet false narratives. In follow-up studies, Ceci and his colleagues showed video clips of the children's eleventh session to professionals (clinicians and researchers who were specialized in interviewing children) to see if they could determine which events had actually been experienced by the children and which were fictitious (Ceci, Huffman, Smith & Loftus, 1994; Ceci, Loftus, Leichtman & Bruck, 1994). These professionals were no better than would be expected by chance at distinguishing between accurate and inaccurate reports (although they were not trained in using CBCA).

In summary, fabricated stories could be very detailed, vivid and rich in information. It is therefore not surprising that CBCA evaluators are sometimes incorrect, as they consider details, vividness and richness to be indicators of veracity. In this respect, it is a pity that CBCA assessments focus solely on 'truth criteria', as the inclusion of 'lie criteria' (verbal indicators of deception) might make the instrument less vulnerable in assessing these types of fabrications.

Subjective Evaluations

I mentioned earlier that SVA assessments are subjective—that is, the outcomes are dependent on the interpretation of the evaluator. It is therefore necessary that, in applied settings, not one but at least two evaluators assess a statement independently from each other. At present this is not common practice. For example, the current German practice is for only one expert to evaluate a statement (Köhnken, 1997, personal communication).

The Only Piece of Evidence

Accuracy rates of CBCA evaluations which have been published to date are too low to introduce such evaluations as evidence in court, given the fact that SVA evaluations often represent a major piece of evidence in a criminal case (Steller & Köhnken, 1989). Sexual offences are often characterized by a lack of evidence, and the statements of the alleged victim and suspect are sometimes the only information available. As a result, jurors and judges might rely heavily on decisions made by SVA experts, which makes it crucial that they are accurate. Personally, I believe that an accuracy rate of less than 90–95% is unacceptable. Moreover, inaccurate judgements may lead to false confessions. Suppose that an innocent suspect cannot prove his innocence and that the SVA expert makes an incorrect decision and informs the court that he or she believes the child's accusation. The suspect might then think that he cannot now avoid a conviction, and might decide to plead guilty and to make a false confession in order to obtain a reduced sentence. It is difficult to verify an expert's decision because there is often no information available to check the accuracy of that decision. The only way to provide some insight into the accuracy of SVA decisions is by using several independent SVA evaluators.

What Do We Know about the Effectiveness of SVA Decisions?

To date, CBCA has attracted the attention of numerous researchers. Many CBCA studies have been published recently, and several scholars are conducting more research at the moment. I approve of this development, as many issues still need to be resolved (as will be discussed in the following section). However, all of the studies published so far are CBCA studies. As yet not a single SVA study has been published. This is alarming given the fact that SVA decisions are presented in court. One might say that SVA research is a two-step process. First, the effectiveness of CBCA should be examined under well-controlled conditions, such as laboratory experiments. These studies have shown that CBCA assessments are not 100% accurate. I therefore agree with Lamb and his colleagues who concluded, on the basis of their field study, that:

> 'Although the results are consistent with Raskin and Esplin's prediction that more CBCA criteria should be present in accounts that are independently deemed credible than in accounts of incidents that appear unlikely to have happened, the level of precision clearly remains too poor to permit the designation of CBCA as a reliable and valid test suitable for the courtroom' (Lamb, Sternberg, Esplin, Hershkowitz, Orbach & Hovav, 1997, p.262) (see also Lamb, Sternberg, Esplin, Hershkowitz & Orbach, 1997).

However, their view is somewhat misleading as they are referring to CBCA decisions, whereas experts present SVA decisions in court. This makes the second step essential. In this stage, SVA decisions—that is,

CBCA assessments combined with the influence of external factors—should be examined. Are decisions more accurate when external factors which are listed in the Validity Check-list are taken into account? In other words, are SVA outcomes more accurate than CBCA outcomes? They might be, and again they should be if SVA evaluators are to present their evaluations as a substantial piece of evidence in court.

Although I believe that at present SVA evaluations should not be allowed in court as a substantial piece of evidence, SVA evaluators appear to be able to detect truths and lies more accurately than would be expected by chance. This makes their assessments valuable. They might be useful in police investigations—for example, to guide those investigations. If other substantial pieces of evidence are presented in court, their assessments might be introduced as additional evidence. In such a case, problems related to SVA (such as the truth bias in CBCA assessments and the fact that evaluations are subjective) should be presented as well. I also believe that more research should be conducted in order to obtain a more detailed view of the effectiveness of SVA assessments. I shall outline in the next section what I have in mind.

FURTHER RESEARCH INTO SVA

- Research should focus not only on CBCA assessments but also on SVA assessments.
- Before people can actually conduct SVA assessments, they need to be trained in how to score statements. Raskin and Esplin (1991b) pointed out that making CBCA evaluations is a skill that can be learned in 2 or 3 days. Horowitz (1991) found that the General Characteristics (criteria 1, 2 and 3) are particularly difficult to teach to new coders, perhaps because they are less specific than the other criteria. However, research has indicated that 45 to 90 minutes of training is sufficient to enable college students to improve their accuracy in differentiating between truthful and fabricated statements given by children (Steller, 1989) and by adults (Landry & Brigham, 1992).

    Akehurst, Bull and Vrij (2000) recently trained different groups of people (police officers, social workers and college students) in the use of CBCA. Training involved a 45-minute session based on materials supplied by David Raskin and John Yuille. Our findings revealed that training did not improve students' and social workers' detection accuracy, and that police officers performed significantly less well after the training session. Köhnken (1987) also found that police officers performed less well after being trained in the use of CBCA. He suggested that the training programme was too difficult for them to understand and apply. These findings are worth noting as CBCA assessments may be particularly useful for police officers. Therefore training programmes that are appropriate for them need to be developed.

- Although SVA has been developed to assess the veracity of statements made by children, only a few studies have been conducted with children to date. More research with children is therefore needed.

- As mentioned earlier, it has been suggested that CBCA assessments can also be used to evaluate statements made by suspects. This would be particularly useful for the police. However, only one study with suspects has been published to date.

- So far, the effectiveness of CBCA has only been studied in a judicial context. It might be useful to investigate whether the technique has relevance in a range of other situations. Steller suggested that CBCA assessments are possible when the statements under investigation are related to events which are negatively emotional, involve a loss of control and directly involve the interviewee (Steller, Wellershaus & Wolf, 1988). Many situations outside the judicial context fulfil these criteria, such as the patient who recalls a traumatic but not sexually or criminally related experience in his childhood during a therapeutic session, people who claim to have witnessed men wearing white uniforms and searching the debris directly after an airplane crash (as happened in The Netherlands directly after the crash with the Boeing 737 in Amsterdam which was discussed earlier), the holiday-maker who claims that the tour guide was responsible for the fact that he lost his way, and therefore wants his money back from the travel agency, and the employee who claims that his colleague is responsible for the fact that a job was not finished on time. Obviously, making complete CBCA assessments is very time-consuming and perhaps not possible in many situations. However, it might be that a quick assessment, using only some criteria, may give a rough idea of the veracity of statements. Criterion 2 (unstructured production) might be useful for this purpose, as the study by Zaparniuk and colleagues showed that 90% of the truths and 70% of the lies could be classified on the basis of this criterion (Zaparniuk, Yuille & Taylor, 1995). I would like to emphasize the use of the words 'a rough idea'. Using only a limited number of criteria is almost certainly going to make the accuracy of judgements lower. Bearing this in mind, one might question the strength of the argument used by the (German) prosecution in a recent case against a woman suspected of supplying the weapons used in a hijacking of a Lufthansa airliner in Mogadishu in 1977. The prosecution relied heavily on a witness whose account was 'so detailed as to be beyond reproach' (*The Independent*, 17 November 1998, p.18). Looking at details alone sounds to me to be a risky way of assessing the veracity of a witness's statement.

• An issue which has not been widely addressed in CBCA-related literature is to what extent people are able to mislead evaluators. That is, to what extent are liars who realize that their statements will be assessed via the CBCA method able to give false accounts which include enough CBCA criteria to make a reliable impression on CBCA evaluators? It seems plausible to assume that some CBCA criteria are easier for deceivers to manipulate than others. For instance, it is probably easier to admit lack of memory (criterion 15) than to tell a fabricated story in an unstructured way (criterion 2). Criterion 15 is therefore more likely to occur in manipulated statements than criterion 2. Other criteria, such as reproduction of conversation (criterion 6), unusual details (criterion 8) and superfluous details (criterion 9) may create problems, too. Not everyone will be inventive enough to incorporate such details in their false statements, and those who are able to do this may have difficulty in remembering these details once they have been included in a fabricated statement. Adequate memory of these fabricated details is important both to avoid inconsistencies in the statement and to avoid forgetting these details in a subsequent interview.

We recently completed a study investigating college students' ability to fool CBCA evaluators (Vrij, Kneller & Mann, in press). Participants were asked either to tell the truth or to lie about a videotaped event. Prior to this task, half of the liars (the so-called informed liars) were informed about nine CBCA criteria. Information was given about criterion 2 (unstructured production), criterion 3 (quantity of details), criterion 4 (contextual embedding), criterion 8 (unusual details), criterion 9 (superfluous details), criterion 13 (attribution of perpetrator's mental state), criterion 14 (spontaneous corrections), criterion 15 (admitting lack of memory) and criterion 16 (raising doubts about one's own memory). Other liars were not informed (so-called 'uninformed liars'). The statements of the participants were scored via the CBCA method. The results indicated that the total CBCA score of uninformed liars was significantly lower than the total CBCA score of truth-tellers and informed liars, whereas the total CBCA scores of informed liars and truth-tellers did not differ significantly from each other. However, this does not necessarily mean that the informed liars were successful in fooling CBCA evaluators.

Including CBCA criteria in a statement is not in itself enough. They have to be included in a convincing way. It may be possible that CBCA experts will become suspicious when they read the statements of informed liars. Liars might exaggerate when they include CBCA criteria in their accounts, and as a result some CBCA criteria might be too obviously present. For example, it is possible that liars could admit lack of memory so often during their accounts that this would make a CBCA expert suspicious. We therefore asked an English CBCA expert to assess the veracity of each statement, without informing the expert that we had informed some liars about CBCA. The expert performed very poorly in detecting lies of the informed liars, and was accurate in only 27% of the cases. We subsequently informed the expert about our manipulation, and asked the expert to reassess the statements. This time 40% of the lies of informed liars were detected—still below the level expected by chance. These findings showed that our college students were able to fool a CBCA expert. However, I do not assume that everyone will succeed in doing this. For example, it is doubtful whether very young children are able to fool CBCA evaluators, as they probably lack the necessary cognitive skills. The issue of misleading CBCA evaluators therefore seems to be a particularly relevant question in assessing the statements of older children and adults.

- As Ruby and Brigham (1997, 1998) correctly pointed out, CBCA research has not yet addressed possible cultural differences. Studies have primarily used the statements of European and American white people, whose expressive style of verbal behaviour may differ from the verbal behaviour of people from other cultural and racial groups. As was mentioned in Chapter 3, research has revealed differences in non-verbal behaviour between white American and Afro-American people, and between native (white) Dutch people and black Dutch people originating from Surinam. Research into verbal differences between black and white people during both truth-telling and deception needs to be conducted as well.
- All CBCA criteria are indicators of truthfulness. For the reasons mentioned above, it would be useful to include some lie criteria and to examine whether this will increase the accuracy scores. Some lie criteria were introduced in the previous chapter, such as the presence of self-references and the giving of indirect answers. Another possible lie criterion consists of 'cognitive operations'. This is part of Reality Monitoring, which will be discussed in the next chapter.

CHAPTER 6

Reality Monitoring

INSIGHT INTO PEOPLE'S MEMORY

Chapter 5 revealed some important limitations of CBCA assessments. First, although CBCA evaluators can detect truths and lies above the level of chance, the method is not perfect and mistakes are made, especially in detecting lies. Secondly, CBCA is a truth-verifying method and not a lie detection method. It contains criteria to check whether someone is telling the truth, but criteria to investigate whether someone is lying are lacking. Thirdly, CBCA is in principle contextually bound, and was specifically developed for child (sexual) abuse cases. These three limitations make the development of an alternative method desirable, particularly a method which includes 'lie criteria' and which can be used in settings other than child sexual abuse cases. Reality Monitoring potentially fulfils these criteria. It deals with memory characteristics of perceived (actually experienced) and imagined events. The core of Reality Monitoring is that memories based on real experiences differ from memories based on fiction. Although Reality Monitoring has nothing to do with telling lies, its principle is relevant for deception, too. It implies that a truthful *memory* (experienced event) will differ in quality from remembering an event that has been made up. Do people therefore also *speak* differently when telling the truth to the way they do when lying? This chapter shows that this is indeed the case.

In 1981, Marcia Johnson and Carol Raye published their ideas and findings about memory characteristics. They argued that memories of real experiences are obtained through perceptual processes and are therefore likely to contain *perceptual information* (visual details, sounds, smells, tastes, and physical sensations), *contextual information* (such as details about where and when the event took place) and *affective information* (details about how someone felt during the event). These memories are usually clear, sharp and vivid. Memories about imagined events are derived from an internal source and are therefore likely to contain *cognitive operations*, such as thoughts and reasonings ('I can only remember my thinking of what my friend would like to have for a present'). They are usually more vague and less concrete (see also Johnson, Hashtroudi & Lindsay (1993) and Johnson & Raye (1998) for a more recent review of Reality Monitoring).

People often try to determine whether they have actually experienced an event they have in mind, or whether this memory is based on imagination. The processes by which a person attributes a memory to an actual experience (external source) or imagination (internal source) is called Reality Monitoring. We normally use the above-mentioned cues to discriminate between memories of actual experiences and imagined experiences. For example, when a memory is vivid and contains a lot of perceptual information, we are inclined to believe that we have experienced the event, but we are more likely to assume that we have imagined the event if our memories are dim and contain many thoughts and reasonings (Johnson, Foley, Suengas & Raye, 1988). In their study, Johnson and her colleagues asked participants to remember one perceived event and one that they had imagined, and asked them to describe how they distinguished in their minds between the event that actually happened and the one that occurred only in their imagination. Perceived events elicited responses such as 'I can remember what the dentist's office looked like', 'I remember how long this event took', 'I remember what time I went' and 'I remember having strong feelings about the situation at the time', whereas imagined events led to responses such as 'This must be a fantasy, I was too young to be a doctor' (Johnson, Foley, Suengas & Raye, 1988, p.374).

Suppose that someone asks you whether a particular woman was in your car on a certain day. This question can result in different types of memory. First, you may remember several details of that event, such as the colour of the dress she was wearing, the smell of her perfume and the fact that she asked you to close the window because she was cold. Secondly, this question may result in thoughts such as 'She must have been in the car, because Thomas, her boyfriend, was there and I remember me thinking that they are always together.' In the latter case you would probably be less certain that the woman was actually in the car than in the former case.

People use the same decision rules when they are asked to indicate whether or not they think that somebody else has actually experienced an event. That is, when the story contains much perceptual, contextual and affective information, they believe that the person is talking about an actual experience, but they believe that the person is only imagining the event if the story contains a lot of reasoning (Johnson & Suengas, 1989). Coming back to the example of the woman in the car, people are more likely to believe that the woman was actually in your car if you describe details of the event than if you reason that she was in your car.

REALITY MONITORING AND DECEPTION

Is it the case that, compared to truth-tellers, liars include less perceptual, contextual and affective information and more cognitive operations in their accounts? The answer to this question cannot be obtained from Johnson's research. First, her research deals with the question of how people determine whether or not they are imagining things. This is not relevant to deception, as liars know that their stories are fabricated. Secondly, Johnson's work primarily deals with how people *remember* events, not how they *describe* them. She believes that how people describe their memories of events differs from how they actually remember these events. People have a tendency to make their stories sound interesting and coherent. If necessary, they will fill gaps in their memory by including some information that they do not actually remember, but which they think makes sense and is probably true (for example, when you know that someone always wears a green scarf, you might include in the description of a particular event the fact that the person was wearing a green scarf, although in fact you can no longer actually remember this detail). This tendency to fill gaps is particularly likely to happen with imagined events, as they are less clear and vivid. As a result, differences between perceived and imagined events become smaller when people are asked to put their memories into words (Johnson, 1988). It seems plausible that the desire to make stories interesting and cohesive will be even stronger when people tell lies, making it unclear whether differences between truth-tellers and liars will actually occur.

Reality Monitoring research in a deception context is relatively new. A standardized set of criteria has not yet been developed. In fact, different researchers use different criteria. In this chapter I shall use the criteria employed by Sporer (1997, see Table 6.1), as this is the only set of criteria published in English. There is an overlap between some of the Reality Monitoring criteria and some of the Criteria-Based Content

Table 6.1. Reality Monitoring criteria

---

1 Clarity
2 Perceptual information
3 Spatial information
4 Temporal information
5 Affect
6 Reconstructability of the story
7 Realism
8 Cognitive operations

Analysis criteria (see Chapter 5), which will be mentioned in the text. Sporer's list contains eight criteria. Criteria 1 to 7 are truth criteria and are expected to occur more often in truthful statements, whereas criterion 8 is a lie criterion and is expected to occur more often in deceptive statements.

1   *Clarity.* This refers to the clarity and vividness of the statement. This criterion is present if the report is clear, sharp and vivid (instead of dim and vague).

2   *Perceptual information.* This criterion is present if the statement includes sensorial experiences such as sounds (e.g. 'He really shouted at me'), smells (e.g. 'It had a smell of rotten fish'), tastes (e.g. 'The chips were very salty'), physical sensations (e.g. 'It really hurt') and visual details (e.g. 'I saw the nurse entering the ward').

3   *Spatial information.* This criterion is present if the statement includes information about locations (e.g. 'It was in a park') or the spatial arrangement of people and/or objects (e.g. 'The man was sitting left from his wife' or 'The lamp was partially hidden behind the curtains'). This criterion is related to 'contextual embedding' (CBCA criterion 4).

4   *Temporal information.* This criterion is present if the statement includes information about when the event happened (e.g. 'It was early in the morning') or explicitly describes a sequence of events (e.g. 'When he heard all that noise, the visitor became nervous and left', 'As soon as the guy entered the pub, the girl started smiling'). This criterion is related to 'contextual embedding' (CBCA criterion 4) as well.

5   *Affect.* This criterion is present if information is included about how the participant felt during the event (e.g. 'I was very scared'). This criterion is similar to 'accounts of subjective mental state' (CBCA criterion 12).

6   *Reconstructability of the story.* This criterion is present if it is possible to reconstruct the event on the basis of the information given. This criterion is related to 'logical structure' (CBCA criterion 1), 'unstructured production' (CBCA criterion 2) and 'amount of details' (CBCA criterion 3).

7   *Realism.* This criterion is present if the story is plausible, realistic and makes sense. This criterion is related to 'logical structure' (CBCA criterion 1).

8   *Cognitive operations.* This criterion is present if there are descriptions of inferences made by the participant at the time of the event (e.g. 'It appeared to me that she didn't know the layout of the building', 'Her reactions gave me the impression that she was upset').

REALITY MONITORING AS A LIE DETECTION INSTRUMENT

Table 6.2 provides an overview of Reality Monitoring deception studies conducted so far.

Almost all of the studies were experimental ones in which the participants (mostly adults) were asked to describe something that had or had not actually happened to them. For example, participants in Höfer, Akehurst and Metzger's (1996) truth condition took part in a photo-session and were interviewed afterwards about what had happened. Participants in the deception condition did not take part in the photo-session, but were verbally coached by a confederate about what had happened. In the subsequent interview they had to pretend that they had actually had their photograph taken. The study by Roberts and colleagues (1998) is an exception. They examined statements of 26 allegedly sexually abused children whose cases were confirmed ($n=10$) or unconfirmed ($n=16$). Cases were judged to be confirmed if the suspect confessed to the alleged incidents before plea bargaining and/or there was medical or physical evidence. If there was a lack of substantiating evidence, the suspect persistently denied the allegations and/or polygraph tests showed a truthful outcome regarding the denial of the allegation, the allegations were judged to be unconfirmed.

Table 6.2. Objective indicators of truth-telling (Reality Monitoring)

				Criteria				
	1	2	3	4	5	6	7	8
Alonso-Quecuty (1992) (adults)		>	>[1]			>		
Alonso-Quecuty (1996) (adults)		—	>[1]		>			—
Alonso-Quecuty (1996) (children)		>	<[1]		<			—
Alonso-Quecuty et al. (1997) (adults)[2]		>	>[1]					—
Alonso-Quecuty et al. (1997) (children)[2]		>	>[1]					—
Hernandez-Fernaud & Alonso-Quecuty (1997) (adults)		>	>					<
Höfer et al. (1996) (adults)	>	—	—	>	—	>	>	>
Manzanero & Diges (1996) (adults)		<	<[1]					
Roberts et al. (1998) (children)	—	>	>	>	—			—
Sporer (1997) (adults)	—	—	>	>	>	—	>	—
Vrij et al. (1999) (adults)		>	>	>	—			—

[1] Spatial information (criterion 3) and temporal information (criterion 4) combined.
[2] The audio-recording-event condition.
>, verbal characteristic occurs more frequently in truthful than in deceptive statements;
<, verbal characteristic occurs more frequently in deceptive than in truthful statements;
—, no relationship between verbal characteristic and lying/truth-telling.

Table 6.2 shows that statements about actually experienced events included more perceptual information (information about visual details, sounds, tastes, and so on; criterion 2), more spatial information (criterion 3) and more temporal information (criterion 4) than statements about imagined events. Table 6.2 further shows that, compared to lies, truthful stories were easier to reconstruct by Reality Monitoring judges on the basis of the information given (criterion 6).

However, there is no support for the lie criterion. There is no evidence so far that liars include more cognitive operations in their accounts than truth-tellers. Moreover, Johnson did not always find that imagined events contained more cognitive operations than experienced events (Suengas & Johnson, 1988). One explanation is that people use cognitive operations in experienced events in order to facilitate and enhance later memory for these events (Roediger, 1996). For example, someone who drove fast in Germany might try to remember this in two different ways. First, he could remember that he had actually looked at his speedometer to find out how fast he was driving. Alternatively, he could remember this by logical reasoning (e.g. by thinking that he must have driven fast because he drove on the motorway). The latter alternative, in which a cognitive operation is included, is an easier way of remembering that he drove fast than the first alternative. If this person is asked a couple of years later whether he drove fast through Germany it is therefore more likely that he will remember this by thinking that he drove on the motorway than by remembering that he checked his speedometer. As a result, that person's memory about this experienced event will contain a cognitive operation.

To date, Sporer, Höfer and colleagues and Vrij and colleagues are the only researchers to have calculated accuracy rates for detecting lies and truths on the basis of Reality Monitoring assessments. The study by Vrij and colleagues revealed accuracy rates of 71% for detecting truths and 74% for detecting lies. The study by Höfer *et al.* showed a 61% hit rate for classifying truths and a 70% hit rate for classifying lies. The hit rates in Sporer's study were 75% and 68%, respectively. The accuracy rates in all three studies were above the level that would be expected by chance (i.e. 50%).

LIMITATIONS IN USING REALITY MONITORING

Johnson, Foley, Suengas and Raye's (1988) research has revealed that differences in the quality of memories between perceived and imagined events decrease as a function of time. They found larger differences for adults' recent memories than for their childhood memories. It may well be that if people talk or think about an event, external memories

(memories of experienced events) become more internal, and internal memories (memories about fictitious events) become more external. As already mentioned, people will add reasoning to memories about experienced events in order to facilitate their memory. Imagined memories, on the other hand, will become more vivid and concrete as people try to visualize what might have happened (Manzanero & Diges, 1996). This explains why some researchers have found differences between liars and truth-tellers only when their responses were immediate and spontaneous, and not when they could hesitate for a while before giving an answer, or when they were allowed to prepare their answers (Alonso-Quecuty, 1992; Manzanero & Diges, 1996). However, Sporer (1997) found more differences between truthful and deceptive responses if they were given after a short delay than if they were given immediately.

It has also been found that children do not differentiate between ongoing fact and fantasy as clearly as adults do. One explanation is that their memories of these two kinds of experiences might not differ from one another in the way that adults' memories do (Ceci & Bruck, 1995; Lindsay & Johnson, 1987). This might explain why Alonso-Quecuty (1992) found the predicted differences between perceived and imagined events only in adults' statements, and not in children's statements.

In summary, Reality Monitoring might be more useful for analysing adults' statements than for studying children's statements, and might be particularly useful for analysing statements about events which happened recently rather than a long time ago.

CONCLUSION

Initial findings have shown that Reality Monitoring can be used to detect truths and lies, especially when the responses are given by adults and when they refer to events which happened recently. It makes sense to compare Reality Monitoring with CBCA (discussed in Chapter 5), as there are some overlaps between the two methods. To date it is unclear which method is preferable. Höfer, Akehurst and Metzger (1996) obtained slightly higher hit rates with CBCA (70% truths, 73% lies and 71% overall) than with Reality Monitoring (61% truths, 70% lies and 65% overall), whereas Sporer was slightly more successful in detecting truths and lies with Reality Monitoring (75% truths, 68% lies and 71% overall) than with CBCA (70% truths, 60% lies and 65% overall). Vrij, Edward, Roberts and Bull (1999) obtained hit rates which were similar for CBCA (77% truths, 74% lies, 75% overall) and Reality Monitoring (71% truths, 74% lies and 72% overall). All three studies used adults' statements. As mentioned above, there are reasons to believe that

Reality Monitoring is more effective with adults' statements, whereas CBCA is specifically designed for use with children. The present comparison between CBCA and Reality Monitoring may therefore be somewhat unfair with regard to CBCA. More research is needed to make a better judgement about which method is most appropriate.

Suppose, however, that future studies demonstrate similar findings to the three studies conducted to date, and do indicate that there is no difference in accuracy between CBCA and Reality Monitoring assessments. In that case I believe that Reality Monitoring is preferable. First, it is easier to apply than CBCA because it contains fewer criteria. Secondly, as Sporer suggested, it is probably easier to train observers to make Reality Monitoring assessments than to make CBCA assessments (Sporer, 1997; Vrij, Edward, Roberts & Bull, 1999). Thirdly, and perhaps most importantly, Reality Monitoring is more theoretically based than CBCA. Reality Monitoring is a theoretical approach which deals with memory and (cognitive) memory processes. The benefit of the theoretical underpinning of Reality Monitoring is that this makes it possible to predict those situations in which the method can be used, namely situations in which memory and memory processes are involved. Obviously deception has a lot to do with memory and memory processes, which suggests that Reality Monitoring could be used in virtually all deception situations.

A logical step is to combine both methods. The experiments of Sporer and Vrij *et al.* showed a (small) beneficial effect of combining both methods (Sporer: CBCA overall, 65%; Reality Monitoring overall, 71%; combined overall, 79%; Vrij *et al.*: CBCA overall, 75%; Reality Monitoring overall, 72%; combined overall, 78%), whereas Höfer's study showed no beneficial effect of combining the two assessment techniques. An interesting addition to the CBCA list of criteria would be the Reality Monitoring criterion 'perceptual information' (criterion 2). For example, pornographic films may increase children's knowledge about sexual acts. As a result, an unexperienced child may give a detailed account of a non-experienced sexual encounter after watching a pornographic film. However, in such an account details about smell and taste will be missing, as genuine experiences are required for such details. Details about smell and taste in statements about sexual abuse may therefore be a strong indication that the statements are based on real experiences (unless smell and taste were mentioned by people in the pornographic film).

In addition, the cognitive operations criterion (criterion 8) could be added to the CBCA list as well. I am aware that this criterion has not yet been found to be reliable in differentiating between truths and lies. In this respect, adding this criterion would seem to be unwarranted.

However, this criterion may be useful for differentiating between statements which the story-teller believes to be true, but which are in fact imagined, and statements about real experiences. In the previous chapter I pointed out that there are problems in CBCA differentiating between these two types of experience. Research has indicated that people include more reasoning in their accounts when they are talking about events they think they have experienced, but which were in fact imagined, than when they are describing an event which they actually have experienced (Schooler, Gerhard & Loftus, 1986). Looking at cognitive operations may therefore be a useful tool for distinguishing between fact and fantasy when using CBCA.

PART III

PROFESSIONAL DETECTION OF DECEPTION

CHAPTER 7

The Polygraph

Example 1. In 1986, CBS (a US television station) enlisted the help of four polygraph-testing firms in New York to ascertain which of four of its employees had stolen a valuable camera. As the polygraph examiners arrived (on different days) to do the testing, each one was told that the manager's suspicions were focused on one particular individual; a different individual was specified for each polygraph examiner.

This was a charade. There was no missing camera and the four employees were aware of this. They were merely instructed to deny that they had stolen any camera (i.e. to tell the truth). As an incentive they were each offered 50 dollars if they succeeded in passing the polygraph test. The outcome was that each of the four polygraphers positively and confidently identified a culprit—in each case the one employee whom that polygrapher had been told was suspected of being the culprit (Lykken, 1988).

Example 2. A bomb exploded in Centennial Park in Atlanta during the Olympic Games in 1996. Two people were killed and 111 people were injured. Thirty-three-year-old Richard Jewell became the main suspect, because he had warned the police about the bomb just before the attack. In order to prove his innocence, Jewell volunteered to undergo a polygraph test. After 15 hours of testing, the polygrapher came to the conclusion that Jewell was innocent. Subsequently, the FBI cleared Jewell as a suspect (Van Koppen, Boelhouwer, Merckelbach & Verbaten, 1996).

WHAT IS A POLYGRAPH?

Apart from looking at speech content and non-verbal behaviour, there is in principle a third way of detecting lies, namely by examining the physiological reactions of deceivers. Throughout history it has been assumed that lying is accompanied by physiological activity within the liar's body. For example, the Chinese used to force suspected liars to chew rice powder and then to spit it out. If the resultant powder was dry, then the person was judged to have been lying (Kleinmuntz & Szucko, 1984).

The modern way of detecting physiological activity in liars is by using a polygraph. The polygraph—from two Greek words, namely 'poly' (= many) and 'grapho' (= to write)—is an accurate scientific measuring device which can display, via ink pens on to charts or via a computer's visual display unit, a direct and valid representation of various types of bodily activity (Bull, 1988). The most commonly measured activities are palmar sweating, blood pressure and respiration (Ben-Shakhar & Furedy, 1990). In scientific polygraph research, measures of brain electrical acitivity (event-related brain potentials) are investigated as well (Allen & Iacono, 1997; Bashore & Rapp, 1993; Farwell & Donchin, 1991; Johnson & Rosenfeld, 1991; Rosenfeld, 1995; Rosenfeld, Angell, Johnson & Qian, 1991; Rosenfeld, Reinhart, Bhatt, Ellwanger, Gora, Sekera & Sweet, 1998). However, this is not (yet) common practice in applied settings. The polygraph accurately records changes in palmar sweating, blood pressure and respiration, and is able to measure even very small differences. It does this by amplifying signals picked up from sensors that are attached to different parts of the body. In the typical use of the polygraph, four sensors are attached to the subject. Pneumatic tubes are stretched around the person's chest and stomach in order to measure changes in the depth and rate of breathing. A blood-pressure cuff placed around the bicep measures changes in blood pressure, and metal electrodes attached to the fingers measure palmar sweating (Ekman, 1992).

The polygraph measures physiological activity and changes in these activities. Changes in physiological activity are often associated with changes in arousal. It is assumed that liars will be more aroused than truth-tellers. This may be the result of feeling guilty or—and in a polygraph context more likely—because examinees will be afraid that the polygraph will detect their lies.

People sometimes call a polygraph a lie detector, but this term is misleading. A polygraph does not detect lies, but only arousal which may be a result of telling a lie. There is no other option than to attempt to detect lies in this indirect way, because a pattern of physiological activity that is typical of lying does not exist (Saxe, 1991).

It is easy to imagine that this indirect way of detecting lies could lead to incorrect decisions—for example, when liars are not aroused, or when truth-tellers are very aroused. A good example of a truth-teller being very aroused, even more so than a liar, is the biblical story of two women who each claimed one particular baby as her own. They both appeared before King Solomon, who suggested cutting the infant in half and dividing it between them by way of solution. One mother agreed with this solution, whereas the other was distraught. Noticing this arousal in the latter woman, King Solomon realized that she was the real mother and gave her the child (Ford, 1995). Another example in which an aroused person might not necessarily have been lying is the case of Roger Keith Coleman, who was convicted of the rape and brutal murder of his sister-in-law (Ford, 1995). Coleman insisted that he was innocent, and there were some weaknesses in the case against him. For example, after his conviction, four people came forward to testify that they had heard someone else confess to the crime. In a last attempt to prove his innocence, Coleman asked for a polygraph examination. The polygraph test was administered 12 hours before the scheduled execution. It was announced that Coleman failed the test and he was put to death later that night. It is perhaps not surprising that Coleman failed the polygraph test. It is difficult to believe how he could not have been extremely aroused when answering the crucial questions during this polygraph test, whether he was guilty or innocent. I shall return to the issue of incorrect decisions later.

Polygraph tests are currently used in criminal investigations in countries all over the world, including Canada, Israel, Japan, South Korea, Mexico, Pakistan, the Philippines, Taiwan, Thailand and the USA (Lykken, 1998). In most countries, however, the use of the polygraph is limited, except in the USA where many polygraph tests take place (Barland, 1988). In the USA polygraph tests are mostly used in criminal and forensic investigations, and in security screening (Gale, 1988). The Polygraph Protection Act (introduced in 1988) has limited the use of polygraph tests for personnel screening. Outcomes of polygraph tests are sometimes used as evidence in court in criminal cases in the USA (Honts & Perry, 1992), although not in all US states (Patrick & Iacono, 1991) (see Cohen (1997) and Faigman, Kaye, Saks and Sanders (1997) for a recent review of the history and current legal status of polygraph evidence in the USA). In many courts in the USA polygraph evidence is still inadmissible, but not necessarily because it is felt that the test is inaccurate. Another reason is that juries may be overwhelmed by the scientific nature of the evidence (Honts, 1994). However, a recent experimental study conducted by Myers and Arbuthnot (1997) does not support this claim. Mock jurors (college students from Ohio University, USA) were asked to give verdicts on the basis of several pieces of evidence, namely forensic evidence (hair samples and fingerprints which matched the suspect were found in the victim's apartment), medical evidence (semen found on the scene matched that of the suspect), eyewitness evidence (an eyewitness testified that he saw the suspect leaving the victim's building and that the suspect appeared to be hiding something under his jacket) and polygraph evidence (a polygraph test revealed that the suspect was guilty). The jurors found the latter piece of evidence the least convincing.

In other countries, such as The Netherlands and the UK, polygraph tests are not used. In the UK, following a well-known spy case, the Government announced its intention to undertake pilot studies of the effectiveness of the polygraph. A number of distinguished psychologists from the UK formed a Working Group chaired by Professor Tony Gale. Their aim was to provide a report on the status of polygraphic examination. Their conclusion was devastating. The psychologists doubted whether polygraph outcomes were accurate enough (this and the other issues mentioned in their conclusion will be discussed in this chapter). The procedures involved were not standardized to the extent that they might be described as satisfactory in psychometric terms. They expected difficulties in checking on the practices and procedures employed by individual polygraphers. Finally, they thought that some aspects of a polygraph test, particularly deceiving an examinee, were contrary to British Law, making polygraph outcomes unlikely to be admissible in a British court of law (Report of the Working Group of the British Psychological Society on the use of the polygraph, British Psychological Society, 1986, p.92). Subsequently, the UK Government abandoned its plans to introduce polygraph examinations.

In other words, the use of the polygraph is disputed. Supporters and opponents challenge each other in the media and in scientific and professional journals and books, and their debate about the polygraph is lively and heated. In addition to the debate between opponents and supporters, there are also disagreements within the polygraph community. The two leading and probably most distinguished scientific polygraph researchers, David Raskin and David Lykken, have engaged in prolonged controversy over the reliability and validity of various polygraph tests. They have come into conflict in the scientific literature, as expert witnesses in court and as possible opponents in the legal process against each other. More recently, others such as Furedy and Iacono (Lykken camp) and Honts (Raskin camp) took over the Lykken–Raskin dispute (Furedy, 1993, 1996a,b; Honts, Kircher & Raskin, 1996; Iacono & Lykken, 1997). Again, both camps are in favour of polygraph tests, and the dispute is related to the question of which test should be used. This chapter provides an overview of the existing scientific literature regarding polygraph tests, and the arguments of both camps will be presented.

I shall discuss the polygraph in detail for the following two reasons. First, many people have heard about the polygraph (for instance via the (American) media and film industry) but probably do not know how polygraph tests work. Therefore this chapter can be used to increase their knowledge. Secondly, many people (including those who work in a judicial context) have a very negative attitude towards the polygraph. 'I don't believe in it, it is entirely unreliable' are comments that are often heard. In my view, such an attitude is somewhat exaggerated. Polygraph tests can be used in certain circumstances to detect lies, as I shall illustrate in this chapter. Much attention will be paid to the role of the polygraph examiners. Their role is crucial, especially in developing and conducting the test, and also in evaluating test outcomes. Properly conducted polygraph tests require skilled examiners, and their task is far from easy, as will be shown in this chapter.

RELEVANT/IRRELEVANT TECHNIQUE

Several different polygraph test procedures exist. One of the first procedures to be widely used was the relevant/irrelevant technique (RIT) developed by Larson in 1932. In the RIT, two types of questions are asked, namely crime-relevant questions and crime-irrelevant questions. Crime-relevant questions are related to the crime under investigation, such as 'Did you break into a black Mercedes last night?' Obviously, all suspects—both innocent and guilty—will answer 'no' to this question, otherwise they are admitting to having committed the crime. Irrelevant questions have nothing to do with the crime, and the examiner knows for sure that the examinee will tell the truth when answering these questions. An example of a crime-irrelevant question is 'Is it Tuesday today?'. The examiner will then compare the physiological responses to both types of questions. The rationale behind the RIT is that larger responses to relevant crime-related questions than to irrelevant questions indicate that the examinee was lying while responding to the crime-relevant questions. However, it is obvious that the premise used in RIT polygraph tests is incorrect. The strong physiological response might be caused by the fact that the person is lying, but this is not necessarily the case. Suppose a woman is attached to a polygraph in order to find out whether she stole money from the office in the company where she is employed. She is innocent, but she realizes that a large response on the polygraph might imply that she will lose her job. Hence the relevant question 'Did you steal the money?' has major consequences for her, and might therefore arouse her. Thus it is possible that this relevant question will result in a larger response on the polygraph than an irrelevant question about, say, the colour of her shirt. However, a positive score in this case, is a result of fear of losing her job and being branded a thief, and not the result of deception!

A similar case was broadcast on Dutch television a while ago (in a Veronica-programme entitled *Berg je voor Berg*). The cyclist and former world champion Gerrie Knetemann was attached to a polygraph. A voice-stress analyser was used in this programme, which is an unreliable instrument for detecting deceit (Merckelbach, 1990). The aim of the polygraph test was to find out whether Knetemann had ever used illegal drugs in his career in order to enhance his performance. Both crime-irrelevant questions such as 'Are you wearing a watch at the moment?' and 'Are you now in Amsterdam?' and crime-relevant questions such as 'Did you ever use performance-enhancing illegal drugs in your career as a cyclist?' were asked. Knetemann answered 'no' to the relevant question, and was subsequently accused of lying by the examiner, as his physiological response to this question was stronger than his physio-logical responses to the crime-irrelevant questions. This conclusion was, of course, premature. Performance-enhancing drugs are a sensitive issue for professional cyclists, and questions about this matter will almost automatically increase their arousal, whether they have actually used such drugs or not. In other words, all competitive cyclists—both those who use drugs and those who do not, are likely to show strong responses to such relevant questions.

The opposite situation, in which guilty suspects do not become aroused when they answer relevant questions, may occur as well. In this case, the polygraph test will not show differences in arousal concerning crime-relevant and crime-irrelevant questions, and the examiner will incorrectly assume that the suspect is not guilty. These examples make it clear that RIT is an inappropriate technique for polygraph testing, and there is agreement among polygraph researchers that such a test should not be used (Honts, 1991; Lykken, 1998; Raskin, 1986; Saxe, 1994). Larson himself acknowledged the limitations of his technique and declared that he was not particularly happy with the importance others gave to the technique. He said in 1961:

> 'I originally hoped that instrumental lie detection would become a legit-imate part of professional police science. It is little more than a racket. The lie detector, as used in many places, is nothing more than a psychological third-degree aimed at extorting confessions as the old physical beatings were. At times I'm sorry I ever had any part in its development' (cited in Lykken, 1998, p.28–29).

The two polygraph tests that are used most often nowadays are the Control Question Test (CQT) and the Guilty Knowledge Test (GKT). The CQT was initially developed by Reid in 1947, and was further conceptualized within the framework of current concepts in psychology and psychophysiology by Raskin (Raskin, 1979, 1982, 1986). The GKT was developed and described in detail by Lykken (Lykken, 1959, 1960, 1991, 1998). In the USA, the CQT is much more often used than the GKT (Honts & Perry, 1992). On the other hand, GKT polygraph testing is more frequently used than CQT polygraph testing in Israel and Japan (Lykken, 1991).

THE POLYGRAPH: HOW DOES IT WORK?

The Procedure

It is important that examinees are not distracted during the polygraph test. Every distraction may result in a physiological response which will be detected by the polygraph and may influence the results. Therefore tests should preferably take place in sound-isolated locations—to prevent noises from outside being heard—and the examiner and equipment are preferably located behind the examinee. Moreover, examinees should not move and are only allowed to answer questions with a simple 'yes' or 'no' answer, as movements and speech may lead to unwanted physiological responses. Therefore it is clear that it is necessary for the examinee to co-operate when using the polygraph test. Not surprisingly, examinees only participate in polygraph testing on a voluntary basis, and can decide to withdraw during the test any time. However, examinees are perhaps reluctant to do so, as this would make them seem more suspicious. Withdrawal might easily lead to reactions such as 'if you are innocent, why don't you prove this in the polygraph test?'.

The Control Question Test

The typical control question polygraph test consists of four phases (Furedy, 1991b). In phase one, the questions which will be asked during the polygraph test are formulated by the examiner and discussed with the examinee. There are two reasons for discussing the questions with the examinee beforehand. First, the examiner wants to make sure that the examinee understands the questions, so that no further discussion about the content of the questions will take place during the test or afterwards. Secondly, the examiner wants to make sure that the examinee is willing to answer the questions with a simple 'yes' or 'no' answer (and not with 'yes, but...' or 'it depends...' answers). Table 7.1 provides an example of a typical CQT question sequence in a case where someone is suspected of stealing a camera. The example is derived from Raskin, Kircher, Horowitz and Honts (1989).

There are three types of question, namely neutral questions, relevant questions and control questions. *Neutral questions* are general questions

Table 7.1. An example of a control question sequence

N1: Do you live in the USA? 'Yes'
C1: During the first 20 years of your life, did you ever take something that did not belong to you? 'No'
R1: Did you take that camera? 'No'
N2: Is your name Rick? 'Yes'
C2: Prior to 1987, did you ever do something dishonest or illegal? 'No'
R2: Did you take that camera from the desk? 'No'
N3: Were you born in the month of November? 'Yes'
C3: Before the age of 21 did you ever lie to get out of trouble or to cause a problem for someone else? 'No'
R3: Did you participate in any way in the theft of that camera? 'No'

and are not expected to create any arousal (e.g. 'Do you live in the USA?', 'Is your name Rick?', and so on) (see also Table 7.1). Neutral questions are used as fillers. The physiological responses to these questions are disregarded when the polygraph charts are scored. Fillers can be used to check whether the examinee is paying attention to the questions asked by the examiner, as will be discussed in the section on 'countermeasures' below.

Relevant questions are specific questions about the crime. For example, 'Did you take that camera?' is a question that can be asked in a case involving theft of a camera. Obviously, both innocent and guilty examinees will answer 'no' to this question, otherwise they would admit to the theft of the camera. Relevant questions are expected to create more arousal in guilty suspects (because they are lying) than in innocent suspects (because they are telling the truth).

Control questions deal with acts that are related to the crime under investigation, but do not refer to the crime in question. They are always general in nature, deliberately vague, and cover long periods of time. They are intended to embarrass the suspects (both guilty and innocent) and to evoke arousal. This is facilitated by on the one hand giving the suspect no choice but to lie when answering the control questions, and on the other hand making it clear to the suspect that the polygraph will detect this lie. The examiner formulates a control question for which, in his or her view, the examinee's answer 'no' is deceptive. The exact formulation of the question will depend on the examinee's circumstances, but a control question in an examination regarding theft might be 'During the first 20 years of your life, did you ever take something that did not belong to you?' where the examiner believes that the examinee did indeed steal something before the age of 21 years (which many people have done). Under normal circumstances, some examinees might admit this wrongdoing. However, during a polygraph examination they will not do this because the examiner will tell the examinee that admitting such a theft would cause the examiner to conclude that the examinee is the type of person who would commit the crime in question and is therefore considered guilty. Therefore the examinee has no other choice than to deny this earlier wrongdoing and thus to be untruthful in answering the control questions. If, nevertheless, subjects admit some wrongdoing, then the wording of the control question will be reformulated (e.g. 'Apart from what you have told me...') (O'Toole, Yuille, Patrick & Iacono, 1994). Furthermore, the examiner will tell the subject that deceptive answers to control questions will result in physiological reactions during the test, which will be detected by the polygraph. The examinee will then be led to think that lying in response to the control questions indicates that the examinee was also deceptive with regard to the relevant issues concerning the crime in question and, going back to the example, will be found guilty of the theft of a camera. In fact, as will be described later on, the examiner will actually interpret strong physiological reactions to a control question as a sign of being *truthful*, but he will not inform the examinee about this!

Overall, control questions and relevant questions may evoke different patterns of physiological responses in guilty and innocent suspects, as is shown in Figure 7.1.

Control questions may generate more arousal than the relevant questions in the *innocent suspect* for two reasons. First, the innocent suspect gives deceptive responses to the control questions but honest responses

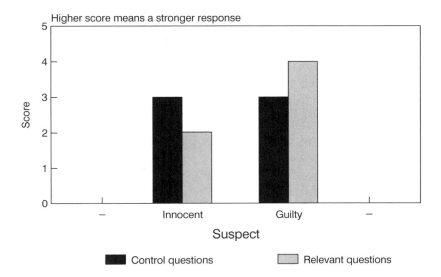

Figure 7.1. Physiological profile for guilty and innocent suspects (CQT).

to the relevant questions. Secondly, because the examiner puts so much emphasis on the control questions to which the examinee will respond deceptively and because the examinee knows he or she is answering the relevant questions truthfully, the examinee will become more concerned about his or her answers to the control questions. However, the same control questions are expected to elicit less arousal in *guilty suspects* than the relevant questions. A guilty suspect gives deceptive responses to both types of question, which in principle should lead to similar physiological responses to both types of question. However, relevant questions represent the most immediate and serious threat to the examinee, which will lead to a stronger physiological response than do the control questions. The guilty suspect might think 'If the examiner catches my lie concerning the relevant questions the game is over, but there is still some hope left if the examiner notices that I lied to the control questions.'

After designing the questions, and after the examiner is sure that the examinee understands the questions and will answer them with simple 'yes' or 'no' answers, the second phase starts, namely the so-called *stimulation test*. The stimulation test is intended to convince the examinee that the technique is highly accurate and that the polygraph is able to detect every lie. It is crucial for a polygraph test that the examinee believes that the test is infallible. The notion that the polygraph test is 100% accurate will augment fear of detection in the guilty suspect when answering the relevant questions ('There is no way to beat this machine'), and will increase confidence in innocent people when answering the relevant questions ('The machine works accurately and, as I am innocent, I will therefore be exonerated'). The opposite situation may occur if examinees do not trust the accuracy of the polygraph. It may then make guilty suspects more confident ('Nothing is lost yet, there is still a chance that I will beat the polygraph') and will make innocent suspects more afraid ('I know I am innocent, but what is this machine going to tell? I really hope the machine is not going to make a mistake').

A card game is often used in the stimulation test. The subject is asked to pick a playing card from a deck of cards, to take note of it, and to return it to the deck. The polygrapher then shows several cards, and the subject is instructed to respond with a 'no' answer to each card. As the subject does so, the examiner evaluates the polygraphic response and will inform the subject which card he or she selected. The examiner's choice of card will very often be correct. Showing the correct card will almost automatically lead to a physical response in the examinee—for example, due to some tension concerning whether or not the examiner will find out that the examinee is lying in this particular case. The card test gives the examiner insight into the examinee's pattern of reaction when lying and when telling the truth. The examiner informs the examinee explicitly about this. (In fact the card game is a Guilty Knowledge Test, as will become clear in the section about GKT.)

Examiners always run the risk of making the wrong decision, which would have catastrophic consequences. They would look extremely foolish and the continuation of the polygraph test would probably be worthless if they inform the examinees that the card they have seen was the Four of Hearts whereas in fact the card they were shown was the Five of Spades! In order to avoid such a gaffe, examiners sometimes use tricks—for example, by marking the correct card or by using (unbeknown to the examinee) a deck of cards which contains only one type of card (Bashore & Rapp, 1993). Obviously, in this case the examiner does not actually show the cards to the examinee but calls out the supposed card names. Other examiners may not play card games but persuade the examinee of the effectiveness of their procedures by having a well-appointed office with various framed diplomas and certificates adorning the walls (Bull, 1988).

After the stimulation test, phase three—the test proper—is carried out. Table 7.1 shows an example of a polygraph test in the case of theft of a camera, but again the exact wording of the control questions depends on the examinee's circumstances. The same question sequence is presented at least three times, in order to exclude accidental differences in physiological responses between control questions and irrelevant questions. That is, it might occur that an innocent examinee accidentally gives a particularly large response to one of the relevant questions. The more questions the examiner asks, the smaller will be the influence of such accidental responses on the final outcome.

The final phase of the test, phase four, consists of the interpretation of the polygraph charts. There are two interpretation approaches, namely the global approach and the numerical scoring approach. In the global approach the examiner forms an impression of the examinee's physiological responses to the test. This information is then combined in some unspecified manner with evaluations of the case facts (the examinee's criminal history, evidence in the case) and the examinee's behaviour during the test in order to reach an overall decision about the truthfulness of the examinee.

Raskin is strongly against the global scoring method, and advocates the numerical scoring approach. The numerical method attempts to minimize the influences of sources other than the polygraph charts in the decision-making, and also attempts to score the charts systematically. In the numerical method comparisons are made between the reactions to the relevant questions and subsequent control questions (R1 compared to C1, R2 compared to C2, and R3 compared to C3). There are four possibilities. If there is no difference in physiological response, the score 0 will be assigned. If there is a noticeable difference the score 1 will be allocated, whereas the scores 2 and 3 are assigned to strong differences and dramatic differences, respectively. However, there are no standardized rules about what a 'noticeable', 'strong' or 'dramatic' difference means. According to Raskin, most assigned scores are 0 or 1, scores of 2 are less common, and scores of 3 are unusual (Raskin, Kircher, Horowitz & Honts, 1989). If the observed reaction is *stronger* to the relevant question than to the control question, a negative score (–1, –2, or –3) is assigned. If the observed reaction is *weaker* to the relevant question than to the control question, a positive score (+1, +2 or +3) is allocated. The scores are then summed to give a total score for the test. The outcome of the test is based on this total. If the total is –6 or lower (–7, –8, and so on), the examiner will conclude that the suspect failed the test and is guilty. If the total is +6 or higher (+7, +8, and so on), the examiner will conclude that the suspect passed the test and is innocent. Scores between –5 and +5 indicate an inconclusive outcome. The responses to the first control and relevant question are often disregarded, as examinees sometimes show disproportionately strong responses to the first questions, due to unfamiliarity with the polygraph machine or being nervous about the investigation.

An unofficial fifth phase of the test involves telling the examinee directly after the test that he or she is lying, and asking the examinee to think about why it is possible that the charts show that he or she is lying (Lykken, 1998). In order to facilitate this thinking process the examiner will leave the room for a while. The aim of the fifth phase is to obtain a confession. The examinee might become nervous at this stage and think that the game is up, and so may confess to having committed the crime. This happened in one particular case in which, after making the accusation, the examiner left the room for a while to watch the examinee from another room via a one-way mirror (Lykken, 1998). The examinee, obviously upset, kept looking at the polygraph charts, then made up his mind and started to eat the charts—a total of 6 feet of paper, 6 inches wide. After he had finished this meal, the examiner returned as if nothing had happened, leaned his ear down to the polygraph and said: 'What's that? He ate them?' The examinee responded by saying 'My God, you mean the thing can talk, too?', and then confessed to having committed the crime.

Criticisms Concerning the Control Question Test

The Control Question Test evokes major criticisms among its opponents. The most important of these are described below.

Innocent Suspects and Control Questions

The CQT assumes that innocent suspects give larger physiological responses to control questions than to relevant questions. Ekman (1992) cites five reasons why some innocent suspects may do the reverse and will become more aroused in their responses to the relevant questions than to the control questions.

- Innocent suspects may think that the police are fallible. Innocent suspects who have been asked to take a polygraph test know that the police have already made one mistake, namely suspecting them of a crime that they did not commit. Perhaps they have already tried to convince the police of their innocence, without any success. Although, on the one hand, they could see the test as an opportunity to prove their innocence, on the other hand it is also possible that they could fear that those who made the mistake of suspecting them will make further mistakes. In other words, if police methods are fallible enough to make them falsely suspicious, could not their polygraph tests also be fallible?
- The innocent suspect may think that the police are unfair. People may dislike or distrust the police and will therefore expect and fear that the polygraph examiner will misjudge them or cheat them.
- The innocent suspect may think that machines are fallible. For example, they may have had difficulties with their own personal computer or other technical equipment, and therefore do not believe that a machine can ever be infallible.
- The innocent suspect is a fearful person. Someone who is generally fearful might respond more to the relevant questions than to the control questions.
- As mentioned earlier, the suspect—even though innocent—has an emotional reaction to the events involved in the crime. Suppose an innocent man is suspected of murdering his wife. When asked about the murder in the relevant questions, the memory of his late wife might reawaken his strong feelings about her, which will be recorded on the polygraph charts.
- A sixth reason can be added. A test whose validity depends on deception is vulnerable in the sense that the deception must be successful in order to make the test effective. Thus examinees must believe that the test is infallible, and must believe that the control questions are crucial. According to Elaad (1993) and Lykken (1988), it is unlikely that all examinees believe this. There are probably dozens of books and articles about the CQT in which the test is described, including details about the stimulation test, the nature of control questions, and the fact that the test does sometimes make mistakes.

Even popular newspaper articles appear about the test (Furedy, 1996b). Of course, those who are taking polygraph tests have access to this literature, and may well have read some of it. It is unlikely that those who know about the procedures and/or fallibility of the test will be deceived by the examiner's lies about the importance of the control questions and about the fact that the test never makes mistakes. The polygraph test will probably become increasingly ineffective with those who do not believe the examiner. Unbelieving innocent suspects have valid reasons to be very nervous during the relevant questions, as incorrect test outcomes—which are always possible if the test is not infallible—will result in them being further accused of committing a crime of which they are innocent.

Guilty Suspects and Relevant Questions

If the efforts of the examiner during the pre-test interview are successful, then all examinees will be concerned about the control questions. As Ben-Shakhar and Furedy (1990) pointed out, it is not clear why a guilty suspect should be less concerned with the control questions, given that this suspect is under the impression that a deceptive response to those questions might be harmful to his or her case.

A Difficult and Crucial Role for the Examiner

Preparing a polygraph test might perhaps be considered a masterpiece. For the polygraph examination to work, the examiner should formulate control questions that, on the one hand, elicit in innocent suspects *stronger* physiological responses than the relevant questions. On the other hand, in guilty suspects, these control questions should elicit *weaker* physiological responses than the relevant questions. Obviously it is not easy for the examiner to formulate questions that meet these criteria. If the examiner scares the examinee too much with the control questions, they will run the risk that guilt will not be detected in guilty examinees. In such a case, physiological responses to control questions might be equal to physiological responses to relevant questions, resulting in an inconclusive test outcome. A further problem with asking too 'heavy' control questions is that this might damage the examinee's psyche (Furedy, 1996a). On the other hand, if examiners do not embarrass the examinees enough with the control questions, they run the risk of innocent examinees being found guilty, as in such a case their physiological responses to the relevant questions might be higher than their physiological responses to the control questions. Lykken (1998) referred to the examiner's task in phase one as 'a very sophisticated piece of psychological engineering'. Furedy (1991a) considers the fact that much depends on the skills of the examiner to be the major criticism of CQT.

Raskin acknowledges this problem. He addressed this issue as follows:

> 'The traditional CQT is difficult to administer, and the level of psycho-logical sensitivity, sophistication, and skill of the examiner are crucial to obtaining an accurate outcome. Unfortunately, many polygraph examiners lack adequate training in psychological methods and do not understand the basic concepts and requirements of a standardized psychological test. These problems are exacerbated when the examiner formulates and intro-duces the control questions to the subject, because it is very difficult to standardize the wording and discussion of the questions for all subjects. A great deal depends on how the subject perceives and responds to the control questions when they are introduced and discussed during the pre-test interview' (Raskin, Kircher, Horowitz & Honts, 1989, p.8).

Barland (1984) has also expressed concern about the quality of many polygraphers in the USA.

An additional problem is that the examiner can never find out in the pre-test whether the control and relevant questions which the examiner is going to ask are appropriate to achieve the desired effect. Reid and Inbau (1977) stated that examiners should check the examinee's behav-ioural symptoms during the pre-test. However, this is a very difficult and risky task. As we saw in Chapter 3, people are not very good at detecting lies by paying attention to someone's non-verbal behaviour. Ekman and O'Sullivan (1991) specifically tested polygraph examiners and found that they were not particularly good at detecting lies on the basis of behavioural cues.

Finally, the examinee's responses to the control questions are often not 'known' lies but 'assumed' lies (Lykken, 1998). The examiner believes that the examinee's answers to these questions are untrue, but often cannot be absolutely certain about this. Obviously, when the assumptions made by the examiner are incorrect the control questions will not achieve the desired effect, since in that case the examinee is actually telling the truth.

The important role of the examiner may lead to a situation in which the examiner's beliefs about the examinee's guilt prior to the polygraph test will influence the test outcome. The examinee is usually not a complete stranger to the examiner, who usually knows important details about him or her (including case-file information) and will form an impression of him or her in the pre-test interview in which the control and relevant questions are formulated. If the examiner believes that the suspect is *innocent*, the result may be that he or she puts the suspect under much pressure during the control questions, increasing the likelihood that the polygraph outcome will indicate 'not guilty'. On the other hand, in a case where the examiner believes the suspect is *guilty*, this may result in not putting so much emphasis on the control questions, leading to a 'guilty' outcome of the polygraph test. The result will be that the test outcome reflects the examiner's prior beliefs about the examinee's guilt. This may well have happened in the very first example, namely the CBS study. In that case study the manager told the examiners beforehand which suspect he considered to be the culprit, and the examiners identified those suspects as the culprits after conducting the polygraph tests. This does not necessarily imply that the examiners intentionally aimed at this outcome. They may have been unconsciously influenced by this pre-information. Apart from beliefs about the possible guilt of examinees, other impressions may influence polygraph outcomes as well, such as liking the suspects or feeling sorry for them. In these circumstances 'guilty outcomes' are perhaps less likely to occur.

Lack of Clarity in How to Score the Polygraph Outcomes

Differences between the control and relevant questions are scored as (1) noticeable difference, (2) strong difference or (3) dramatic difference. However, there are no rules about what constitutes a noticeable, strong or dramatic difference, as mentioned above. In fact, it is impossible to make decision rules because this depends on the examinee. The same difference may be strong in one examinee but only noticeable in another. Figure 7.2 makes this point clear.

Both examinees in Figure 7.2 showed a stronger response to the relevant questions than to the control questions. The absolute difference in responses between the control and relevant questions is the same in both examinees. However, the relative difference is much larger in examinee 2 than in examinee 1, due to the fact that examinee 2's overall physiological responses were smaller than examinee 1's overall responses. The examiner will therefore assign a higher number to the difference in examinee 2 than to the difference in examinee 1.

Scoring Polygraph Charts is a Subjective Matter

In the global approach, the examiner forms a global impression of the examinee's polygraph charts and combines this information in some unspecified manner with non-polygraphic sources of information—such as case-file information, the examinee's criminal history or the examinee's demeanour throughout the test—in order to reach an overall decision. This means that the decision-making process is subjective, as it

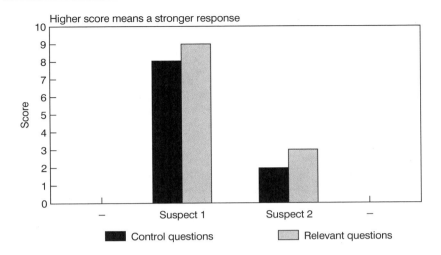

Higher score means a stronger response

■ Control questions ▢ Relevant questions

Figure 7.2. Individual differences in physiological responses.

depends on the examiner. Moreover, it is not verifiable. It is difficult for other people to find out why a particular examiner has reached a particular conclusion. Raskin acknowledges this problem and introduced the numerical scoring approach. However, even this approach is subjective, for the following two reasons.

First, even in the numerical scoring approach some contamination can occur. The examiner usually knows important details about the examinee. It is possible that this will influence the scoring of the polygraph charts, particularly because this scoring is not standardized, as mentioned above. In a recent study using experienced polygraph examiners as participants, Elaad, Ginton and Shakhar (1994) showed that contamination does occur. In their experiment they manipulated prior expectations about the examinee (in the guilt–expectation condition the examiners were told that the examinee ultimately confessed to being responsible for the crime, while in the innocent–expectation condition they were informed that another person had confessed to the crime). The outcomes revealed that these manipulated prior expectations affected the examiners' decisions about the guilt of the examinees, but only if the polygraph charts did not include clear indications of guilt or innocence. If the charts included strong indications that clearly contradicted these expectations, judgements were not affected by these expectations. Honts (1996) acknowledges that this type of contamination also takes place in real-life settings, as I shall discuss later.

Secondly, as it is impossible to define whether a score of 1, 2 or 3 should be allocated to polygraph charts, it may be the case that different examiners may reach different conclusions by judging the same charts. That is, one examiner may assign a total score of –5 to the test, and will therefore decide that the test was inconclusive, whereas another examiner may assign a score of –6, which indicates that the examinee failed the test (and will be considered as deceptive). Again this emphasizes the important role of the examiner. These problems may be overcome by using a computer-based method for scoring polygraph data, as developed by Kircher and Raskin (1988) and more recently by Olsen and his colleagues (Olsen, Harris, Capps & Ansley, 1997). Another solution is to introduce independent evaluators who are blind to the examinee and the crime under investigation. Barland (1988) states that most federally administered polygraph tests in the USA are checked by quality-control officers who review the charts without having seen the behaviour of the examinees. Unfortunately, in field studies inter-agreement rates between different examiners are not usually available, whereas inter-agreement rates between examiners in laboratory studies range from modest (0.61) to satisfactory (0.95) (Carroll, 1988).

Whatever solution is found, it is unlikely to please the opponents of CQT. One of those opponents is John Furedy (who is in favour of GKT, which will be discussed below). In a recent article he expressed his opinion about these solutions in the following way: 'data based on flawed procedures will still yield flawed output...or in less technical and polite words: garbage in, garbage out' (Furedy, 1996a, p.57) (this quotation refers to utilizing computer-based methods for scoring polygraph charts).

Is the Control Question Test Unethical?

Misleading the examinee plays a crucial role in the Control Question Test. One may argue how appropriate it is to use deceptive procedures. Supporters will probably say that the end justifies the means, and that it is important to convict serious criminals, if necessary by deceiving them. Supporters might also argue that polygraph tests sometimes benefit innocent suspects, namely when the test confirms that they are innocent, as was the case with Richard Jewell (see Example 2).

Opponents might point out that deceiving suspects is always inappropriate, and that this can have negative consequences. For example, it may undermine public confidence and social trust in the police and other agencies that conduct polygraph tests, or suspects may think that they are allowed to lie because the police examiner is allowed to lie to them. Finally, suspects may decide not to co-operate with the investigation any longer when they find out that they have been cheated (co-operation is sometimes needed to obtain further evidence because polygraph outcomes often do not count as evidence in court).

Apart from the debate as to whether it is *appropriate* or *desirable* to lie to suspects, it is often *illegal* to do this, as deceptive investigative procedures are not acceptable under law in many countries. This implies that in these countries information obtained via CQT polygraph tests almost certainly could not be used as evidence in court.

As mentioned above, the debate about the polygraph is heated. Indeed, it is probably one of the most heated debates in psychology at present. The following quote by Furedy and Heslegrave, two opponents of the CQT, illustrates the sharpness with which CQT opponents attack the technique:

> 'It is also important to recognize the important role played by the attitudes of evaluators toward accepting errors, and weighing these errors depending upon the circumstances. Because the circumstances are known by the evaluator prior to the administration of the polygraph, and because the test is not standardized, it is likely that not only will the outcome be judged on the basis of examinee circumstances and examiner attitude, but also the administration of the test will be shaped by these prejudices. Because the test is psychological in the sense of involving a complex interview-like interaction between examiner and examinee, any biases in designing and administering the test are likely to produce outcomes that are consistent with those biases. So different individuals accused of different crimes may be given quite different tests, even though all of those tests are called by a single name: polygraph test. Indeed, the term test itself is potentially misleading, because it suggests relatively standardized instruments such as the IQ test that, although controversial, give essentially the same results across competent operators' (Furedy & Heslegrave, 1988, p.224).

The Guilty Knowledge Test

The aim of the Guilty Knowledge Test is to examine whether examinees possess knowledge about a particular crime which they do not want to reveal. For example, suppose that the examinee killed someone with a knife, left the knife at the murder scene, and tells the police that he is not involved in the crime in any way. The police might then try to find out via a Guilty Knowledge Test whether the suspect is telling the truth or not when he denies any involvement in the crime. In a Guilty Knowledge Test the examiner will show the suspect several types of knife, including the one used in the murder. For each knife the examinee will be asked whether he recognizes it as the one that was used by him. Both innocent and guilty examinees will deny each time that they have used such a knife. However, a guilty examinee will recognize the knife he has used. It is assumed that this so-called *guilty knowledge* will produce a heightened physiological response which will be detected by the polygraph. The playing-card game which, as mentioned before, is often used in the Control Question Technique as a stimulation test, is based on this principle.

Figure 7.3 shows the predicted physiological responses in a Guilty Knowledge Test for innocent and guilty suspects. In this example the third alternative represents guilty knowledge.

Lykken (1988) gives the following example of a Guilty Knowledge Test (see Table 7.2). The questions are always asked in a multiple-choice format, and the suspect is instructed to say 'no' to each response alternative. The example refers to a bank robber who, whilst escaping, runs through an alley and accidentally drops and leaves behind his hat.

Theoretically, an innocent suspect has about one chance in five of reacting most strongly to the correct alternative in any of these questions. However, he has only about two chances (1.6 exactly) in 1000 of reacting most strongly to the correct alternative in all four questions. Hence the more questions that are asked, the less likely it is that an innocent suspect will be falsely accused. Examinees usually give a slightly stronger response to the first alternative than to the others. The first alternative is therefore usually an incorrect alternative (not the guilty knowledge alternative) (Bashore & Rapp, 1993).

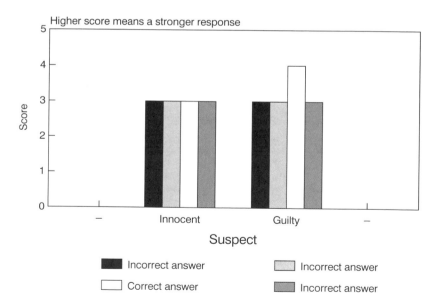

Figure 7.3. Physiological profile for guilty and innocent suspects (GKT).

Table 7.2. An example of a guilty knowledge sequence

1	'The robber in this case dropped something while escaping. If you are that robber, you will know what was dropped. Was it a weapon? A face mask? A sack of money? A hat? Car keys?'
2	'Where was the hat dropped? Was it in the bank? On the bank steps? On the sidewalk? In the parking lot? In an alley?'
3	'What colour was the hat? Was it brown? Red? Black? Green? Blue?'
4	'I'm going to show you five red hats or caps, one at a time. If one of them is your hat, you will recognize it. Which of these hats is yours? Is it this one? This one? (etc.)'

It is probably preferable that the examiner who conducts the actual test does not know the correct answers, as it is possible that, if the examiner knows the correct response, this will influence his or her behaviour. For example, the examiner may become excited about whether or not the suspect will give a stronger response to the correct item. This subtle change in the examiner's behaviour might be noticed (consciously or unconsciously) by the examinee, who might then become nervous when answering the correct item, which could increase their physiological responses (Rosenthal & Rubin, 1978). However, Elaad (1997) has recently shown that participants do not give stronger responses when the examiner knows the answers to the Guilty Knowledge Test.

It is possible that different alternatives elicit different responses in examinees because of the nature of the responses. For instance, it is possible that the alternative 'weapon' elicits more arousal in subjects (guilty and innocent) than the alternative 'keys' or that the alternative 'black knickers' are more arousing than the alternative 'pink knickers' (in a case where the examinee is a suspect in a rape case). It is also possible that some responses will evoke stronger responses because they are more likely to be the correct answer. For example, it is more likely that a bank robber will lose his hat than one of his shoes, and the alternative 'hat' may therefore evoke a larger response in an innocent person than the alternative 'shoe'. This problem can be minimized by pre-testing the set of alternatives on mock suspects—that is, on known innocent people. They should give similar responses to all of the alternatives, and another set of alternatives needs to be chosen if this is not the case (Lykken, 1988).

Criticism Concerning the Guilty Knowledge Test

The Guilty Knowledge Test is less disputed among scientists than the Control Question Test. Iacono and Lykken (1997) recently published a survey of scientific opinion about both types of polygraph testing. They asked members of the American Society of Psychophysiological Research (who can be regarded as experts) and fellows of the American Psychological Association (division 1, general psychology) about their opinions on CQT and GKT polygraph tests. The findings, which have been published in the prestigious *Journal of Applied Psychology*, revealed that the opinions of both groups of psychologists were very similar, and that they favoured the Guilty Knowledge Test. The majority of interviewees (about 75%) considered the Guilty Knowledge Test to be based on scientifically sound psychological principles or theory, whereas a minority (about 33%) thought that this was the case for the Control Question Test. Moreover, only 22% would advocate that courts admit as evidence the outcome of control question polygraph tests.

However, there are criticisms concerning the Guilty Knowledge Test. They are all related to its limited applicability. The problem with GKT is that questions can only be asked to which *the person who designs the test and the guilty examinee alone know the answers.* The person who designs the test should know the correct answer, otherwise there is a risk that the correct answer will not be included in the set of alternatives. Moreover, the GKT only works if questions are asked about details which are actually known to the culprit, otherwise there is no guilty knowledge to detect. This is not always the case. The guilty suspect may not have perceived the details the examiner is asking about, or may have forgotten them by the time the test takes place. For instance, it might be the case that when the examiner asks a question about the colour of the hat which has been found at the scene of the crime, the guilty suspect has simply forgotten the colour of his hat! The longer the period between the crime and the polygraph test, the more likely it is that the suspect has forgotten certain details. The problem is that the person who designs the test can never be sure that the culprit knows the answer to the question. For example, one can never be sure that the bank robber actually knows that he lost his hat in the alley. It can only be assumed that the guilty suspect will know this.

Moreover, a suspect may admit to having guilty knowledge but nevertheless deny guilt. This happens if the suspect admits being present but denies the specific alleged acts. The most common example is an alleged sexual assault in which the witness claims that force was used and the suspect admits the sexual act but claims that it was consensual. Similar problems arise in cases where several suspects were involved in the crime and all of them deny having been the principal player (Raskin, 1988, pp.102–103).

Finally, questions can only be asked about items to which innocent suspects do not know the answer (otherwise they will have guilty knowledge as well). However, this is not always the case. In many cases the salient details of the crime are made available by the media, investigators or attorneys. In order to minimize this problem, questions could be asked about minor details which are not widely known, although this increases the likelihood that the guilty suspect does not know the answers either.

The result is that the number of cases in which the GKT can be used is limited. Podlesny analysed criminal case files of the American Federal Bureau of Investigation (FBI) and found that in fewer than 9% of the cases in which CQTs were used, a GKT could have been used as well (Podlesney, 1995). Bashore and Rapp (1993) believe that the limited applicability of the test is the principal obstacle to broader use of the technique. Given its limited applicability, recent findings of Elaad and Ben-Shakhar (1997) are promising. Their experimental GKT study showed that instead of asking several questions to obtain reliable accuracy rates (as in the example shown in Table 7.2), asking the same question more than once could achieve this. Their study was the first attempt to demonstrate this, so we should be cautious when drawing conclusions. However, should this finding be replicated in different studies and in different settings, it might increase the applicability of the GKT, as it is easier to formulate one question than many. On the other hand, asking one question may emphasize the problems just mentioned. For example, if a guilty suspect does not know the answer to one of the four different questions that have been asked, the scores on the other three questions may correct this deficiency. However, if a suspect does not know the answer to the only question that has been asked, no correction can take place.

Lykken (1998) rejects the idea that the GKT cannot be used in many cases. He pointed out that at present FBI investigators are not trained to search fresh crime scenes for usable GKT items. If they were so trained, then the test could be used more often. Lykken made a comparison with the search for fingerprints and stated that:

'had Podlesny (*who analysed the FBI case files, just mentioned*) been working at Scotland Yard in 1900 at the time of the introduction of the Galton-Henry system of fingerprint identification, it is likely that he would also have found very few cases in the records of the Yard that included fingerprints of suspects' (Lykken, 1998, p.305) (the information in italics has been added by me).

To support his argument, Lykken (1998) described how the GKT could have been used in the O.J. Simpson murder case and in the bomb attack on the Murrah building in Oklahoma City in the USA on 19 April 1995, in which the building was destroyed and 168 men and women were killed. Questions which could have been used in a GKT immediately after the body of Simpson's wife was found include the following: (i) 'You know that Nicole has been found murdered, Mr Simpson. How was she killed? Was she drowned? Was she hit on the head with something? Was she shot? Was she beaten to death? Was she stabbed? Was she strangled?'; and (ii) 'Where did we find her body? Was it in the living-room? In the driveway? By the side gate? In the kitchen? In the bedroom? By the pool?' (Lykken, 1998, p.298).

THE POLYGRAPH: DOES IT WORK?

The number of publications in scientific journals concerning actual, real-life polygraph examination is disappointing, given the number of tests that are conducted each year. However, case examples are easy to find in professional journals, and two are mentioned at the beginning of this chapter. Case examples include both 'success stories' (e.g. Example 2) and 'failures' (e.g. Example 1).

All of the case studies published to date were conducted in a judicial setting. This is not surprising given the fact that CQT and GKT are specifically designed for this purpose. In practice tests were (and probably still are) conducted for personnel purposes as well—for example, in attempts to investigate whether an applicant will be a reliable employee. In fact, the GKT cannot be used for personnel selection purposes. In selection procedures, employers are interested in general information—for example, whether the applicant has ever stolen anything. A GKT cannot answer that question, because only specific questions about specific events can be asked.

The non-applicability of GKT in selection procedures may be one of the reasons why CQTs were normally used, but this technique is not suitable either. It is possible to ask general questions in a control-question sequence. However, the number of incorrect outcomes increases if the questions become more general (Barland, 1988).

Moreover, while a polygraph test could reveal information about how someone behaved *in the past* (for example, it could reveal whether a candidate lied when filling in his application form), perhaps of more importance to employers is how someone will behave *in the future*. A polygraph test cannot answer this question, and this restricts the use of polygraph tests for personnel purposes.

In order to test the accuracy of polygraph testing, both field studies and laboratory studies have been conducted. Field studies deal with real-life criminal cases and suspects. The advantage of field studies is that they are realistic. Suspects do really care about the polygraph outcome, and therefore strong emotions are likely. Another advantage is that real suspects are studied instead of college students (who are usually the participants in laboratory studies). The main disadvantage of field studies is the ambiguity about ground truth—that is, it is very difficult to establish the actual guilt or innocence of the subjects. Confessions are usually used as ground truth, but are not 100% reliable. On the one hand, people who do not confess and who are considered to be innocent may actually be guilty, as cases may be dismissed due to lack of sufficient evidence rather than to innocence. On the other hand, people who are considered to be guilty by virtue of a confession may actually be innocent, as some innocent people do confess (Gudjonsson, 1992). Polygraph tests may actually lead to false confessions. Innocent suspects sometimes make false confessions after they have been found to be guilty by a polygraph test. One reason is that they see little further opportunity to convince the jury or judges of their innocence, and they therefore decide to confess in order to receive a lesser sentence. Alternatively, it might be that as a result of failing a polygraph test suspects actually believe that they are guilty. This happened to Peter Reilly and Tom Sawyer. Their cases are described in Box 7.1.

Box 7.1. The Reilly and Sawyer cases

Peter Reilly Eighteen-year-old Peter Reilly returned home one night to find his mother dead. He realized that she had been murdered and called the police. The police interviewed Reilly and suspected him of killing his mother. They conducted a polygraph test. The police told him that he had failed the test, thus indicating that he was guilty even though he had no memory of the incident. Transcripts of the interrogation sessions revealed that Reilly underwent a remarkable transformation from denial to confusion and finally to conversion ('Well, it really looks like I did it') and a full written confession. Two years later, independent evidence revealed that Reilly could not have committed the murder, and that the confession that even he had come to believe in was in fact false (Kassin, 1997).

Tom Sawyer Tom Sawyer's next-door neighbour was murdered by manual strangulation. The police became suspicious of Sawyer solely because he seemed to them to be nervous when they spoke to him during routine interviews with him as one of the murdered woman's neighbours. Sawyer was invited to the police station for a second interview. In response to questions about his general background, Mr Sawyer discussed both his social anxiety and the fact that he had been an alcoholic. In trying to engage Mr Sawyer in conversation about the crime, the detectives asked him to help them to create a scenario of how the murder might have happened. Mr Sawyer, who loved to watch detective shows on television, was eager to help and joined in. The police let Mr Sawyer explain several scenarios and accused him at the end of having committed the murder. The police claimed that he mentioned nine

(continued overleaf)

Box 7.1. (*continued*)

facts that only the killer could have known. Subsequent analysis of the interrogation transcripts showed that all of the crucial information was
introduced into the interrogation by the police. (Being confused about the
source of information occurs more frequently, and is called *source-moni-
toring error* (Raye & Johnson, 1980). People sometimes become confused
about whether they themselves or others presented some information, or
about which out of a number of people presented the information. This sometimes happens during meetings. People disagree afterwards about who took
the initiative regarding a particular proposal, and so on.)

Following the accusation, Mr Sawyer strongly denied his guilt. The police
obtained fingerprint and hair samples from him and suggested a polygraph
examination. Mr Sawyer believed that the polygraph examination would
prove his innocence and agreed with the examination. After the test, the
examiner told Mr Sawyer that the test had proved he was lying (subsequent
re-scoring of the test by a polygraph expert later on revealed that the test
outcome was inconclusive). Once he had been told that the polygraph showed
him to be lying, Mr Sawyer's confidence began to erode. He was no longer
able to express firm denials of guilt, and could only say that he still did not
believe he had committed the crime. His main defence against the police's
demands to confess was his lack of memory of having committed the crime.
The police replied by saying that he was blocking out his memory of the
crime, that he had a black-out, just as he often had when he had been
drinking. At this point, Mr Sawyer still refused to accept fully that he had
committed the crime, and pinned his hopes on the other tests (fingerprints
and hair test) revealing his innocence. The detectives decided to lie to him
and told him that his hair samples matched hairs found on the victim's body.

On receipt of this information, Mr Sawyer's resistance collapsed, and he
agreed that 'all the evidence was in' and that he must have committed the
crime. During the next period of the interrogation the detectives wanted to
obtain an accurate description of the crime, which was impossible for Mr
Sawyer because he had not commited it. The police helped Mr Sawyer
somewhat by suggesting to him what they knew had happened or what they
thought might have happened. For example, the police believed that the
victim had been sexually assaulted. Encouraged by the police detectives, Mr
Sawyer confessed to having raped the victim. When the medical examiner's
report was received, no evidence of sexual assault was indicated (Ofshe,
1989).

Suspects might start to doubt their innocence because they trust the
polygraph and believe that it is infallible. This perhaps sounds naive, but
you must bear in mind that the examiner assures the suspect that the
polygraph is infallible, and that no mistakes have been made. Moreover,
the police will tell the suspect afterwards that the outcome was accurate.
Some suspects believe this.

In a typical laboratory polygraph experiment, participants are
randomly assigned to an innocent or guilty condition. Those in the guilty

condition commit a mock crime, such as the theft of an object. Those in the innocent condition are given a description of the crime but do not commit it. All of the participants are told to deny the theft. They may be promised a reward if they can convince the examiner of their innocence, or they may be threatened with punishment if they cannot. For instance, Bradley and Janisse (1981) threatened their guilty and innocent subjects with a 'painful but not permanently damaging electric shock' if they failed the test. The subject is then given a polygraph test by an examiner who is blind with respect to guilt or innocence. The examiner's task is to find out via the polygraph test who is guilty and who is not. The major advantage of such a laboratory study is that there is absolute certainty about the ground truth—that is, absolute certainty about who is actually guilty or innocent. However, there is almost inevitably a lack of realism in laboratory studies. For instance, in real-life situations the stakes are much higher than in laboratory studies. It is never possible to elicit in a laboratory study the strong emotions that may possibly be felt by a person who is accused of murder and whose guilt or innocence may be established by means of a polygraph test. For these reasons, Lykken (1988, 1998) and Kleinmuntz and Szucko (1982) have argued that laboratory polygraph tests are not useful for estimating field accuracy. Raskin has suggested that laboratory studies might be useful as long as certain criteria are met, namely representative subject populations (not only college students) and realistic polygraph practices (including expert examiners and some motivation for the examinee to deceive the examiner) (Kircher, Horowitz & Raskin, 1988; Raskin, 1989). In a recent experimental study, Elaad and Ben-Shakhar (1997) provided some evidence that highly motivated examinees were indeed easier to detect than poorly motivated examinees.

A unique attempt to conduct a polygraph study in a realistic setting and maintaining certainty about the ground truth was made by Ginton, Daie, Elaad and Ben-Shakhar (1982). The participants in this study were 21 Israeli policemen who took a paper-and-pencil test that was presented as a requirement for a police course in which they were enrolled. They were asked to score their own tests, which provided an opportunity to cheat by revising their initial answers. However, the test answer sheets were chemically treated so that cheating could be detected. It turned out that seven of the 21 subjects cheated. Later, all of them were told that they were suspected of cheating. They were offered a polygraph examination, and were told that their future careers in the police force might depend on the outcome of this examination (the option to allow the police officers to refuse to take the test was a realistic one. As mentioned earlier, in criminal investigations taking a polygraph test is an option and not an absolute requirement for a suspect). Although initially all 21 policemen agreed to undergo a polygraph examination, one guilty officer did not turn up for the actual examination, and two (one guilty and one innocent) refused to take the polygraph test. Three other guilty subjects confessed just before the polygraph interrogation[1], so the final sample included only two guilty and 13 innocent participants. The Control Question Test was used, and the outcomes were rather accurate. Both guilty officers were accurately detected. However, two of the 13 innocent officers were mistakenly judged to be lying. Although the findings appear to provide impressive support for the Control Question Test, in fact they did not. The examiner (who made the decisions about the guilt or innocence of the examinees) had access to both polygraph data and the subjects' general demeanour during questioning. His accuracy with regard to innocent subjects (11 out of 13 correct) was equal to the accuracy of an observer who had access only to the suspects' demeanour! (The observer, who watched the polygraph examinations but who had no access to the polygraph data, also classified 11 out of 13 innocent examinees' correctly). A blind evaluator who had access only to the polygraph data classified only 7 out of 13 cases correctly, and classified 3 innocent examinees as guilty and 3 outcomes as inconclusive. These results seriously challenge the efficiency of polygraph testing in this particular case (Carroll, 1991).

CQT and GKT Accuracy Rates: Laboratory Studies

In principle, six outcomes are possible in a Control Question Test. A *guilty suspect* might show stronger physiological responses to relevant questions than to control questions. In this case, the suspect has failed the test, which is an accurate outcome. It is also possible that they show similar responses to relevant and control questions. In this case, the outcome is inconclusive. Finally, they might show stronger physiological responses to control questions than to relevant questions. In this case they have passed the test, which is an incorrect outcome.

An *innocent suspect* might show stronger reactions to control questions than to relevant questions. In this case, the suspect has passed the test, which is the correct outcome. It is also possible that the innocent suspect shows similar responses to control questions and relevant questions. In this case, the outcome is inconclusive. Finally, the innocent suspect might react more strongly to relevant questions than to control questions. The suspect has then failed the test, which is the incorrect outcome.

In GKT polygraph tests six outcomes are also possible. The *guilty suspect* shows stronger physiological responses to the correct answers

---

[1] Ekman (1992) pointed out that these figures support what polygraph examiners claim, namely that the threat of taking a polygraph examination does produce confessions among guilty suspects. However, the findings also suggest that refusal to take the test is no certain guarantee of guilt.

than to the incorrect ones. In this case, the suspect fails the test, which is the correct decision. It is also possible that a guilty suspect shows similar responses to all of the alternatives (correct and incorrect). In this case, the suspect has passed the test, which is an incorrect outcome. Finally, a guilty suspect may show the strongest responses to the incorrect answers. In this case, the examiner will make an incorrect decision and will classify the suspect as innocent.

An *innocent suspect* may show similar responses to all of the alternatives (correct and incorrect). In this case, the suspect has passed the test, which is the right decision. An innocent suspect may show the strongest response to an incorrect answer. In this case again the suspect has passed the test. Finally, the suspect may show the strongest responses to the correct answers. This time, the suspect has failed the test, which is an incorrect decision.

In short, there are two types of error, namely the classification of a guilty subject as innocent, which is called a *false-negative error*, and the false accusation of an innocent suspect, which is called a *false-positive error*. Although both types of error are undesirable, a false-positive error is probably the most serious error. In such a case, the result may be that an innocent suspect will be convicted and/or lose their job. A false-negative error may result in a guilty person being released.

Figure 7.4 provides a summary of laboratory-based polygraph tests. The scores are calculated on the basis of several reviews which have been published and also some recent studies (published after 1995) concerning laboratory tests examining the accuracy of CQTs and GKTs. Appendices 7.1 and 7.2 provide an overview of the (review) studies used in this summary and the accuracy scores for individual reviews and studies.

Outcomes with regard to *laboratory Control Question Tests* show that these tests are rather accurate in detecting guilty subjects. The majority of guilty suspects (73%) were detected, and relatively small numbers of guilty suspects (9%) were incorrectly classified as innocent. A less positive picture emerges with regard to proving the innocence of innocent subjects. In total, 66% of these were correctly classified as innocent, and a rather high percentage of subjects (13%) were falsely accused of being guilty. The test outcomes for guilty and innocent suspects were inconclusive in about 20% of the cases.

Outcomes with regard to *laboratory Guilty Knowledge Tests* show that the test is very accurate with regard to innocent subjects. The vast majority of innocent people (96%) were correctly classified, and only a small percentage of innocent people (4%) were falsely accused. However, the test is less accurate when detecting guilt in guilty subjects. In total, 82% of guilty suspects were classified as such, but relatively high

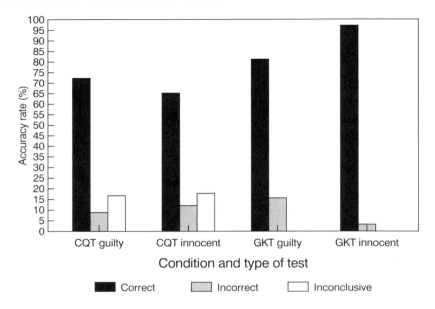

Figure 7.4. Results of laboratory studies testing the accuracy of the CQT and GKT.

percentages of guilty subjects (18%) were classified as innocent. The GKT does not have an inconclusive category.

A comparison between the two types of test shows that GKTs are more accurate both in detecting truth and in detecting deceit. Moreover, the CQT has more false-positive errors than the GKT, but the GKT has more false-negative errors than the CQT.

CQT and GKT accuracy rates: field studies

Figure 7.5 provides a summary of CQT and GKT polygraph tests in applied settings. The scores are calculated on the basis of several reviews and also some recent studies which were not included in the literature reviews. Only recent studies were included which fulfilled the following four criteria: (i) the participants were suspects in real-life criminal cases; (ii) the evaluations were based on the physiological data alone; (iii) the evaluations were conducted by people trained and experienced in performing 'blind' chart evaluations; and (iv) a criterion for who was innocent and who was guilty was developed independently of the polygraph test. Most of the studies used confessions as the criterion. I have already noted that confessions never provide certainty about the actual

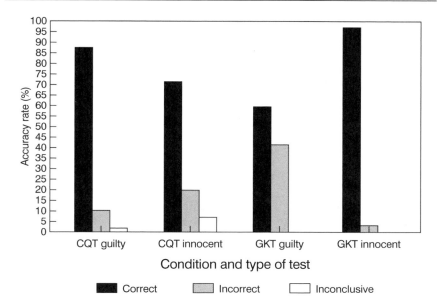

Figure 7.5. Results of field studies testing the accuracy of the CQT and GKT.

guilt or innocence of suspects. The criterion used by Honts (1996) is not clear (although criterion (iv) was fulfilled). Appendices 7.3 and 7.4 provide an overview of the (review) studies used in the summary and the accuracy scores of the individual reviews and studies.

Outcomes with regard to *field studies with the Control Question Test* show that accuracy scores concerning the classification of guilty suspects are rather high. The vast majority of guilty suspects (87%) were correctly classified as guilty, whereas relatively small numbers of guilty suspects (10%) were incorrectly classified as innocent. As in the laboratory studies, the picture for innocent suspects is less optimistic. Only 72% of innocent suspects were classified as such, and 21% of innocent suspects failed the polygraph test and were wrongly accused. The test results were inconclusive for about 7% of guilty and innocent suspects.

The findings reveal that the CQT is susceptible to false-positive errors—the false accusation of an innocent suspect. This is perhaps not surprising. A false-positive error occurs if a subject shows more emotional arousal when answering the relevant questions than when answering the control questions. Apparently, despite the examiner's efforts, innocent suspects do not always show more concern for the control questions than for the relevant questions. It might be that they realize the major consequences of the relevant questions and therefore show emotional arousal when answering this type of question, even when they are answering truthfully.

The percentages of false-positive errors are higher in field studies than in laboratory studies, which is not surprising. In field studies the stakes are high, and suspects will realize the major consequences of relevant questions.

Outcomes with regard to *field studies with the Guilty Knowledge Test* show that, as was the case in laboratory studies, accuracy rates for innocent suspects are very high. Correct decisions were made in 96% of cases, and in only 4% of the cases was an innocent suspect wrongly accused. Again the accuracy rates for guilty suspects are much lower. In total, 59% of the guilty suspects were classified as such, and 41% of the guilty suspects were classified as innocent.

A comparison between field studies with regard to CQT and GKT shows that GKT is more accurate in classifying innocent suspects whereas CQT is more accurate in classifying guilty suspects. In fact, accuracy rates for guilty suspects are low in GKT field studies and many false-negative errors (41%) are made (classifying guilty suspects as innocent). The occurrence of false-negative errors in GKT is not surprising. It implies that guilty suspects do not always show stronger physiological responses to correct answers than to incorrect ones. This might be because, as I explained earlier, the suspect has forgotten the details that the examiner was asking about, or had never known these details. This may well be the result of the questions asked in the Guilty Knowledge Test. As I pointed out above, the police are not well trained in the use of GKT, and therefore perhaps lack the skills to search for crime scenes which are appropriate for GKT polygraph examinations. Trained police officers may well be able to find crime scenes which are more suitable for guilty knowledge testing—that is, crime scenes which will be recognized by guilty suspects in subsequent Guilty Knowledge Tests.

The incidence of false-negative errors is higher in field studies than in laboratory studies, which is not surprising either. In laboratory studies all guilty examinees have guilty knowledge (as the experimenter makes sure that this is achieved), whereas in field studies this is not necessarily the case, for the reasons just mentioned.

In CQT field studies, usually several examiners score the polygraph charts, namely the original examiners (those who conducted the polygraph test) and independent examiners who were not present during the test. The main difference between the two types of examiner is that independent examiners only have access to the polygraph charts, whereas the original examiners have more information to rely on, such as the demeanour of the examinee during the test, case-file information and the examinee's criminal history. The percentage figures presented so far are the accuracy scores obtained by independent examiners. In three recent studies, accuracy rates for both independent and original examiners were reported (see Appendix 7.5) (Honts, 1996; Honts, Raskin, Kircher & Hodes, 1988; Patrick & Iacono, 1991). This makes a comparison between the two types of examiner possible. This comparison is illustrated in Figure 7.6.

Figure 7.6 shows that with regard to guilty suspects the difference is marginal. Independent examiners made slightly more 'correct' classifications, but they also made more errors. The difference with regard to the classification of innocent suspects is particularly remarkable. The original examiners correctly classified 82% of the innocent suspects, but the independent examiners only classified 49% correctly. Overall, the original examiners seem to be more accurate than the independent examiners. Honts, Raskin, Kircher and Hodes (1988) obtained very high hit rates with original examiners—among the highest hit rates ever found in deception research. Their accuracy rates for guilty and innocent classifications were 92% and 91%, respectively!

There are two possible reasons why original examiners are more accurate than independent examiners. First, original examiners might

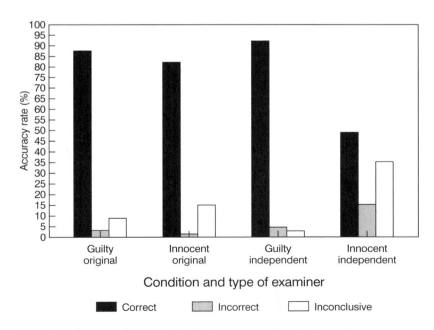

Figure 7.6. Results of CQT field studies: original and independent examiners.

be more skilful in scoring charts. This explanation is unlikely, as independent examiners are usually experienced and skilful polygraphers. Secondly, original examiners use extra non-polygraph information in addition to make their decision, such as the examinee's demeanour during the test, case-file information, and so on. Honts (1996) acknowledged that this indeed happens. In his study he found that in four cases—involving two innocent and two guilty suspects—the examiner made a decision on the basis of the polygraph outcomes, whereas a decision should not have been made because the test outcomes for these four cases were inconclusive. In all four cases, however, the decisions made by the examiners (guilty or innocent) were correct, indicating that extra non-polygraph information led the examiners to make the correct decision. Bearing this in mind, it is worth looking at how much accuracy is added by polygraph tests. To what extent are polygraph examiners who assess both an examinee's behaviour and their physiological responses more accurate than observers who only observe that person's behaviour? This issue will be discussed in Chapter 8.

COUNTERMEASURES

So far, it has been assumed that examinees comply with all of the examiner's demands during polygraph tests. This is obviously not always the case. Sometimes examinees try to influence the polygraph outcomes and to produce physiological responses which will lead the examiner to conclude that they are telling the truth. Methods used to achieve this are called 'countermeasures'. If such techniques could be shown to be effective, this might have major implications for polygraph testing, because it would make the technique less effective.

Different countermeasures can be distinguished, such as tongue biting, foot tensing (by pressing the toes against the floor), counting sheep or counting backwards. Tongue biting or foot tensing will result in a physiological response which will be detected by the polygraph. By doing this, examinees can artificially increase their physiological reactions during control questions, thereby increasing the likelihood that they will pass the test. The result of counting sheep or counting backwards (obviously, not aloud but silently) will be that examinees do not process the questions asked (CQT) or the alternatives listed (GKT) by the examiners. As a result, a similar physical response to each question or answer alternative is likely, which will lead to an inconclusive test outcome in CQTs and to a pass in GKTs. The introduction of fillers (used in CQTs) may counteract this technique, as examinees are supposed to answer 'yes' to fillers but 'no' to the other questions. This forces the examinee to listen to and process the questions, as answering 'no' to a filler may reveal that they are not paying attention to the questions.

The most famous countermeasure test was probably conducted by Floyd 'Buzz' Fay, a man who was falsely convicted of murder on the basis of a failed polygraph examination. He took it on himself to become a polygraph expert during his two and a half years of wrongful imprisonment. He coached 27 inmates, who all freely confessed to him that they were guilty, in how to beat the control question polygraph test. After only 20 minutes of instruction, 23 of the 27 inmates were successful in beating the polygraph test (Ford, 1995; Kleinmuntz & Szucko, 1984).

Reid and Inbau (1977) do not seem to be concerned about the effectiveness of countermeasures. They argue that it is highly improbable that countermeasures can succeed because a properly trained examiner would notice that the examinee was trying to fool them. However, several studies have shown that training in countermeasures can be very effective in beating polygraph tests (Ben-Shakhar & Dolev, 1996; Elaad, 1987, cited in Ben-Shakhar & Furedy, 1990; Honts, Devitt, Winbush & Kircher, 1996; Honts, Hodes & Raskin, 1985; Honts, Raskin & Kircher, 1994). In the study conducted by Honts, Raskin and Kircher (1994), subjects were trained for 30 minutes in the use of either physical countermeasures (biting the tongue or pressing the toes against the floor) or a mental countermeasure (counting backwards from seven). After this training session they underwent a CQT polygraph test. The mental and physical countermeasures were equally effective, each enabling approximately 50% of the subjects to beat the polygraph test. Moreover, the examiner (who was experienced in control-question polygraph tests) only detected 12% of the physical countermeasure users, whereas none of the mental countermeasure users showed behaviour or physiological responses that raised the suspicion of the examiner. These findings contradict Reid and Inbau's claim that experienced examiners will detect the use of countermeasures[2], and they have serious implications. For example, in the USA, CQT polygraph tests are still performed in the defence industry, perhaps in order to catch and deter spies. It is possible that these spies are trained to beat the polygraph. Lykken cites the example of Aldrich Ames, the CIA agent who sold secrets to the Soviets for many years and who passed several polygraph tests during these years. He stated that Ames 'succeeded in his spy career for as long as he did because his ability to beat the lie detector deflected official

---

[2] It is perhaps possible to detect countermeasures with counter-countermeasures. Honts, Raskin and Kircher (1987) placed electrodes in the area of the gastronemius muscle and in the area of the temporalis muscle and could correctly identify 90% of the countermeasure users.

suspicions' (Lykken, 1998, p.3). Recently, Ames' KGB controller Viktor Cherkashin explained in an interview with the British newspaper *The Sunday Times* (8 February 1998, p.21) how he helped Ames to pass polygraph tests. Cherkashin had arranged a lunch between Ames and a Russian diplomat. To Ames' surprise, Cherkashin attended the lunch himself as well. Ames became nervous, as the FBI knew Cherkashin and had him watched. However, Cherkashin attended the lunch on purpose. He knew that the CIA often made its officers undergo routine polygraph tests, and he knew that Ames would be asked 'If he had recently had unoffical contacts with KGB officers', because this was a standard question they always asked. Since contacts between Ames and KGB officers were secret, Ames would then have to lie when answering this question. After the lunch, however, there was no need for Ames to lie about this any longer, and he could safely say that he had been approached.

As with the Control Question Test, the Guilty Knowledge Test is vulnerable to countermeasures, too. However, the situation is different. In CQTs, even innocent suspects may try to beat the polygraph and may try to show strong responses on the control questions, to avoid being mistakenly found guilty. In GKTs, innocent suspects could not systematically use countermeasures even if they wished to, as they do not know which alternatives are correct and which are incorrect (Lykken, 1998).

Obviously, it is difficult to conduct a countermeasures test, as it can only be done in laboratories and never in field studies. It is therefore impossible to find out whether the use of countermeasures outside the laboratory will be as sucessful as the use of these measures inside the laboratory.

PERSONALITY AND THE POLYGRAPH

It is perhaps reasonable to assume that it is difficult for a polygraph to detect lies told by psychopaths. Lies are only detectable with a polygraph if the examinee becomes aroused when they tell a lie. Arousal can be the result of guilt, fear or duping delight, as I pointed out earlier in this book. Psychopaths are less anxious than normal people about danger in general and punishment in particular (Lykken, 1998). Thus it might well be that psychopaths do not become aroused when they are lying, making it impossible to detect their lies. Perhaps surprisingly, Raskin and Hare's (1978) research has shown that psychopaths and non-psychopaths were equally detectable with a polygraph. However, it is too early to draw conclusions on the basis of this one study, particularly as that study has been criticized (Lykken, 1998). In order to motivate the examinees in that study, a prize of 20 US dollars could be won by those who beat the polygraph. Although this prize is likely to motivate examinees and will cause arousal, it is more likely to create duping delight than fear or guilt! This might explain why the study did not find differences between psychopaths and non-psychopaths. Although a psychopath is less anxious than normal people about punishment, there is no reason to expect that psychopaths would be any less interested in winning. In order to investigate the differences between psychopaths and non-psychopaths, tests in which examinees face punishment instead of incentives are therefore required. Such tests have not yet taken place. It therefore remains unclear whether or not psychopaths are better able to beat polygraph tests than normal examinees in criminal investigations.

To my knowledge, apart from differences between psychopaths and non-psychopaths, differences between introverts and extraverts in polygraph testing are the only personality factors to have been examined (Steller, Haenert & Eiselt, 1987; Watson & Sinka, 1993). These studies did not reveal any differences between introverts and extraverts.

CONCLUSION

Field studies examining the accuracy of polygraph tests have shown that these tests (both CQTs and GKTs) make substantial numbers of mistakes. The proponents of the CQT tests will probably argue that this conclusion is incorrect, and they will then refer to the accuracy scores obtained by original examiners in their field studies. The problem is that independent examiners were much less accurate. This suggests that extra, non-polygraph information, known to the original examiner but not to the independent evaluator, is essential for making an accurate decision. The accuracy of the test *itself* can only be reliably determined by using evaluators who have access solely to the test results, and their accuracy rates appeared to be less accurate.

Given the numbers of mistakes made in polygraph tests, I think that polygraph outcomes should not be allowed as a substantial piece of evidence in court. Raskin is in favour of admitting CQT outcomes in court, and Lykken is against this. Lykken also does not advocate the admissibility of his own Guilty Knowledge Test as evidence in court (Iacono & Lykken, 1997). However, polygraph tests may make a valuable contribution to the detection of deceit. Polygraph outcomes might therefore be used as an additional piece of evidence in court (as long as more substantial evidence is presented as well), or as a tool in police investigations to eliminate potential suspects, to check the truthfulness of informants, or to examine contradictory statements of witnesses and suspects in the same case (Boelhouwer, Merckelbach, Van Koppen & Verbaten, 1996; Van Koppen, Boelhouwer, Merckelbach & Verbaten, 1996).

For this purpose, I prefer and advocate the use of guilty knowledge polygraph tests. I do not do this for reasons of accuracy. Research has shown that Control Question Tests can be accurate, and their accuracy rates (at least in field studies) do exceed the accuracy rates of Guilty Knowledge Tests. I reject control question polygraph tests, because part of the procedure involves deceiving examinees. First, deception makes the test vulnerable, as people who read about a CQT will come to know, which will probably make the test less efficient. Secondly, in many countries the use of deception in criminal investigations is illegal. For example, in both the UK (the country where I work) and The Netherlands (my native country) it is illegal to lie to suspects in criminal investigations. This makes it illegal to conduct control question polygraph tests in these countries, and impossible to use the outcomes of such tests as evidence in criminal trials. This 'deception is illegal' argument may be a typical European one. For example, Lykken, whose book *A Tremor in the Blood* (the first edition of which was published in 1981, and the second in 1998) might be regarded as a continuous plea against CQT polygraph testing, does not use this deception argument.

Before guilty knowledge polygraph tests can be widely introduced in police investigations, several issues need to be clarified.

- More field studies with GKT are needed to test its accuracy. In these tests, the multiple repetition of one item technique (asking about one detail several times) instead of the multiple item technique (asking about several details) might be worth testing, because this will probably improve the applicability of the test, as it is probably easier to design a test about one detail than a test about several details.
- It is important to ensure the quality of polygraph examiners, as they have such an important role in polygraph testing. It might be a good idea to introduce university grades in polygraph testing, and only people with a 'polygraph examination degree' would then be allowed to conduct tests.
- Polygraph tests should be carried out by institutions that are independent of the police force. There are several reasons to support this view. First, police officers often have pre-conceived ideas about the guilt of suspects, which might influence the test. Secondly, police officers might make up polygraph outcomes in order to put suspects under pressure. This is not so likely to occur if the tests are carried out by an independent organization. Thirdly, suspects may distrust the police or may not have confidence in them. This may be particularly so with regard to innocent suspects who are falsely accused by

the police of having committed a crime. It seems fair and reasonable that suspects should be given an independent test.

- It is necessary to check carefully confessions made by suspects after they have failed a polygraph test. Polygraph tests may result in false confessions, either because suspects are going to believe that they have committed the crime (see the Reilly and Sawyer cases; Box 7.1), or because they no longer see much opportunity to convince others of their innocence.

Appendix 7.1. Results of laboratory study reviews and recent studies testing the accuracy of the control question polygraph test

	Guilty condition			Innocent condition		
	Guilty (%)	Innocent (%)	Inconclusive (%)	Guilty (%)	Innocent (%)	Inconclusive (%)
Ekman (1992) (*n*=13)	68	10	22	15	55	30
Honts (1995) (*n*=8)	77	10	13	8	84	8
Kircher *et al*. (1988) (*n*=14)	74	8	18	12	66	22
Ben-Shakhar & Furedy (1990) (*n*=9)	80	7	13	15	63	22
Studies published after 1995						
Bradley *et al*. (1996)	60	10	30	10	80	10
Horowitz *et al*. (1997)	53	20	27	13	80	7

n = number of studies reviewed.

Appendix 7.2. Results of laboratory study reviews and a recent study testing the accuracy of the Guilty Knowledge Test[1]

	Guilty condition		Innocent condition	
	Guilty (%)	Innocent (%)	Guilty (%)	Innocent (%)
Ekman (1992) (*n*=6)	78	22	5	95
Honts (1995) (*n*=5)	86	14	1	99
Ben-Shakhar & Furedy (1990) (*n*=10)	84	16	6	94
Study published after 1995				
Elaad (1997)	76	24	0	100

[1] The GKT does not have an inconclusive category
n = number of studies reviewed.

Appendix 7.3. Results of field study reviews and recent field studies testing the accuracy of the Control Question Test: blind scoring of the polygraph charts

	Guilty condition			Innocent condition		
	Guilty (%)	Innocent (%)	Inconclusive (%)	Guilty (%)	Innocent (%)	Inconclusive (%)
Reviews						
Ekman (1992) (n=10)	88	10	2	20	78	2
Ben-Shakhar &						
Furedy (1990) (n=9)	84	13	3	23	72	5
Individual recent field studies which were not included in the previous reviews						
Honts (1996)	91	5	4	9	55	36
Honts & Raskin						
(1988)	92	8	0	15	62	23
Patrick & Iacono						
(1991)	92	2	6	24	30	46

n = number of studies reviewed.

Appendix 7.4. Results of field studies testing the accuracy of the Guilty Knowledge Test[1]

	Guilty condition		Innocent condition	
	Guilty (%)	Innocent (%)	Guilty (%)	innocent (%)
Elaad (1990)	42	58	2	98
Elaad et al. (1992)	76	24	6	94

[1] The GKT does not have an inconclusive category.

Appendix 7.5. Results of field study reviews testing the accuracy of the Control Question Test: scoring was by the original examiners

	Guilty condition			Innocent condition		
	Guilty (%)	Innocent (%)	Inconclusive (%)	Guilty (%)	Innocent (%)	Inconclusive (%)
Honts (1996)	71	5	24	0	82	18
Honts et al. (1988)	92	8	0	0	91	9
Patrick & Iacono (1991)	98	0	2	8	73	19

CHAPTER 8

Guidelines and Implications for Detecting Lies in Professional Practice

Finally, I shall discuss three issues which I have not yet explicitly addressed. First, there are differences between individuals regarding how good they are at lying. Some people tell transparent lies which are easy to discover, whereas others are very skilful liars. Everyone can probably think of examples of both types of liar. An example of someone who told a transparent lie was Jonathan Aitken, a former English conservative politician who served under John Major, first as Defence Procurement Minister and then as First Secretary to the Treasury. While serving as Minister for Defence Procurement, Aitken spent some time in the Ritz hotel in Paris. The British newspaper *The Guardian* and the television programme *World in Action* reported that the hotel bill was paid by a businessman. Aitken strongly denied this. He claimed that his wife and not a businessman paid the bill, and he sued the newspaper and television station for libel. The libel trial collapsed when the accused parties revealed evidence showing that Aitken's wife was not in Paris during his visit to the hotel and that therefore she could not have paid the bill. Aitken faced a jury trial and admitted charges of perjury and perverting the course of justice. On 8 June 1999 he was jailed for 18 months (*The Independent*, 9 June 1999, front page). By lying about the whereabouts of his wife, Aitken told a lie which he knew could be discovered. By suing the newspaper and television programme he probably increased the likelihood of getting caught, as this would stimulate the accused parties to search for evidence that he was lying. Aitken may be a poor liar. In this chapter I shall describe what characterizes a good liar.

Secondly, I shall summarize the three different ways of catching a liar (analysing non-verbal behaviour, speech content and physiological responses) which were discussed throughout this book. Instead of discussing the three techniques separately, as I have done so far, I shall now compare the three techniques.

Thirdly, my aim in this book was to advise the lie detector on how to detect lies. Inevitably, a book for lie detectors will benefit liars as well. It describes how liars respond and what lie detectors should pay attention to in order to catch a liar. After reading this book, liars might decide to change their response strategy, which will make the task for the lie detector even more difficult. This will always happen. Liars and lie detectors are in an 'arms race' with each other to improve their techniques, and improvements made by lie detectors will result in liars changing their strategy. This was seen most clearly in Chapter 7. The development of polygraph techniques resulted in the development of countermeasures in order to beat the polygraph. I explained in Chapter 7 how the KGB helped Russian spies to fool CIA lie detectors. It will never be possible to detect all lies, nor will this be desirable. People often prefer to remain ignorant and do not wish to find out whether someone is lying to them. However, those who want to catch liars can make the task more difficult for liars. In this chapter I shall describe how to do this.

WHO ARE GOOD LIARS?

Characteristics of the Good Liar

I believe that liars are caught because it is cognitively too difficult to continue lying, or because the way in which they deal with their emotions gives away their lies. Good liars are those people who do not find it cognitively difficult to lie and who do not experience any emotions when they are lying. More precisely, at least seven aspects characterize a good liar: (i) being well prepared; (ii) being original; (iii) thinking quickly; (iv) being eloquent; (v) having a good memory; (vi) not experiencing feelings of fear, guilt or duping delight while lying; and (vii) being good at acting.

Liars are often caught because they are not well enough prepared. Lie detectors will search for evidence which contradicts the liar's statement. Liars should therefore be careful about what they say. Ideally, they should only say things which are impossible for others to verify. Concealing information is therefore better than telling an outright lie. Telling someone that you 'honestly can't remember' what you did a couple of days ago is preferable to making up a story, as the latter gives the observer the opportunity to check the story. However, concealment is not always possible, and sometimes a statement needs to be provided.

The more difficult it is to verify that statement, the better the statement is from a liar's point of view. By lying about the whereabouts of his wife, Jonathan Aitken told a lie which could be verified—but he is not the only one. We recently described five cases of people who were deemed to have killed their relatives and who initially denied having done so (Vrij & Mann, 1999) (see also Chapter 3). Some of those people made serious mistakes when they planned their stories, which made it easy to find out that they were probably hiding the truth. For example, one person could not account for the considerable time period between starting the journey which eventually led to the death of the victim and calling the police. Moreover, blood stains suggested that the victim was actually killed somewhere other than the place claimed. Another person claimed to have been knocked out for 10 hours, but anaesthetists say that this was impossible. Moreover, a reconstruction that included going 'back' into the pub where that person claimed he was on the night of the crime showed that no one who was there on that particular night could confirm that the accused had been there.

With regard to originality, a liar can be faced with unexpected situations which require an immediate response. For example, a wife may confront her husband with the telephone number and address of a woman—unknown to her—which she found in his pocket, or the police detective may tell the suspect that he was seen by a witness at the scene of the crime directly after the crime occurred. To lie successfully in these situations—or in similar ones—the liar needs to give a convincing answer, which requires original thinking. Returning to the example just given, the accused who was not recognized by anyone in the pub during the reconstruction could have challenged the memory of these other customers. However, he did not do this. Instead he admitted defeat.

Liars should not only be original, but should also be able to come up with answers quickly. It is essential that they do not wait too long before giving an answer, because a delay may make the observer suspicious. Rapid thinking is therefore required.

It will benefit the liar to be an eloquent speaker, as eloquence can help them to get out of awkward situations. People who usually use many words to express themselves are in an advantageous position. They can commence by giving a long-winded response, which in fact does not answer the question. Meanwhile, they can think about the appropriate answer. Or they can use their eloquence to fool the observer, by giving a response which sounds convincing but which, in fact, does not provide an answer to the question. Some politicians are very good at this.

Liars always run the risk that lie detectors will ask them to repeat or clarify what they have just said. They should then be able to repeat the same story or to add some information without contradicting themselves. Thus a good memory is required. Repeating the same story or adding extra information is especially difficult when there is some delay between telling the lie and the request to repeat or clarify the lie. For example, it often happens that when people lie about why they were unable to attend a social gathering, they can no longer remember the excuse they gave when the issue is raised again one week later.

People differ in the emotions that they experience while they are lying. One guilty suspect may be very scared when presenting a fake alibi, whereas another may remain calm. One applicant may feel guilty when exaggerating the salary they receive from their present employer, whereas another applicant may not experience any guilt at all while doing this. One pupil may be delighted on realizing that the head-teacher is about to believe their excuse for being too late, whereas another does not experience such 'duping delight'. Deceiving others is easier when the liar does not experience feelings of fear, guilt or delight. As long as the liar does not experience any of these emotions (or indeed any other emotion), there will not be any emotional behaviour that has to be suppressed while they are lying, and therefore they can react naturally. Furthermore, the control question polygraph test will not be able to detect lies if the examinee does not experience any emotion. An absence of emotions during deception may be caused by the frequency of lying. The more often a person lies, the less duping delight they will experience and the less guilty they will feel about lying. Lying frequently will also probably make someone a more skilful liar, which reduces the likelihood of being caught, and thereby reduces the fear of getting caught.

Being good at acting might be helpful, too. It may even may reduce the presence of emotions associated with deception. Good actors will be good at controlling their behaviour and probably also know how to make an honest impression on others. This makes them confident while lying, and they will often get away with their lies. Noticing this will eventually decrease their fear of getting caught. The less fear that liars experience, the easier it is for them to lie convincingly.

DePaulo and DePaulo (1989) conducted a deception study with sales personnel as participants. They did not find any behavioural differences between sales personnel who were lying and those who were telling the truth, suggesting that the sales personnel were very good liars. DePaulo and DePaulo gave several explanations for these findings, and these explanations correspond with what I have stated above. First, sales personnel often stretch the truth when they sell their products, which means that they become experienced in telling lies. These experiences can make them better liars, as customers' reactions give them insight into how successful they are at lying. If they fail to convince customers, they can change their demeanour. They can continue doing this until they make an honest impression on customers. Secondly, sales personnel will probably not experience guilt during deception, as they might consider stretching the truth to be part of their job. Thirdly, sales personnel probably know that they are good liars, because they will often experience getting away with their lies. Therefore they are probably confident in their ability to lie, and will not worry unduly that they might be caught lying.

Good and Perfect Liars

A distinction could be made between good liars and perfect liars. Perfect liars are liars who do not show any cues to deception, either verbally or non-verbally. Such liars might exist, but they are exceptional. In my own research (see Chapter 2), participants are usually interviewed twice. In one interview they tell the truth and in the other interview they lie. Afterwards we compare the behaviour displayed during the two interviews. Incidentally, we do come across perfect liars—some participants show identical behaviour during both interviews. However, the majority of participants show behavioural cues to deception. Many of them are good liars (at least in my experiments). They are good liars because observers are often unable to detect their lies, but they are not perfect liars because they do show behavioural cues to deception. They do not get caught because they exhibit only a few cues to deception, or because the cues which they show are subtle and therefore difficult to detect, or because the cues which they display are not the cues that lie detectors expect liars to show. Therefore, although they are detected, these cues do not lead the lie detector to believe that the person is lying. My research (discussed in Chapter 3) shows that liars who sit still while being interviewed usually make an honest impression on observers. They are not perfect liars, however, because they usually show an unnatural rigidity during deception.

THREE WAYS OF DETECTING LIES

In principle there are three different ways to catch a liar. The first is by observing liars' non-verbal behaviour, such as the movements they make, whether or not they smile or show gaze aversion, the pitch of their voice, their speech rate, whether or not they stutter, and so on. The second way is by analysing what is being said. The third way is by examining physiological responses (blood pressure, heart rate, palmar sweating, and so on). Table 8.1 shows some aspects of these three techniques for detecting lies.

Table 8.1. A schematic overview of the three methods for detecting lies

	Non-verbal	Verbal	Physiological
What should a liar experience?	Cognitive difficulty/emotions	Emotions/cognitive difficulty	Emotions/guilty knowledge
How does the lie express itself?	• Stutters • Pauses during speech • Slower speech rate • Rigidity • Higher-pitched voice • Emotional facial expression	• Implausible answers • Negative statements • Indirect answers • Lack of personal experiences • Structured production • Lack of detail	• Physiological reactions
Are there individual differences?	Yes	Yes	Unknown
Does the method require equipment to detect lies?	Yes	No	No
How good are lay people at detecting lies?	Poor	Unknown	Not applicable
How good are experts at detecting lies?	68% truths—92% lies[a]	76% truths—68% lies[b]	72% truths—87% lies[c] 96% truths—59% lies[d]
Can people be trained to become good lie detectors?	Unknown	Yes	Yes
Is it difficult to fool observers?	Probably	Perhaps not	No

[a] Average hit rates obtained by Frank and Ekman (1997), and Vrij et al. (1999), the only two studies in which truth and lie classifications were made on the basis of detailed analyses of nonverbal behaviour.

[b] Average hit rates obtained in CBCA studies which were presented in Table 5.4, Chapter 5, excluding accuracy rates obtained by Esplin et al., due to the fact that their results have been heavily criticized. Accuracy rates for white and black adults were combined (Ruby et al., 1998). Accuracy rates obtained with CBCA expert and discriminant analysis were combined (Vrij, Kneller & Mann, in press).

[c] Average hit rates of field studies with the Control Question Technique using independent examiners (see also Figure 7.5, Chapter 7).

[d] Average hit rates of field studies with the Guilty Knowledge Test (see also Figure 7.5, Chapter 7).

Non-verbal Cues to Deception

Non-verbal cues to deception are more likely to occur if the lie is difficult to fabricate. When telling a difficult lie, liars tend to speak more slowly, include more pauses in their speech and stutter more. For example, the convicted murderer (described in Chapter 2) showed this behavioural pattern.

Emotions, such as feelings of guilt, fear or excitement when lying might influence someone's behaviour, too. The stronger these emotions, are, the more likely it is that non-verbal cues to deceit will appear. Liars who are very anxious about getting caught will try to make an honest impression on observers. Chapter 2 showed that the behaviour they tend to show in these situations often appears rigid, planned and rehearsed. Moreover, experience of emotions often results in a higher pitch of voice, which is an automatic response beyond the control of the liar. However, the increase in pitch is very small and very difficult to detect. Finally, emotions may lead to emotional facial expressions. For example, fear automatically results in eyebrows being raised and pulled together, and a raised upper eyelid and tensed lower eyelid. Liars who do not want to show that they are scared will try to suppress these emotional expressions. They often achieve this within 1/25th of a second after the expression appears. This means that the expression is present for 1/25th of a second, which could be just long enough for it to be detected by skilled observers.

Verbal Cues to Deception

Sometimes a liar says something which the observer knows is not true. Such a lie is easy to detect by listening to what the liar is saying. However, not all liars tell transparent lies. Even when a lie is not transparent, it is often possible to detect by paying attention to the speech content. As was described in Chapters 4, 5 and 6, liars sometimes tell stories which sound implausible. Moreover, their statements are often negative and indirect, and lack descriptions of personal experiences. In addition, truth-tellers, especially if they are emotional, tend to tell their stories in an unstructured way, whereas liars describe events in a more chronological order. Finally, liars often include fewer details in their statements than truth-tellers. There are several reasons for these findings (see also Chapters 4 and 5). For example, negative emotions (e.g. guilt, anger) may result in negative statements, and being upset may result in the liar telling a story in an unstructured way. Not mentioning many details may be the result of a lack of imagination to invent such details, not having enough knowledge to provide certain details, or not wanting to mention many details as this will increase the likelihood of contradiction, or that observers will discover the lie when they check what has been said.

Physiological Responses When Lying

Fear of being caught, feelings of guilt when lying, excitement when lying and guilty knowledge during deception are associated with (small) physiological reactions such as increased blood pressure, increased heart rate and increased palmar sweating. A polygraph is able to measure these physiological responses.

A COMPARISON OF THE THREE WAYS TO DETECT DECEIT

Individual Differences

Analyses of non-verbal behaviour and speech content are often hampered by the fact that individuals differ from one another in their non-verbal and verbal behaviour during deception. For example, eloquent speakers make fewer speech disturbances while lying than less eloquent speakers, and children include fewer details in their stories than adults, regardless of whether they are lying or not. It is unclear whether personality has an impact on polygraph outcomes. Individual differences in physiological reactions during polygraph tests have not yet been found.

Equipment Necessary to Detect Deception

Unlike analyses of verbal behaviour and physiological reactions, analyses of non-verbal behaviour do not require any equipment. All the observer has to do is to look carefully and to listen carefully. Examinations of verbal behaviour require written transcripts of statements, and physiological reactions can only be investigated with the use of technical equipment. This implies that analyses of physiological responses or verbal behaviour are not possible in circumstances where immediate observations are required, as is the case in the majority of situations. Obviously, parents will never ask their son to perform a polygraph test in order to find out whether he smokes secretly, nor will customs officers transcribe the conversations they have with customers and decide on the basis of analyses of these transcripts whether or not to search someone's luggage. Moreover, in order to analyse verbal behaviour or physiological responses, it is necessary for the potential liar to say something. A verbal response is not required when analysing behaviour. Such analyses can take place even when a person decides to remain silent. In short, in many situations observers are dependent on analyses of non-verbal behaviour to find out whether someone is lying.

How Good Are Lay People at Detecting Lies?

Experimental research has revealed that lay people are not very good at detecting lies. In a typical deception experiment, observers are exposed to a videotape consisting of a number of people (strangers, friends or partners) who are either telling the truth or not. Observers have to indicate for each person on the videotape whether or not he or she is lying. The accuracy rate (percentage of correct answers) in these studies usually varies between 45% and 60%, when a 50% accuracy rate could be expected by chance alone. This means that observers only just (if at all) exceed the level expected by chance in detecting deceit when they pay attention to someone's non-verbal behaviour. It is unclear how good lay people are at detecting lies when they are exposed to written transcripts, although there is some evidence that lay people are more accurate in detecting lies when they read transcripts than when they observe a person's behaviour (DePaulo, Stone & Lassiter, 1985). A proper polygraph test can only be conducted by skilful polygraph examiners.

How Good Are Professional Lie-catchers at Detecting Lies?

Ekman and his colleagues are the only researchers who have developed a non-verbal method for detection of deception and who have published accuracy rates when applying this method. They looked at facial microexpressions which result from the emotions that people experience, and they were able to detect 70% of the truths and 90% of the lies using their method (Frank & Ekman, 1997). However, it is unclear whether or not the 20% of misses included inconclusive outcomes. Ekman, O'Sullivan, Friesen and Scherer (1991) claimed an even higher hit rate (86%), but they disregarded inconclusive outcomes. In that study, they obtained 19 hits, 3 misses and 9 inconclusive outcomes. The accuracy rate when inconclusive outcomes are disregarded is therefore 86%, but the accuracy rate is much lower, at 61%, when the inconclusive outcomes are taken into account as well.

Most professional lie-catchers, such as customs officers and police officers, achieve lower accuracy rates than Ekman when they pay attention to a person's non-verbal behaviour. On average, they detect 54% of the truths and 49% of the lies (see Table 3.3 in Chapter 3). These hit rates are about the level that would be expected by chance, and similar to the accuracy rates obtained by lay people. Research has further shown that professional lie-catchers are more confident than lay people in their ability to detect lies, suggesting that being a professional lie-catcher makes someone more confident but not more accurate in detecting lies.

Research has indicated that people who are trained in CBCA—the verbal detection of deception technique which was discussed in Chapter 5—are able to detect truths and lies above the level of chance. On average, 76% of truths and 68% of lies were correctly classified with CBCA assessments.

Field studies examining the accuracy of polygraph testing have revealed reasonably high accuracy rates for the Control Question Test—72% of the truths and 87% of the lies were correctly classified. Field studies concerning the Guilty Knowledge Test revealed an extremely high hit rate (96%) for detecting truths, but a relatively poor hit rate (59%) for detecting lies.

In short, experts are able to detect truths and lies above the level that would be expected by chance by using non-verbal, verbal or physiological techniques for detection of deception. The accuracy rates, however, are definitely not perfect. Therefore, outcomes of the use of these techniques should not constitute substantial evidence in court, and they could only be used as additional evidence at most. In addition to presenting such evidence, experts should inform the courts that these techniques are not perfect, and that there are several problems associated with using them. These problems have been discussed throughout this book. The main problems with analysing non-verbal behaviour are that a typical non-verbal behaviour of deception does not exist, but that deceptive behaviour differs according to the person and the situation, and that differences between truth-tellers and liars are usually small. Problems with SVA include the vulnerability to false-negative errors in CBCA assessments (the tendency to believe liars), the fact that evaluations are subjective, and the fact that not much research has yet been conducted into testing the accuracy of this technique. Problems with polygraph testing include deceiving examinees, the use of countermeasures by examinees, and the vulnerability to false-positive errors—that is, disbelieving truth-tellers (in the case of the Control Question Test), and the occurrence of false-negative errors and the fact that hardly any field research has been conducted on the accuracy of the technique to date (in the case of the Guilty Knowledge Test).

Can People Be Trained to Become Good Lie Detectors?

Research has indicated that observers who are trained in the use of CBCA are better lie detectors than untrained observers. Obviously, performing a polygraph test requires training in how to conduct the test and how to interpret the polygraph charts. It is unclear whether people can be trained to analyse non-verbal behaviour. The training programmes which have been evaluated to date were not very successful. However, as I have already mentioned in Chapter 3, these training programmes had severe limitations. They focused too much on informing observers about actual non-verbal indicators of deception. This is not particularly useful, as not every liar will show these behaviours. Despite the fact that typical deceptive behaviour does not exist, some people are good at detecting lies when they observe someone's behaviour. A more fruitful approach would be to consult these good lie detectors and to learn from their experiences. Unfortunately, as yet it is unclear what makes them good at detecting lies and what cues they pay attention to. Further research will be necessary to discover this.

Is it Difficult to Fool Observers?

Obviously, lie detection methods will be less accurate if liars are able to fool observers when they are aware of the techniques that these observers use in order to detect deceit. Some people might wonder what the relevance of this issue could be. How likely is it that liars will seek information about the latest lie detection techniques and train themselves to beat these techniques? It probably depends on the liars' motivation to avoid getting caught, and on the likelihood that the technique will be used against them. Highly motivated liars, such as criminals, spies and adulterous partners, will probably show more interest in ways to fool lie detectors than less motivated liars. Whether they will actually obtain information about the techniques and train themselves to beat the techniques will probably depend on the perceived likelihood that the technique will be used against them. It is therefore unlikely that adulterous partners would seek information about such techniques, as they will think it unlikely that their partners will ever use them. On the other hand, criminals and spies might think that they run the risk that examiners will use these techniques, and therefore they might practise in order to fool them. As was described in Chapter 7, the CIA uses polygraph tests in attempts to catch spies, but spies are trained to try to fool CIA polygraph examiners.

Research has indicated that polygraph examinees are able to fool polygraph examiners and are able to beat the polygraph. Several examples of this were given in Chapter 7. Hardly any research has been conducted to investigate liars' ability to beat verbal and non-verbal lie detection techniques, probably because these techniques are relatively new and not yet widely used (CBCA) or do not even exist (valid non-verbal lie detection techniques).

To my knowledge, our own study was the first to examine liars' ability to fool CBCA judges (Vrij, Kneller & Mann, in press). As was described in Chapter 5, liars were successful in deceiving a CBCA expert. However, it is difficult to draw conclusions on the basis of a single study, and more research is therefore needed. I expect future studies to reveal that many liars are capable of fooling CBCA experts. People are well practised in controlling their speech content, as speech is often vital for expressing ideas, thoughts, feelings and opinions. This practice makes us good at controlling our speech content.

There is perhaps no need for liars to practise their non-verbal presentation style, given the fact that observers are generally unskilled in detecting deceit when they pay attention to someone's behaviour. I doubt whether liars will be found to be good at controlling their behaviour if they wish to do so. Liars sometimes give away their lies via brief emotional facial expressions. However, it is very difficult if not impossible to suppress these emotional expressions completely, as they occur automatically when the emotion is felt. There is some evidence that liars also have difficulty in controlling behaviours which are rather easier to control than emotional expressions, such as hand and arm movements. In our study, we informed half of the participants that a decrease in subtle hand and finger movements often indicates deception (Vrij, Semin & Bull, 1996). No information was given to the remaining participants. All of the participants were instructed to lie, and were asked afterwards how they thought they had behaved when they were lying. Compared to the uninformed liars, the informed liars thought that they made more subtle hand and finger movements during deception. However, analyses of the participants' actual behaviour showed that both groups of participants exhibited the same number of subtle hand and finger movements. In other words, although the informed liars thought that they managed to show an increase in subtle hand and finger movements, in fact they did not succeed in doing this, suggesting that it is a difficult thing to do.

Combination of Different Lie Detection Techniques

Different ways of detecting lies—via analyses of speech content, non-verbal behaviour or physiological responses—have been discussed separately so far. One obvious way of attempting to increase the accuracy of detecting deceit is to combine several methods. However, not all combinations are feasible, as it is impossible to combine verbal lie detection techniques with polygraph examinations. As I explained in Chapter 7, in polygraph tests examinees are only allowed to give simple 'yes' or 'no' answers because speech may result in undesired physiological responses.

Obviously, such short answers are insufficient for the purposes of verbal lie detection techniques. Only combinations of a non-verbal behavioural lie detection technique and either a polygraph examination or a verbal lie detection method are therefore possible. However, it cannot be guaranteed that this will prove successful. For example, polygraph examiners who use the control question technique and lie detectors who observe facial expressions of emotions try to detect emotions. Both types of lie detector will therefore fail to detect deceit when the liar is not emotional. Liars who do not experience emotions cannot be caught by lie detectors who look at emotional facial expressions, because these liars will not show these emotional expressions. These liars also cannot be caught with a control question polygraph test, as they will not show the physiological reactions that liars are expected to display during the test.

In addition, lie detectors seem to be reluctant to combine detection techniques. For example, both David Raskin (a leading polygraph expert) and Günter Köhnken (a leading CBCA expert) are against analysing non-verbal behaviour, because they are pessimistic about the possibility of detecting deceit via behavioural cues (personal communication, 1996). To what extent are observers who analyse both polygraph outcomes and non-verbal behaviour more accurate than those who analyse non-verbal behaviour alone? Ekman and O'Sullivan (1991, see also Chapter 3, Table 3.3) showed that polygraph examiners who only analyse non-verbal behaviour achieve 56% accuracy, whereas polygraph research revealed that examiners who evaluate polygraph charts achieve up to 80% accuracy (Table 8.1). However, we should bear in mind that this is not a fair comparison, as polygraph examiners are not trained in detecting deceit via non-verbal cues. As I mentioned in Chapter 3, good lie detectors are able to achieve 80% accuracy rates by observing non-verbal behaviour alone. Accuracy rates for detecting lies might therefore increase when trained observers pay attention to the behavioural cues exhibited by examinees during polygraph examinations. The stakes are usually high for examinees in polygraph tests, implying that they might display emotional expressions. Their behavioural cues can provide information about which emotions are felt during the test, such as fear, anger, surprise, distress or excitement (Ekman, 1992). Moreover, guilty examinees are probably highly motivated to get away with their lies, which makes them prone to the motivational impairment effect (a tendency to show planned and rigid behaviour). Research to investigate these ideas has not been carried out to date.

To my knowledge, research combining verbal and non-verbal lie detection methods has not been published to date either. The results of our current research project suggest that such an approach might be fruitful (Vrij, Edward, Roberts & Bull, 1999). In one experiment, 36 nursing students either told the truth or lied about a film they had just seen. The interviews were videotaped and audiotaped, and the non-verbal behaviour and speech content of the liars and truth-tellers were analysed, the latter utilizing both CBCA and Reality Monitoring. The results revealed that 81% of truths and lies could be detected on the basis of analyses of non-verbal behaviour alone. The accuracy rates for CBCA and Reality Monitoring were 75% and 72%, respectively. However, a combination of the three lie detection techniques (non-verbal behaviour, CBCA and Reality Monitoring) resulted in a 94% accuracy rate! It is not difficult to explain the surplus value of a combined lie detection technique. A non-verbal lie detection method considers different aspects of liars and truth-tellers (i.e. non-verbal behaviours) to a verbal detection method (i.e speech content), and therefore a combination of non-verbal and verbal techniques results in a more detailed observation of liars and truth-tellers than either component alone.

GUIDELINES FOR CATCHING A LIAR

On the one hand, lie detectors might conduct a polygraph test when they want to find out whether someone is lying. On the other hand, they could decide to focus on verbal and non-verbal behaviour in order to detect deceit. In the latter case, several aspects are important.

Be Suspicious

Lies often remain undetected because observers have too much good faith—too often they assume that people speak the truth. It is essential for a lie detector to be *suspicious* and to distrust what people are saying. This is sometimes difficult. Conversational rules in daily life prevent the observer from showing suspicion. Conversations would become awkward if the observer expressed their doubts, because the speaker would then become irritated if the observer consistently interrupted and challenged everything they said ('I do not believe this', 'Do you have evidence for this?', 'I would like to check what you are saying', and so on). Expressing doubt is particularly difficult if the speaker is someone to whom the observer feels emotionally close, such as a friend or partner. This could explain why people are less skilled at detecting lies told by friends and partners than we might expect. Obviously, not being allowed to show suspicion only applies to daily life conversations. Professional lie catchers, such as police detectives in police interviews and customs officers in interviews with overseas travellers, are allowed to be suspicious and to challenge what a person is saying.

Probing

Furthermore, observers should *keep on asking questions about the topic* as soon as they suspect someone is telling a lie. It will become increasingly difficult to continue lying when the observer keeps on asking questions about the topic. There are several reasons for this. Liars must avoid self-contradiction, should not say things which the observer already knows to be untrue, and must remember the things they have already said in case the observer asks for information they have just given to be repeated or clarified. Moreover, liars should control their behaviour all the time in order to prevent the possibility that clear behavioural signs of nervousness and cognitive load will give their lies away.

However, it is not easy to keep on asking questions. First, as just mentioned, asking many questions is not compatible with social conversation rules. Secondly, research has shown that, in the first instance, liars make an honest impression as a result of further questioning. That is, when liars—after being challenged by observers—persist in lying, observers have a tendency to believe them. One explanation might be that observers expect to put liars in an awkward position by further questioning and therefore expect liars to show nervous behaviour (start stuttering, fidgeting, and so on). Liars will therefore make an honest impression as long as they successfully avoid displaying nervous behaviour.

Do Not Reveal Important Information

It is important for lie detectors *not to reveal too much of their knowledge to the liar*. Liars should not say things which the observer knows to be untrue. This is easy if the liar knows what the observer knows, but becomes more difficult if the liar is unaware of the observer's knowledge. In such circumstances, liars cannot know what they can say, and they always run the risk that they will get caught by saying things which contradict the observer's knowledge. This continuous threat of getting caught might make them nervous, too, which increases the likelihood that they may show behavioural cues while lying.

Be Informed

It is easier for the observer to catch a liar if he or she is *well informed about the topic of the lie*. The more details the observer already knows, the more likely it is that he or she will notice that what the liar is saying is untrue.

Ask Liars to Repeat What they Have Said Before

A useful technique for lie detectors is *to ask liars to repeat what they have said before*. This has two advantages. First, liars sometimes make a suspicious impression or even get caught because they may no longer remember what they said before, and start to contradict themselves when they try to repeat their stories. Secondly, when liars realize that observers use this technique, they may decide not to include too many fabrications in their lies, because the more they say the more they run the risk of forgetting what they have said and contradicting themselves. This might make deceptive statements poor in quality, and might make detection techniques which look at the richness of statements (such as CBCA) more accurate.

Watch and Listen Carefully and Abandon Stereotypes

There is no typical non-verbal behaviour that indicates deception, nor do all liars say specific things or avoid saying certain things. It is therefore not useful to make judgements about deceit on the basis of stereotypical beliefs (e.g. 'liars show gaze aversion', 'liars fidget', 'liars stutter'). Instead, observers should judge each case individually. *To look carefully at how someone is behaving and to listen carefully to what they are saying* is thus essential. A brief emotional expression, an inhibition of subtle movements, a verbal contradiction—all of these signs may indicate deception. Lie detectors should therefore try to explain why the person showed these particular signs, but should bear in mind that such signs might occur for reasons other than that the person was lying.

Looking carefully at someone's behaviour may cause a problem. Looking at movements of the hands, fingers, legs and feet can be particularly useful in detecting lies. This means that the observer has to scrutinize the potential liar carefully and observe them almost literally from head to foot. This is very unusual behaviour in conversations, and makes an odd impression, as we usually restrict ourselves to looking into the eyes of the conversation partner. However, eye movements do not give reliable information about deception. It may therefore be a good idea if during police interviews one or more police officers watch the suspect via a video-link system while sitting in a different room. This could provide the opportunity to observe the suspect from head to foot, which might not be possible if these officers were in the same room as the interviewer.

Compare Liars' Behaviour with their Natural Behaviour

Detecting subtle non-verbal cues of deception is often easier if the lie detector is familiar with the potential liar's natural behaviour. In such a case, (subtle) changes in behaviour can be more easily spotted. Lie detectors should therefore try to get to know the person's natural behaviour, look for deviations from this 'baseline' behaviour, and try to explain these deviations (they may occur for reasons other than that the person is lying). However, this 'baseline comparison approach' will only work if the person's potential deceptive behaviour is compared with their natural behaviour shown *in similar circumstances*. For example, it is not useful to compare a suspect's behaviour while denying having committed the crime with his or her behaviour displayed during the casual chat at the beginning of the interview, as suspects (both guilty and innocent) are likely to show different behaviours during the casual chat and during the actual interview (when they are under suspicion and the stakes are high) (Vrij, 1995). A fair comparison is to contrast the suspect's behaviour during this particular denial with his or her behaviour during another denial regarding a similar crime (of which it is certain that the denial is truthful).

FINAL COMMENT

In this book I have attempted to provide an overview of psychological research and theory concerning the relationship between deception and non-verbal behaviour, speech content and physiological responses, as well as what the lie detector should do in order to detect deceit. The extent to which this is a valid and honest account is for you to decide.

References

Akehurst, L. & Vrij, A. (1999). Creating suspects in police interviews. *Journal of Applied Social Psychology*, **29**, 192–210.

Akehurst, L., Bull, R. & Vrij, A. (2000). *Training British police officers, social workers and students to detect deception in children using criteria-based content analysis*. Manuscript submitted for publication.

Akehurst, L., Köhnken, G. & Höfer, E. (1995). *The analysis and application of Statement Validity Assessment*. Paper presented at the Fifth European Conference on Psychology and Law, Budapest, Hungary.

Akehurst, L., Köhnken, G., Vrij, A. & Bull, R. (1996). Lay persons' and police officers' beliefs regarding deceptive behaviour. *Applied Cognitive Psychology*, **10**, 461–471.

Allen, J.J.B. & Iacono, W.G. (1997). A comparison of methods for the analysis of event-related potentials in deception detection. *Psychophysiology*, **34**, 234–240.

Alonso-Quecuty, M.L. (1991). *Post-event information and reality-monitoring: when the witness cannot be honest*. Paper presented at the First Spanish and British Meeting on Psychology, Law and Crime in Pamplona, Spain.

Alonso-Quecuty, M.L. (1992). Deception detection and Reality Monitoring: a new answer to an old question? In F. Lösel, D. Bender. & T. Bliesener (Eds), *Psychology and law: international perspectives* Berlin: Walter de Gruyter, 328–332.

Alonso-Quecuty, M.L. (1996). Detecting fact from fallacy in child and adult witness accounts. In G. Davies, S. Lloyd-Bostock, M. McMurran & C. Wilson (Eds), *Psychology, law and criminal justice: international developments in research and practice*. Berlin: Walter de Gruyter, 74–80.

Alonso-Quecuty, M.L., Hernandez-Fernaud, E. & Campos, L. (1997). Child witnesses: lying about something heard. In S. Redondo, V. Garrido, J. Perez & R. Barbaret (Eds), *Advances in psychology and law*. Berlin: Walter de Gruyter, 129–135.

Anolli, L. & Ciceri, R. (1997). The voice of deception: vocal strategies of naive and able liars. *Journal of Nonverbal Behavior*, **21**, 259–284.

Anson, D.A., Golding, S.L. & Gully, K.J. (1993). Child sexual abuse allegations: reliability of criteria-based content analysis. *Law and Human Behavior*, **17**, 331–341.

Apple, W., Streeter, L.A. & Krauss, R.M. (1979). Effects of pitch and speech rate on personal attributions. *Journal of Personality and Social Psychology*, **37**, 715–727.

Arntzen, F. (1982). Die Situation der Forensischen Aussagenpsychologie in der Bundesrepublik Deutschland. In A. Trankell (Ed.), *Reconstructing the past: the role of psychologists in criminal trials*. Deventer: Kluwer, 107–120.

Arntzen, F. (1983). *Psychologie der Zeugenaussage: Systematik der Glaubwürdigkeitsmerkmale*. Munich: C. H. Beck.

Aune, R.K., Levine, T.R., Ching, P.U. & Yoshimoto, J.M. (1993). The influence of perceived source reward value on attributions of deception. *Communication Research Reports*, **10**, 15–27.

Backbier, E. & Sieswerda, S. (1997). Wanneer en waarom liegen we eigenlijk? *Nederlands Tijdschrift voor de Psychologie*, **52**, 255–264.

Barland, G.H. (1984). Standards for the admissibility of polygraph results as evidence. *University of West Los Angeles Law Review*, **16**, 37–54.

Barland, G.H. (1988). The polygraph test in the USA and elsewhere. In A. Gale (Ed.), *The polygraph test: lies, truth and science*. London: Sage Publications, 73–96.

Bashore, T.R. & Rapp, P.E. (1993). Are there alternatives to traditional polygraph procedures? *Psychological Bulletin*, **113**, 3–22.

Baskett, G.D. & Freedle, R.O. (1974). Aspects of language pragmatics and the social perception of lying. *Journal of Psycholinguistic Research*, **3**, 117–131.

Bell, B.E. & Loftus, E.F. (1988). Degree of detail of eyewitness testimony and mock juror judgments. *Journal of Applied Social Psychology*, **18**, 1171–1192.

Bell, B.E. & Loftus, E.F. (1989). Trivial persuasion in the courtroom: the power of (a few) minor details. *Journal of Personality and Social Psychology*, **56**, 669–679.

Bell, K.L. & DePaulo, B.M. (1996). Liking and lying. *Basic and Applied Social Psychology*, **18**, 243–266.

Ben-Shakhar, G. & Dolev, K. (1996). Psychophysiological detection through the Guilty Knowledge technique: effects of mental countermeasures. *Journal of Applied Psychology*, **81**, 273–281.

Ben-Shakhar, G. & Furedy, J.J. (1990). *Theories and applications in the detection of deception*. New York: Springer-Verlag.

Blaauw, J.A. (1971). 99 tips voor het verhoor. *Algemeen Politie Blad*, **120**, 287–296.

Boelhouwer, A.J.W., Merckelbach, H.L.G.J., Van Koppen, P.J. & Verbaten, M.N. (1996). *Leugendetectie in Nederland* (Rapport aan Minister van Justitie). Tilburg: University of Tilberg.

Bond, C.F. & Fahey, W.E. (1987). False suspicion and the misperception of deceit. *British Journal of Social Psychology*, **26**, 41–46.

Bond, C.F. & Robinson, M. (1988). The evolution of deception. *Journal of Nonverbal Behavior*, **12**, 295–307.

Bond, C.F., Kahler, K.N. & Paolicelli, L.M. (1985). The miscommunication of deception: an adaptive perspective. *Journal of Experimental Social Psychology*, **21**, 331–345.

Bond, C.F., Omar, A., Mahmoud, A. & Bonser, R.N. (1990). Lie detection across cultures. *Journal of Nonverbal Behavior*, **14**, 189–205.

Bond, C.F., Omar, A., Pitre, U., Lashley, B.R., Skaggs, L.M. & Kirk, C.T. (1992). Fishy-looking liars: deception judgment from expectancy violation. *Journal of Personality and Social Psychology*, **63**, 969–977.

Boychuk, T. (1991). *Criteria-Based Content Analysis of children's statements about sexual abuse: a field–based validation study*. Unpublished doctoral dissertation, Arizona State University, Tempe, AZ.

Bradley, M.T. & Janisse, M.P. (1981). Accuracy demonstrations, threat, and the detection of deception: cardiovascular, electrodermal and pupillary measures. *Psychophysiology*, **18**, 307–315.

Bradley, M.T., MacLaren, V.V. & Black, M.E. (1996). The control question test in polygraphic examinations with actual controls for truth. *Perceptual and Motor Skills*, **83**, 755–762.

Brandt, D.R., Miller, G.R. & Hocking, J.E. (1980a). The truth-deception attribution: effects of familiarity on the ability of observers to detect deception. *Human Communication Research*, **6**, 99–110.

Brandt, D.R., Miller, G.R. & Hocking, J.E. (1980b). Effects of self-monitoring and familiarity on deception detection. *Communication Quarterly*, **28**, 3–10.

Brandt, D.R., Miller, G.R. & Hocking, J.E. (1982). Familiarity and lie detection: a replication and extension. *The Western Journal of Speech Communication*, **46**, 276–290.

British Psychological Society (1986). Report of the Working Group on the use of the polygraph in criminal investigation and personnel screening. *Bulletin of the British Psychological Society*, **39**, 81–94.

Brooks, C.I., Church, M.A. & Fraser, L. (1986). Effects of duration of eye contact on judgments of personality characteristics. *The Journal of Social Psychology*, **126**, 71–78.

Brougham, C.G. (1992). Nonverbal communication: can what they don't say give them away? *FBI Law Enforcement Bulletin*, **61**, 15–18.

Bull, R. (1988). What is the lie-detection test? In A. Gale (Ed.), *The polygraph test: lies, truth and science*. London: Sage Publications, 10–19.

Bull, R. (1989). Can training enhance the detection of deception? In J. C. Yuille (Ed.), *Credibility assessment*. Dordrecht: Kluwer, 83–97.

Bull, R. (1992). Obtaining evidence expertly: the reliability of interviews with child witnesses. *Expert Evidence: The International Digest of Human Behaviour Science and Law*, **1**, 3–36.

Bull, R. (1995). Innovative techniques for the questioning of child witnesses, especially those who are young and those with learning disability. In M. Zaragoza *et al.* (Eds), *Memory and testimony in the child witness*. Thousand Oaks, CA: Sage, 179–195.

Bull, R. (1998). Obtaining information from child witnesses. In A. Memon, A. Vrij & R. Bull, *Psychology and law: truthfulness, accuracy and credibility*. Maidenhead: McGraw–Hill, 188–210.

Buller, D.B. & Aune, R.K. (1987). Nonverbal cues to deception among intimates, friends, and strangers. *Journal of Nonverbal Behavior*, **11**, 269–289.

Buller, D.B., Burgoon, J.K., Busling, A.L. & Roiger, J.F. (1994a). Interpersonal deception. VIII. Further analysis of nonverbal and verbal correlates of equivocation from the Bauelas *et al.* (1990) research. *Journal of Language and Social Psychology*, **13**, 396–417.

Buller, D.B., Burgoon, J.K., White, C.H. & Ebesu, A.S. (1994b). Interpersonal deception. VII. Behavioral profiles of falsification, equivocation and concealment. *Journal of Language and Social Psychology*, **13**, 366–395.

Buller, D.B., Comstock, J., Aune, R.K. & Strzyzewski, K.D. (1989). The effect of probing on deceivers and truthtellers. *Journal of Nonverbal Behavior*, **13**, 155–170.

Buller, D.B., Stiff, J.B. & Burgoon, J.K. (1996). Behavioral adaptation in deceptive transactions. Fact or fiction: a reply to Levine and McCornack. *Human Communication Research*, **22**, 589–603.

Buller, D.B., Strzyzewski, K.D. & Comstock, J. (1991a). Interpersonal deception. I. Deceivers' reactions to receivers' suspicions and probing. *Communication Monographs*, **58**, 1–24.

Buller, D.B., Strzyzewski, K.D. & Hunsaker, F.G. (1991b). Interpersonal deception. II. The inferiority of conversational participants as deception detectors. *Communication Monographs*, **58**, 25–40.

Burgoon, J.K. & Newton, D. A. (1991). Applying social meaning model to relational messages of conversational involvement: comparing participant and observer perspectives. *Southern Communication Journal*, **56**, 96–113.

Burgoon, J.K., Buller, D.B., Guerrero, L.K., Afifi, W.A. & Feldman, C.M. (1996). Interpersonal deception. XII. Information management dimensions underlying deceptive and truthful messages. *Communication Monographs*, **63**, 50–69.

Burgoon, J.K., Manusov, V., Mineo, P. & Hale, J.L. (1985). Effects of gaze on hiring, credibility, attraction and relational message interpretation. *Journal of Nonverbal Behavior*, **9**, 133–147.

Carroll, D. (1988). How accurate is polygraph lie detection? In A. Gale (Ed.), *The polygraph test: lies, truth and science*. London: Sage Publications, 20–28.

Carroll, D. (1991). Lie detection: lies and truths. In R. Cochrane & D. Carroll (Eds), *Psychology and social issues: a tutorial text*. London: The Falmer Press, 160–170.

Ceci, S.J. & Bruck, M. (1995). *Jeopardy in the courtroom*. Washington, DC: American Psychological Association.

Ceci, S.J., Huffman, M.L., Smith, E. & Loftus, E.F. (1994). Repeatedly thinking about a non-event. *Consciousness and Cognition*, **3**, 388–407.

Ceci, S.J., Loftus, E.F., Leichtman, M.D. & Bruck, M. (1994). The possible role of source misattributions in the creation of false beliefs among preschoolers. *The International Journal of Clinical and Experimental Hypnosis*, **17**, 304–320.

Chahal, K. & Cassidy, T. (1995). Deception and its detection in children: a study of adult accuracy. *Psychology, Crime, and Law*, **1**, 237–245.

Cody, M.J. & O'Hair, H.D. (1983). Nonverbal communication and deception: differences in deception cues due to gender and communicator dominance. *Communication Monographs*, **50**, 175–193.

Cody, M.J., Lee, W.S. & Chao, E.Y. (1989). Telling lies: correlates of deception among Chinese. In J. P. Forgas & J. M. Innes (Eds), *Recent advances in social psychology: an international perspective*. Amsterdam: Elsevier Science Publishers, 359–368.

Cody, M.J., Marston, P.J. & Foster, M. (1984). Deception: paralinguistic and verbal leakage. In R. N. Bostrom & B.H. Westley (Eds), *Communication Yearbook 8*. Beverly Hills CA: Sage, 464–490.

Cohen, P. (1997). Lie detectors back on trial. *New Scientist*, 15 May.

Comadena, M.E. (1982). Accuracy in detecting deception: intimate and friendship relationships. In M. Burgoon (Ed.), *Communication Yearbook 6*. Beverly Hills, CA: Sage, 446–472.

Conte, J.R., Sorenson, E., Fogarty, L. & Rosa, J.D. (1991). Evaluating children's reports of sexual abuse: results from a survey of professionals. *Journal of Orthopsychiatry*, **61**, 428–437.

Coolbear, J.L. (1992). Credibility of young children in sexual abuse cases: assessment strategies of legal and human service professionals. *Canadian Psychology*, **33**, 151–164.

Craig, R.A. (1995). *Effects of interviewer behavior on children's statements of sexual abuse*. Unpublished manuscript.

Crombag, H.F.M., Wagenaar, W.A. & Van Koppen, P.J. (1996). Crashing memories and the problem of source monitoring. *Applied Cognitive Psychology*, **10**, 93–104.

Davies, G. (1991). Research on children's testimony: implications for interviewing practice. In C. R. Hollin & K. Howells (Eds), *Clinical approaches to sex offenders and their victims*. Chichester: John Wiley, 93–106.

Davis, M. & Hadiks, D. (1995). Demeanor and credibility. *Semiotica*, **106**, 5–54.

DePaulo, B.M. (1988). Nonverbal aspects of deception. *Journal of Nonverbal Behavior*, **12**, 153–162.

DePaulo, B.M. (1991). Nonverbal behavior and self-presentation: a developmental perspective. In R. S. Feldman & B. Rimé (Eds), *Fundamentals of nonverbal behavior* Paris: Cambridge University Press, 351–397.

DePaulo, B.M. (1992). Nonverbal behavior and self-presentation. *Psychological Bulletin*, **111**, 203–243.

DePaulo, B.M. (1994). Spotting lies: can humans learn to do better? *Current Directions in Psychological Science*, **3**, 83–86.

DePaulo, B.M. & Bell, K.L. (1996). Truth and investment: lies are told to those who care. *Journal of Personality and Social Psychology*, **70**, 703–716.

DePaulo, B.M. & Kashy, D.A. (1998). Everyday lies in close and casual relationships. *Journal of Personality and Social Psychology*, **74**, 63–79.

DePaulo, B.M. & Kirkendol, S.E. (1989). The motivational impairment effect in the communication of deception. In J. C. Yuille (Ed.), *Credibility assessment*. Dordrecht: Kluwer, 51–70.

DePaulo, B.M. & Pfeifer, R.L. (1986). On-the-job experience and skill at detecting deception. *Journal of Applied Social Psychology*, **16**, 249–267.

DePaulo, B.M. & Rosenthal, R. (1979). Telling lies. *Journal of Personality and Social Psychology*, **37**, 1713–1722.

DePaulo, B.M., Charlton, K., Cooper, H., Lindsay, J.L. & Muhlenbruck, L. (1997). The accuracy–confidence correlation in the detection of deception. *Personality and Social Psychology Review*, **1**, 346–357.

DePaulo, B.M., Epstein, J.A. & Wyer, M.M. (1993). Sex differences in lying: how women and men deal with the dilemma of deceit. In M. Lewis & C. Saarni (Eds), *Lying and deception in everyday life*. New York: The Guilford Press, 126–147.

DePaulo, B.M., Jordan, A., Irvine, A. & Laser, P.S. (1982) Age changes in the detection of deception. *Child Development*, **53**, 701–709.

DePaulo, B.M., Kashy, D.A., Kirkendol, S.E., Wyer, M.M. & Epstein, J.A. (1996). Lying in everyday life. *Journal of Personality and Social Psychology*, **70**, 979–995.

DePaulo, B.M., Lassiter, G.D. & Stone, J.I. (1982). Attentional determinants of success at detecting deception and truth. *Personality and Social Psychology Bulletin*, **8**, 273–279.

DePaulo, B.M., Rosenthal, R., Eisenstat, R.A., Rogers, P.L. & Finkelstein, S. (1978). Decoding discrepant nonverbal cues. *Journal of Personality and Social Psychology*, **36**, 313–323.

DePaulo, B.M., Rosenthal, R., Rosenkrantz, & Green, C. R. (1982). Actual and perceived cues to deception: a closer look at speech. *Basic and Applied Social Psychology*, **3**, 291–312.

DePaulo, B.M., Stone, J.L. & Lassiter, G.D. (1985). Deceiving and detecting deceit. In B.R. Schenkler (Ed.), *The self and social life*. New York: McGraw-Hill, 323–370.

DePaulo, B.M., Tang, J. & Stone, J.L. (1987). Physical attractiveness and skill at detecting deception. *Personality and Social Psychology Bulletin*, **13**, 177–187.

DePaulo, P.J. & DePaulo, B.M. (1989). Can deception by salespersons and customers be detected through nonverbal behavioral cues? *Journal of Applied Social Psychology*, **19**, 1552–1577.

Desforges, D.M. & Lee, T.C. (1995). Detecting deception is not as easy as it looks. *Teaching of Psychology*, **22**, 128–130.

deTurck, M.A. (1991). Training observers to detect spontaneous deception: effects of gender. *Communication Reports*, **4**, 81–89.

deTurck, M.A. & Miller, G.R. (1985). Deception and arousal: isolating the behavioral correlates of deception. *Human Communication Research*, **12**, 181–201.

deTurck, M.A. & Miller, G.R. (1990). Training observers to detect deception: effects of self-monitoring and rehearsal. *Human Communication Research*, **16**, 603–620.

deTurck, M.A., Feeley, T.H. & Roman, L.A. (1997). Vocal and visual cue training in behavioural lie detection. *Communication Research Reports*, **14**, 249–259.

deTurck, M.A., Harszlak, J.J., Bodhorn, D.J. & Texter, L.A. (1990). The effects of training social perceivers to detect deception from behavioural cues. *Communication Quarterly*, **38**, 189–199.

Dulaney, E.F. (1982). Changes in language behavior as a function of veracity. *Human Communication Research*, **9**, 75–82.

Ebesu, A.S. & Miller, M.D. (1994). Verbal and nonverbal behaviors as a function of deception type. *Journal of Language and Social Psychology*, **13**, 418–442.

Edinger, J.A. & Patterson, M.L. (1983). Nonverbal involvement and social control. *Psychological Bulletin*, **93**, 30–56.

Ekman, P. (1981). Mistakes when deceiving. *Annals of the New York Academy of Sciences*, **364**, 269–278.

Ekman, P. (1988). Lying and nonverbal behavior: theoretical issues and new findings. *Journal of Nonverbal Behavior*, **12**, 163–176.

Ekman, P. (1989). Why lies fail and what behaviors betray a lie. In J. C. Yuille (Ed.), *Credibility assessment*. Dordrecht: Kluwer, 71–82.

Ekman, P. (1992). *Telling lies: clues to deceit in the marketplace, politics and marriage*. New York: W. W. Norton.

Ekman, P. (1993). Why don't we catch liars? *Social Research*, **63**, 801–817.

Ekman, P. (1997). Deception, lying, and demeanor. In D. F. Halpern & A. E. Voiskounsky (Eds), *States of mind: American and post-soviet perspectives on contemporary issues in psychology*. New York: Oxford University Press, 93–105.

Ekman, P. & Frank, M.G. (1993). Lies that fail. In M. Lewis & C. Saarni (Eds), *Lying and deception in everyday life*. New York: Guilford Press, 184–201.

Ekman, P. & Friesen, W.V. (1969). Nonverbal leakage and clues to deception. *Psychiatry*, **32**, 88–106.

Ekman, P. & Friesen, W.V. (1972). Hand movements. *Journal of Communication*, **22**, 353–374.

Ekman, P. & Friesen, W.V. (1974). Detecting deception from the body or face. *Journal of Personality and Social Psychology*, **29**, 288–298.

Ekman, P. & Friesen, W.V. (1982). Felt, false and miserable smiles. *Journal of Nonverbal Behavior*, **6**, 238–253.

Ekman, P. & O'Sullivan, M. (1991). Who can catch a liar? *American Psychologist*, **46**, 913–920.

Ekman, P., Davidson, R.J. & Friesen, W.V. (1990). The Duchenne smile: emotional expression and brain physiology. II. *Journal of Personality and Social Psychology*, **58**, 342–353.

Ekman, P. Friesen, W.V. & O'Sullivan, M. (1988). Smiles when lying. *Journal of Personality and Social Psychology*, **54**, 414–420.

Ekman, P. Friesen, W.V., & Scherer, K.R. (1976). Body movement and voice pitch in deceptive interaction. *Semiotica*, **16**, 23–27.

Ekman, P. O'Sullivan, M., Friesen, W. V. & Scherer, K. (1991). Face, voice, and body in detecting deceit. *Journal of Nonverbal Behavior*, **15**, 125–135.

Elaad, E. (1990). Detection of guilty knowledge in real–life criminal investigations. *Journal of Applied Psychology*, **75**, 521–529.

Elaad, E. (1993). Detection of deception: a transactional analysis perspective. *Journal of Psychology*, **127**, 5–15.

Elaad, E. (1997). Polygraph examiner awareness of crime-relevant information and the guilty knowledge test. *Law and Human Behavior*, **21**, 107–120.

Elaad, E. & Ben-Shakhar, B. (1997). Effects of item repetitions and variations on the efficiency of the guilty knowledge test. *Psychophysiology*, **34**, 587–596.

Elaad, E., Ginton, A. & Jungman, N. (1992). Detection measures in real-life criminal guilty knowledge tests. *Journal of Applied Psychology*, **77**, 757–767.

Elaad, E., Ginton, A. & Shakhar, G. (1994). The effects of prior expectations and outcome knowledge on polygraph examiners' decisions. *Journal of Behavioral Decision-Making*, **7**, 279–292.

Esplin, P.W., Boychuk, T. & Raskin, D.C. (1988). *A field validity study of Criteria-Based Content Analysis of children's statements in sexual abuse cases*. Paper presented at the NATO Advanced Study Institute on Credibility Assessment in Maratea, Italy, June 1988.

Exline, R., Thibaut, J., Hickey, C. & Gumpert, P. (1970). Visual interaction in relation to machiavellianism and an unethical act. In P. Christie & F. Geis (Eds), *Studies in machiavellianism*. New York: Academic Press, 53–75.

Eysenck, H.J. (1984). Crime and personality. In D.J. Muller, D.E. Blackman & A.J. Chapman (Eds), *Psychology and law*. New York: John Wiley, 85–100.

Faigman, D.L., Kaye, D., Saks, M.J. & Sanders, J. (1997). *Modern scientific evidence: the law and science of expert testimony*. St Paul, MN: West.

Farwell, L.A. & Donchin, E. (1991). The truth will come out: interrogative polygraphy ('lie detection') with event-related brain potentials. *Psychophysiology*, **28**, 531–547.

Feeley, T.H. & deTurck, M.A. (1997). *Perceptions of communication as seen by the actor and as seen by the observer: the case of lie detection*. Paper presented at the International Communication Association Annual Conference, Montreal, Canada, 1997.

Feeley, T.H. & deTurck, M.A. (1998). The behavioral correlates of sanctioned and unsanctioned deceptive communication. *Journal of Nonverbal Behavior*, **22**, 189–204.

Feeley, T.H. & Young, M.J. (1997). *Detecting deceptive communication: a narrative review*. Unpublished manuscript.

Feeley, T.H., deTurck, M.A. & Young, M.J. (1995). Baseline familiarity in lie detection. *Communication Research Reports*, **12**, 160–169.

Feldman, R.S., Jenkins, L. & Popoola, O. (1979). Detection of deception in adults and children via facial expressions. *Child Development*, **50**, 350–355.

Fiedler, K. & Walka, I. (1993). Training lie detectors to use nonverbal cues instead of global heuristics. *Human Communication Research*, **20**, 199–223.

Fisher, R.P. & Geiselman, R.E. (1992). *Memory-enhancing techniques for investigative interviewing: the cognitive interview*. Springfield, IL: Charles C. Thomas.

Flavell, J.H., Botkin, P.T., Fry, C.K., Wright, J.C. & Jarvis, P.T. (1968). *The development of role–taking and communication skills in children*. New York: John Wiley.

Foley, M.A. & Johnson, M.K. (1985). Confusions between memories for performed and imagined actions: a developmental comparison. *Child Development*, **56**, 1145–1155.

Ford, Ch.V. (1995). *Lies! Lies!! Lies!!! The psychology of deceit*. Washington, DC: American Psychiatric Press.

Frank, M.G. & Ekman, P. (1997). The ability to detect deceit generalizes across different types of high-stake lies. *Journal of Personality and Social Psychology*, **72**, 1429–1439.

Freedman, J.L., Adam, E.K., Davey, S.A. & Koegl, C.J. (1996). The impact of a statement: more detail does not always help. *Legal and Criminological Psychology*, **1**, 117–130.

Freud, S. (1959). *Collected papers*. New York: Basic Books.

Fugita, S.S., Wexley, K.N. & Hillery, J.M. (1974). Black–white differences in nonverbal behavior in an interview setting. *Journal of Applied Social Psychology*, **4**, 343–351.

Furedy, J.J. (1991a). Alice in Wonderland terminological usage in, and communicational concerns about, that peculiar flight of technological fancy: the CQT polygraph. *Integrative Physiological and Behavioral Science*, **26**, 241–247.

Furedy, J.J. (1991b). On the validity of the polygraph. *Integrative Physiological and Behavioral Science*, **26**, 211–213.

Furedy, J.J. (1993). The 'control' question 'test' (CQT) polygrapher's dilemma: logico-ethical considerations for psychophysiological practitioners and researchers. *International Journal of Psychophysiology*, **15**, 263–267.

Furedy, J.J. (1996a). Some elementary distinctions among, and comments concerning, the 'control' question 'test' (CQT) polygrapher's many problems: a reply to Honts, Kircher and Raskin. *International Journal of Psychophysiology*, **22**, 53–59.

Furedy, J.J. (1996b). The North American polygraph and psychophysiology: disinterested, uninterested, and interested perspectives. *International Journal of Psychophysiology*, **21**, 97–105.

Furedy, J.J. & Heslegrave, R.J. (1988). Validity of the lie detector: a psychophysiological perspective. *Criminal Justice and Behavior*, **15**, 219–246.

Gale, A. (1988). The polygraph test, more than scientific investigation. In A. Gale (Ed.), *The polygraph test: lies, truth and science*. London: Sage, 1–9.

Garratt, G.A., Baxter, J.C. & Rozelle, R.M. (1981). Training university police in black-American nonverbal behavior. *Journal of Social Psychology*, **113**, 217–229.

Garrido, E., Masip, J., Herrero, C., Tabernero, C. & Vega, M.T. (1998). *Policemen's ability to discern truth from deception*. Unpublished manuscript.

Ginton, A., Daie, N., Elaad, E. & Ben-Shakhar, G. (1982). A method for evaluating the use of the polygraph in a real-life situation. *Journal of Applied Psychology*, **67**, 131–137.

Goldman-Eisler, F. (1968). *Psycholinguistics: experiments in spontaneous speech*. New York: Doubleday.

Goodman, G.S. & Schwartz-Kenney (1992). Why knowing a child's age is not enough: influences of cognitive, social, and emotional factors on children's testimony. In H. Dent & R. Flin (Eds), *Children as witnesses*. Chichester: John Wiley, 15–32.

Goodman, G.S., Rudy, L., Bottoms, B. & Aman, C. (1990). Children's concerns and memory: issues of ecological validity in the study of children's eyewitness testimony. In R. Fivush & J. Hudson (Eds), *Knowing and remembering in young children*. New York: Cambridge University Press, 249–284. .

Gordon, R.A., Baxter, J.C., Rozelle, R.M., & Druckman, D. (1987). Expectations of honest, evasive and deceptive nonverbal behavior. *Journal of Social Psychology*, **127**, 231–233.

Gordon, B.N., Schroeder, C.S. & Abrams, J.M. (1990). Age and social class differences in children's knowledge of sexuality. *Journal of Clinical Child Psychology*, **19**, 33–43.

Granhag, P.A. & Strömwall, L.A. (1998). *"Let's go over this again": effects of repeated interrogations on deception detection performance.* Paper presented at the Eighth European Conference on Psychology and Law, Cracow, Poland, September 1998.

Greene, J.O., O'Hair, H.D., Cody, M.J. & Yen, C. (1985). Planning and control of behavior during deception. *Human Communication Research*, **11**, 335–364.

Greuel, L. (1992). Police officers' beliefs about cues associated with deception in rape cases. In F. Lösel, D. Bender & T. Bliesener (Eds), *Psychology and law: international perspectives*. Berlin: Walter de Gruyter, 234–239.

Gudjonsson, G.H. (1992). *The psychology of interrogations, confessions and testimony*. Chichester: John Wiley.

Hale, J.L. & Stiff, J.B. (1990). Nonverbal primacy in veracity judgments. *Communication Reports*, **3**, 75–83.

Hall, J.A. (1979). Gender effects in decoding nonverbal cues. *Psychological Bulletin*, **85**, 845–857.

Hall, J.A. (1984). *Nonverbal sex differences: communication accuracy and expressive style*. Baltimore, MD: The Johns Hopkins University Press.

Hemsley, G.D. & Doob, A.N. (1978). The effect of looking behavior on perceptions of a communicator's credibility. *Journal of Applied Social Psychology*, **8**, 136–144.

Hernandez-Fernaud, E. & Alonso-Quecuty, M. (1997). The cognitive interview and lie detection: a new magnifying glass for Sherlock Holmes? *Applied Cognitive Psychology*, **11**, 55–68.

Hershkowitz, I., Lamb, M.E., Sternberg, K.J. & Esplin, P.W. (1997). The relationships among interviewer utterance type, CBCA scores and the richness of children's responses. *Legal and Criminological Psychology*, **2**, 169–176.

Hocking, J.E. & Leathers, D. G. (1980). Nonverbal indicators of deception: a new theoretical perspective. *Communication Monographs*, **47**, 119–131.

Höfer, E. & Köhnken, G. (1999) *Assessing the credibility of witness statements*. Paper presented at the Ninth European Conference on Psychology and Law, Dublin, Ireland, July 1999.

Höfer, E., Akehurst, L. & Metzger, G. (1996). *Reality monitoring: a chance for further development of CBCA?* Paper presented at the Annual Meeting of the European Association on Psychology and Law in Sienna, Italy, August 1996.

Höfer, E., Köhnken, G., Hanewinkel, R. & Bruhn, C. (1993). *Diagnostik und attribution von glaubwürdigkeit*. Kiel: Final report to the Deutsche Forschungsgemeinschaft, KO 882/4-2 Kiel, Germany: University of Kiel.

Honts, C.R. (1991). The emperor's new clothes: the application of the polygraph tests in the American workplace. *Forensic Reports*, **4**, 91–116.

Honts, C.R. (1994). Assessing children's credibility: scientific and legal issues in 1994. *North Dakota Law Review*, **70**, 879–903.

Honts, C.R. (1995). The polygraph in 1995: progress in science and the law. *North Dakota Law Review*, **17**, 987–1020.

Honts, C.R. (1996). Criterion development and validity of the CQT in field application. *Journal of General Psychology*, **123**, 309–324.

Honts, C.R. & Perry, M.V. (1992). Polygraph admissibility: changes and challenges. *Law and Human Behavior*, **16**, 357–379.

Honts, C. R. & Raskin, D. C. (1988). A field study of the validity of the directed lie control question. *Journal of Police Science and Administration*, **16**, 56–61.

Honts, C.R., Devitt, M.K., Winbush, M. & Kircher, J.C. (1996). Mental and physical countermeasures reduce the accuracy of the concealed knowledge test. *Psychophysiology*, **33**, 84–92.

Honts, C.R., Hodes, R.L. & Raskin, D.C. (1985). Effects of physical countermeasures on the physiological detection of deception. *Journal of Applied Psychology*, **70**, 177–187.

Honts, C.R., Kircher, J.C. & Raskin, D.C. (1996). Polygrapher's dilemma or psychologist's: a reply to Furedy's logico-ethical considerations for psychophysiological practitioners and researchers. *International Journal of Psychophysiology*, **20**, 199–207.

Honts, C.R., Raskin, D.C. & Kircher, J.C. (1987). Effects of physical countermeasures and their electromyographic detection during polygraph tests for deception. *Journal of Psychophysiology*, **1**, 241–247.

Honts, C.R., Raskin, D.C. & Kircher, J. C. (1994). Mental and physical countermeasures reduce the accuracy of polygraph tests. *Journal of Applied Psychology*, **79**, 252–259.

Honts, C.R., Raskin, D.C., Kircher, J.C. & Hodes, R.L. (1988). Effects of spontaneous countermeasures on the physiological detection of deception. *Journal of Police Science and Administration*, **16**, 91–94.

Horowitz, S.W. (1991). Empirical support for statement validity assessment. *Behavioral Assessment*, **13**, 293–313.

Horowitz, S.W. (1998). Reliability of criteria-based content analysis of child witness statements: response to Tully. *Legal and Criminological Psychology*, **3**, 189–193.

Horowitz, S.W., Kircher, J.C., Honts, C.R. & Raskin, D.C. (1997). The role of comparison questions in physiological detection of deception. *Psychophysiology*, **34**, 108–115.

Horowitz, S.W., Lamb, M.E., Esplin, P.W., Boychuk, T.D., Krispin, O. & Reiter-Lavery, L. (1997). Reliability of criteria-based content analysis of child witness statements. *Legal and Criminological Psychology*, **2**, 11–21.

Horowitz, S.W., Lamb, M.E., Esplin, P.W., Boychuk, T.D., Reiter-Lavery, L. & Krispin, O. (1996). Establishing ground truth in studies of child sexual abuse. *Expert Evidence: The International Digest of Human Behaviour Science and Law*, **4**, 42–52.

Hunter, J.E., Gerbing, D.W. & Boster, F.J. (1982). Machiavellian beliefs and personality: construct invalidity of the Machiavellianism dimension. *Journal of Personality and Social Psychology*, **43**, 1293–1305.

Hurd, K. & Noller, P. (1988). Decoding deception: a look at the process. *Journal of Nonverbal Behavior*, **12**, 217–233.

Iacono, W.G. & Lykken, D.T. (1997). The validity of the lie detector: two surveys of scientific opinion. *Journal of Applied Psychology*, **82**, 426–433.

Ickes, W. (1984). Compositions in black and white: determinants of interaction in interracial dyads. *Journal of Personality and Social Psychology*, **47**, 330–341.

Inbau, F.E., Reid, J.E., & Buckley, J.P. (1986). *Criminal interrogation and confessions*. Baltimore, MD: Williams & Wilkins.

Jackson, J. (1996). *Truth or fantasy: the ability of barristers and laypersons to detect deception in children's testimony*. Paper presented at the AP–LS Biennial Conference, Hilton Head Island, South Carolina, USA, March 1996.

Jones, D.P.H. & Krugman, R. (1986). Can a three-year-old child bear witness to her sexual assault and attempted murder? *Child Abuse and Neglect*, **10**, 253–258.

Jones, D.P.H. & McGraw, J.M. (1987). Reliable and fictitious accounts of sexual abuse to children. *Journal of Interpersonal Violence*, **2**, 27–45.

Jones, D.P.H. & McQuinston, M. (1989). *Interviewing the sexually abused child*. London: Gaskell.

Johnson, M.K. (1988). Reality monitoring: an experimental phenomenological approach. *Journal of Experimental Psychology: General*, **117**, 390–394.

Johnson, M.K. & Foley, M.A. (1984). Differentiating fact from fantasy: the reliability of children's memory. *Journal of Social Issues*, **40**, 33–50.

Johnson, M.K. & Raye, C.L. (1981). Reality monitoring. *Psychological Review*, **88**, 67–85.

Johnson, M.K. & Raye, C.L. (1998). False memories and confabulation. *Trends in Cognitive Sciences*, **2**, 137–145.

Johnson, M.M. & Rosenfeld, P.J. (1991). Oddball-evoked p300-based method of deception detection in the laboratory. II. Utilization of non-selective activation of relevant knowledge. *International Journal of Psychophysiology*, **12**, 289–306.

Johnson, M.K. & Suengas, A.G. (1989). Reality monitoring judgments of other people's memories. *Bulletin of the Psychonomic Society*, **27**, 107–110.

Johnson, M.K., Foley, M.A., Suengas, A.G. & Raye, C.L. (1988). Phenomenal characteristics of memories for perceived and imagined autobiographical events. *Journal of Experimental Psychology: General*, **117**, 371–376.

Johnson, M.K., Hashtroudi, S. & Lindsay, D.S. (1993). Source monitoring. *Psychological Bulletin*, **114**, 3–29.

Kalbfleisch, P. (1992). Deceit, distrust and the social milieu: application of deception research in a troubled world. *Journal of Applied Communication Research*, **20**, 308–334.

Kalbfleisch, P.J. (1994). The language of detecting deceit. *Journal of Language and Social Psychology*, **13**, 469–496.

Kalma, A., Witte, M. & Zaalberg, R. (1996). Authenticity: operationalization, manipulation, and behavioural components: an explanation. *Medium Psychologie*, **8**, 49–65.

Kashy, D.A. & DePaulo, B.M. (1996). Who lies? *Journal of Personality and Social Psychology*, **70**, 1037–1051.

Kassin, S.M. (1997). The psychology of confession evidence. *American Psychologist*, **52**, 221–233.

Kircher, J. C. & Raskin, D. C. (1988). Human versus computerized evaluations of polygraph data in a laboratory setting. *Journal of Applied Psychology*, **73**, 291–302.

Kircher, J.C., Horowitz, S.W. & Raskin, D.C. (1988). Meta-analysis of mock crime studies of the control question polygraph technique. *Law and Human Behavior*, **12**, 79–90.

Kleinke, C.L. (1986). Gaze and eye contact: a research review. *Psychological Bulletin*, **100**, 78–100.

Kleinmuntz, B. & Szucko, J.J. (1982). On the fallibility of lie detection. *Law and Society Review*, **17**, 85–104.

Kleinmuntz, B. & Szucko, J.J. (1984). Lie detection in ancient and modern times: a call for contemporary scientific study. *American Psychologist*, **39**, 766–776.

Kline, P. (1993). *The handbook of psychological testing*. New York: Routledge.

Knapp, M.L., Hart, R.P. & Dennis, H.S. (1974). An exploration of deception as a communication construct. *Human Communication Research*, **1**, 15–29.

Köhnken, G. (1985). Speech and deception of eyewitnesses: an information processing approach. In F. L. Denmark (Ed.), *The psychology of women*. Amsterdam: Elsevier Science Publishers, 117–139.

Köhnken, G. (1987). Training police officers to detect deceptive eyewitness statements. Does it work? *Social Behaviour*, **2**, 1–17.

Köhnken, G. (1989). Behavioral correlates of statement credibility: theories, paradigms and results. In H. Wegener, F. Lösel & J. Haisch (Eds), *Criminal behavior and the justice system: psychological perspectives.* New York: Springer-Verlag, 271–289.

Köhnken, G. (1990). *Glaubwürdigkeit: Untersuchungen zu einem psychologischen konstrukt.* Munich: Psychologie Verlags Union.

Köhnken, G. (1996). Social psychology and the law. In G. R. Semin & K. Fiedler (Eds), *Applied Social Psychology.* London: Sage Publications, 257–282.

Köhnken, G. & Wegener, H. (1982). Zur Glaubwürdigkeit von Zeugenaussagen: Experimentelle Uberprüfung ausgewählter Glaubwürdigkeitskriterien (Credibility of witness statements: experimental examination of selected reality criteria). *Zeitschrift für Experimentelle und Angewandte Psychologie,* **29**, 92–111.

Köhnken, G., Milne, R., Memon, A. & Bull, R. (in press). The cognitive interview: a meta-analysis. *Psychology, Crime, and Law.*

Köhnken, G., Schimossek, E., Aschermann, E. & Höfer, E. (1995). The cognitive interview and the assessment of the credibility of adults' statements. *Journal of Applied Psychology,* **80**, 671–684.

Koppelaar, L., Winkel, F.W. & Steen, J.C. van der (1986). Psychologische kanttekeningen bij art 27 Sv.: een experiment rond etnische origine, ritmisch gedrag en verdacht zijn. *Delikt en Delinkwent,* **16**, 25–38.

Krauss, R.M. (1981). Impression formation, impression management, and nonverbal behaviors. In E.T. Higgins, C.P. Herman & M.P. Zanna (Eds), *Social cognition: the Ontario Symposium.* Vol. 1. Hillsdale, NJ: Erlbaum, 323–341.

Kraut, R.E. (1978). Verbal and nonverbal cues in the perception of lying. *Journal of Personality and Social Psychology,* **36**, 380–391.

Kraut, R.E. (1980). Humans as lie detectors: some second thoughts. *Journal of Communication,* **30**, 209–216.

Kraut, R.E. & Poe, D. (1980). On the line: the deception judgments of customs inspectors and laymen. *Journal of Personality and Social Psychology,* **36**, 380–391.

Kuhlman, M.S. (1980). Nonverbal communications in interrogations. *FBI Law Enforcement Bulletin,* **49**, 6–9.

Lamb, M.E. (1998). Mea culpa but caveat emptor! Response to Tully. *Legal and Criminological Psychology,* **3**, 193–195.

Lamb, M.E., Esplin, P.W. & Sternberg, K.J. (1995). Making children into competent witnesses: reactions to the Amicus Brief in re Michaels. *Psychology, Public Policy and Law,* **1**, 438–449.

Lamb, M.E., Hershkowitz, I., Sternberg, K.J., Esplin, P.W., Hovav, M., Manor, M. & Yudilevitch, L. (1996). Effects of investigative utterance types on Israeli children's responses. *International Journal of Behavioral Development,* **19**, 627–637.

Lamb, M.E., Sternberg, K.J. & Esplin, P.W. (1994). Factors influencing the reliability and validity of statements made by young victims of sexual maltreatment. *Journal of Applied Developmental Psychology,* **15**, 255–280.

Lamb, M.E., Sternberg, K.J., Esplin, P. W., Hershkowitz, I., Orbach, Y. & Hovav, M. (1997). Criterion-based content analysis: a field validation study. *Child Abuse and Neglect,* **21**, 255–264.

Lamb, M.E., Sternberg, K.J., Esplin, P.W., Hershkowitz, I. & Orbach, Y. (1997). Assessing the credibility of children's allegations of sexual abuse: a survey of recent research. *Learning and Individual Differences,* **9**, 175–194.

Lamers-Winkelman, F. (1995). *Seksueel misbruik van jonge kinderen: een onderzoek naar signalen en signaleren, en naar ondervragen en vertellen inzake seksueel misbruik.* Amsterdam: VU Uitgeverij.

Lamers-Winkelman, F. & Buffing, F. (1996). Children's testimony in the Netherlands: a study of Statement Validity Analysis. In B. L. Bottoms & G. S. Goodman (Eds), *International perspectives on child abuse and children's testimony*. Thousand Oaks, CA: Sage, 45–62.

Landry, K. & Brigham, J.C. (1992). The effect of training in Criteria-Based Content Analysis on the ability to detect deception in adults. *Law and Human Behavior*, **16**, 663–675.

Lane, J.D. & DePaulo, B.M. (1999). Completing Coyne's cycle: dysphorics' ability to detect deception. *Journal of Research in Personality*, **33**, 311–329.

Larson, J.A. (1932). *Lying and its detection: a study of deception and deception tests*. Chicago, IL: University of Chicago Press.

Levine, T.R. & McCornack, S.A. (1992). Linking love and lies: a formal test of the McCornack and Parks model of deception detection. *Journal of Social and Personal Relationships*, **9**, 143–154.

Levine, T.R. & McCornack, S.A. (1996a). A critical analysis of the behavioral adaptation explanation of the probing effect. *Human Communication Research*, **22**, 575–588.

Levine, T.R. & McCornack, S.A. (1996b). Can behavioral adaptation explain the probing effect? *Human Communication Research*, **22**, 604–613.

Levine, T.R., McCornack, S.A. & Aleman, C.G. (1997). *Ask and you shall believe: behavioral adaptation, confidence, and heuristic-based explanations of the probing effect*. Unpublished manuscript.

Levine, T.R., McCornack, S.A. & Park, H.S. (1999). Accuracy in detecting truths and lies: documenting the 'veracity effect'. *Communication Monographs*, **66**, 125–144.

Lewis, M. (1993). The development of deception. In M. Lewis & C. Saarni (Eds), *Lying and deception in everyday life*. New York: The Guilford Press, 90–105.

Lindsay, D.S. & Johnson, M.K. (1987). Reality monitoring and suggestibility: children's ability to discriminate among memories from different sources. In S. J. Ceci, J. Toglia & D. F. Ross (Eds), *Children's eyewitness memory*. New York: Springer-Verlag, 91–121.

Littlepage, G.E. & Pineault, M.A. (1985). Detection of deception of planned and spontaneous communications. *Journal of Social Psychology*, **125**, 195–201.

Littmann, E. & Szewczyk, H. (1983). Zu einigen Kriterien und Ergebnissen forensisch-psychologischer Glaubwürdigkeitsbegutachtung von sexuell misbrauchten Kindern und Jugendlichen. *Forensia*, **4**, 55–72.

Loftus, E.F. & Palmer, J.C. (1974). Reconstructions of automobile destruction: an example of the interaction between language and memory. *Journal of Verbal Learning and Verbal Behavior*, **13**, 585–589.

Lord, C.G., Ross, L. & Lepper, M.R. (1979). Biased assimilation and attitude polarization: the effects of prior theories on subsequently considered evidence. *Journal of Personality and Social Psychology*, **37**, 2098–2109.

Lykken, D.T. (1959). The GSR in the detection of guilt. *Journal of Applied Psychology*, **43**, 385–388.

Lykken, D.T. (1960). The validity of the guilty knowledge technique: the effects of faking. *Journal of Applied Psychology*, **44**, 258–262.

Lykken, D.T. (1988). The case against polygraph testing. In A. Gale (Ed.), *The polygraph test: lies, truth, and science*. London: Sage, 111–126.

Lykken, D.T. (1991). Why (some) Americans believe in the lie detector while others believe in the Guilty Knowledge Test. *Integrative Physiological and Behavioral Science*, **126**, 214–222.

Lykken, D.T. (1998). *A tremor in the blood: uses and abuses of the lie detector*. New York: Plenum Press.

McClintock, C.C. & Hunt, R.G. (1975). Nonverbal indicators of affect and deception in an interview setting. *Journal of Applied Social Psychology*, **5**, 54–67.

McCornack, S.A. (1997). The generation of deceptive messages: laying the groundwork for a viable theory of interpersonal deception. In J.G. Greene (Ed.), *Message production: advances in communication theory*. Mahwah, N.J.: Erlbaum, 91–126.

McCornack, S.A. & Levine, T.R. (1990). When lovers become leery: the relationship between suspicion and accuracy in detecting deception. *Communication Monographs*, **57**, 219–230.

McCornack, S.A. & Parks, M.R. (1986). Deception detection and relationship development: the other side of trust. In M. McLaughlin (Ed.), *Communication Yearbook 9*. Beverly Hills, CA: Sage, 377–389.

McCornack, S.A. & Parks, M.R. (1990). What women know that men don't: sex differences in determining truth behind deceptive messages. *Journal of Social and Personal Relationships*, **7**, 107–118.

McCroskey, J.C. & Mehrley, S. (1969). The effects of disorganization and nonfluency on attitude change and source credibility. *Speech Monographs*, **36**, 13–21.

Mann, S., Vrij, A. & Bull, R. (1998). *Telling and detecting true lies*. Paper presented at the Eighth Annual Meeting of the European Association on Psychology and Law in Cracow, Poland, September 1998.

Manstead, A.S.R., Wagner, H.L. & MacDonald, C.J. (1986). Deceptive and nondeceptive communications: sending experience, modality, and individual abilities. *Journal of Nonverbal Behavior*, **10**, 147–167.

Manzanero, A.L. & Diges, M. (1996). Effects of preparation on internal and external memories. In G. Davies, S. Lloyd-Bostock, M. McMurran & C. Wilson (Eds), *Psychology, law, and criminal justice: international developments in research and practice*. Berlin: Walter de Gruyter, 56–63.

Markham, R. (1991). Development of reality monitoring for performed and imagined actions. *Perceptual and Motor Skills*, **72**, 1347–1354.

Maxwell, G.M., Cook, M.W. & Burr, R. (1985). The encoding and decoding of liking from behavioral cues in both auditory and visual channels. *Journal of Nonverbal Behavior*, **9**, 239–264.

Mehrabian, A. (1972). *Nonverbal communication*. Chicago, IL: Aldine-Atherton.

Mei-tai Fan, R., Wagner, H.L. & Manstead, A.S.R. (1995). Anchoring, familiarity, and confidence in the detection of deception. *Basic and Applied Social Psychology*, **17**, 83–96.

Memon, A. (1998). Telling it all: the Cognitive Interview. In A. Memon, A. Vrij & R. Bull, *Psychology and law: truthfulness, accuracy and credibility*. Maidenhead: McGraw-Hill, 170–188.

Memon, A. & Bull, R. (1999). *Handbook of the psychology of interviewing*. Chichester: John Wiley.

Merckelbach, H.L.G.J. (1990). Leugendetector kan gevaarlijk zijn. *Intermediair*, **26**, 35–37.

Metts, S. (1989). An exploratory investigation of deception in close relationships. *Journal of Social and Personal Relationships*, **6**, 159–179.

Millar, M.G. & Millar, K. (1995). Detection of deception in familiar and unfamiliar persons: the effects of information restriction. *Journal of Nonverbal Behavior*, **19**, 69–84.

Millar, M.G. & Millar, K. (1997). Effects of situational variables on judgments about deception and detection accuracy. *Basic and Applied Social Psychology*, **19**, 401–410.

Miller, G.R., Bauchner, J.E., Hocking, J.E., Fontes, N.E., Kaminski, E.P. & Brandt, D.R. (1981). '... and nothing but the truth'. In B. D. Sales (Ed.), *Perspectives in law and psychology. Vol. II: The trial process.* New York: Plenum, 145–179.

Miller, G.R., deTurck, M.A. & Kalbfleisch, P.J. (1983). Self-monitoring, rehearsal, and deceptive communication. *Human Communication Research*, **10**, 97–117.

Miller, G.R., Mongeau, P.A. & Sleight, C. (1986). Fudging with friends and lying to lovers: deceptive communication in personal relationships. *Journal of Social and Personal Relationships*, **3**, 495–512.

Milne, R. & Bull, R. (1999). *Investigative interviewing: psychology and practice.* Chichester: John Wiley.

Mitchell, R.W. (1986). A framework for discussing deception. In R.W. Mitchell & N.S. Mogdil (Eds), *Deception: perspectives on human and nonhuman deceit.* Albany: State University of New York Press, 3–4.

Moston, S. (1987). The suggestibility of children in interview studies. *Child Language*, **7**, 67–78.

Mulder, M. & Vrij, A. (1996). Explaining conversation rules to children: an intervention study to facilitate children's accurate responses. *Child Abuse and Neglect*, **20**, 623–631.

Myers. B. & Arbuthnot, J. (1997). Polygraph testimony and juror judgments: a comparison of the guilty knowledge test and the control question test. *Journal of Applied Social Psychology*, **27**, 1421–1437.

Neisser, U. (1981). John Dean's memory: a case study. *Cognition*, **9**, 1–22.

Nigro, G.N., Buckley, M.A., Hill, D.E. & Nelson, J. (1989). When juries 'hear' children testify: the effects of eyewitness age and speech style on juror's perceptions of testimony. In S.J. Ceci, D.E. Ross & M.P. Toglia (Eds), *Perspectives on children's testimony.* New York: Springer-Verlag, 57–70.

Ofshe, R. (1989). Coerced confessions: the logic of seemingly irrational action. *Cultic Studies Journal*, **6**, 1–15.

O'Hair, H.D., Cody, M. & McLaughlin, M.L. (1981). Prepared lies, spontaneous lies, Machiavellianism and nonverbal communication. *Human Communication Research*, **7**, 325–339.

Olsen, D.E., Harris, J.C., Capps, M.H. & Ansley, N. (1997). Computerized polygraph scoring system. *Journal of Forensic Sciences*, **42**, 61–70.

O'Sullivan, M., Ekman, P. & Friesen, W.V. (1988). The effect of comparisons on detecting deceit. *Journal of Nonverbal Behavior*, **12**, 203–216.

O'Toole, D., Yuille, J.C., Patrick, C.J. & Iacono, W.G. (1994). Alcohol and the physiological detection of deception: arousal and memory influences. *Psychophysiology*, **31**, 253–263.

Parham, I.A., Feldman, R.S., Oster, G.D. & Popoola, O. (1981). Intergenerational differences in nonverbal disclosure of deception. *Journal of Social Psychology*, **113**, 261–269.

Parker, J.F. (1995). Age differences in source monitoring of performed and imagined actions on immediate and delayed tests. *Journal of Experimental Child Psychology*, **60**, 84–101.

Patrick, C.J. & Iacono, W.G. (1991). Validity of the control question polygraph test: the problem of sampling bias. *Journal of Applied Psychology*, **76**, 229–238.

Peters, D.P. (1991). The influence of stress and arousal on the child witness. In J. Doris (Ed.), *The suggestibility of children's recollections.* Washington, DC: American Psychological Association, 60–76.

Podlesney, J.A. (1995). *A lack of operable case facts restricts applicability of the Guilty Knowledge Deception Detection Method in FBI criminal investigations.* FBI Technical Report, Quantico, VA.

Poole, D.A. & White, L.T. (1991). Effects of question repetition and retention interval on the eyewitness testimony of children and adults. *Developmental Psychology*, **27**, 975–986.

Porter, S. & Yuille, J.C. (1996). The language of deceit: an investigation of the verbal clues to deception in the interrogation context. *Law and Human Behavior*, **20**, 443–459.

Pynoos, R.S. & Eth, S. (1984). The child as witness to homicide. *Journal of Social Issues*, **40**, 87–108.

Pynoos, R.S. & Nader, K. (1988). Children who witness the sexual assault of their mothers. *Journal of the American Academy of Child and Adolescent Psychiatry*, **27**, 567–572.

Raskin, D.C. (1979). Orienting and defensive reflexes in the detection of deception. In H. D. Kimmel, E. H. Van Olst & J. F. Orlebeke (Eds), *The orienting reflex in humans*. Hillsdale, NJ: Erlbaum, 587–605.

Raskin, D.C. (1982). The scientific basis of polygraph techniques and their uses in the judicial process. In A. Trankell (Ed.), *Reconstructing the past*. Stockholm: Norsted & Soners, 317–371.

Raskin, D.C. (1986). The polygraph in 1986: scientific, professional, and legal issues surrounding acceptance of polygraph evidence. *Utah Law Review*, **29**, 29–74.

Raskin, D.C. (1988). Does science support polygraph testing? In A. Gale (Ed.), *The polygraph test: lies, truth and science*. London: Sage, 96–110.

Raskin, D.C. (1989). Polygraph techniques for the detection of deception. In D.C. Raskin (Ed.), *Psychological methods in criminal investigation and evidence*. New York: Springer-Verlag, 247–296.

Raskin, D.C. & Esplin, P.W. (1991a). Assessment of children's statements of sexual abuse. In J. Doris (Ed.), *The suggestibility of children's recollections*. Washington, DC: American Psychological Association, 153–165.

Raskin, D.C. & Esplin, P.W. (1991b). Statement Validity Assessment: interview procedures and content analysis of children's statements of sexual abuse. *Behavioral Assessment*, **13**, 265–291.

Raskin, D.C. & Hare, R.D. (1978). Psychopathy and detection of deception in a prison population. *Psychophysiology*, **15**, 126–136.

Raskin, D.C., Kircher, J.C., Horowitz, S.W. & Honts, C.R. (1989). Recent laboratory and field research on polygraph techniques. In J. C. Yuille (Ed.), *Credibility assessment*. Dordrecht: Kluwer Academic Publishers, 1–24.

Raye, C.L. & Johnson, M.K. (1980). Reality monitoring vs. discrimination between external sources. *Bulletin of the Psychonomic Society*, **15**, 405–408.

Reid, J.E. (1947). A revised questioning technique in lie detection tests. *Journal of Criminal Law, Criminology, and Police Science*, **37**, 542–547.

Reid, J.E. & Inbau, F. E. (1977). *Truth and deception: the polygraph (lie detector) technique*. Baltimore, MD: Williams & Wilkins.

Reis, H. T., Senchak, M. & Solomon, B. (1985). Sex differences in the intimacy of social interaction: further examination of potential explanations. *Journal of Personality and Social Psychology*, **48**, 1204–1217.

Riggio, R.E. (1986). Assessment of basic social skills. *Journal of Personality and Social Psychology*, **51**, 649–660.

Riggio, R.E. & Friedman, H.S. (1983). Individual differences and cues to deception. *Journal of Personality and Social Psychology*, **45**, 899–915.

Riggio, R.E., Tucker, J. & Throckmorton, B. (1988). Social skills and deception ability. *Personality and Social Psychology Bulletin*, **13**, 568–577.

Roberts, K.P., Lamb, M.E., Zale, J.L. & Randall, D.W. (1998). *Qualitative differences in children's accounts of confirmed and unconfirmed incidents of sexual abuse.* Paper presented at the biennial meeting of the American Psychology-Law Society, Redondo Beach, March 1998.

Robinson, W.P., Shepherd, A. & Heywood, J. (1998). Truth, equivocation/concealment, and lies in job applications and doctor–patient communication. *Journal of Language and Social Psychology*, **17**, 149–164.

Rockwell, P., Buller, D.B. & Burgoon, J.K. (1997). Measurement of deceptive voices: comparing acoustic and perceptual data. *Applied Psycholinguistics*, **18**, 471–484.

Roediger, H.L. (1996). Memory illusions. *Journal of Memory and Language*, **35**, 76–100.

Rosenfeld, P.J. (1995). Alternative views of Bashore and Rapp's (1993) alternative to traditional polygraphy: a critique. *Psychological Bulletin*, **117**, 159–166.

Rosenfeld, P.J., Angell, A., Johnson, M.M. & Qian, J. (1991). An ERP–based, control-question lie detector analog: algorithms for discriminating effects within individuals' average waveforms. *Psychophysiology*, **28**, 319–335.

Rosenfeld, J.P., Reinhart, A.M., Bhatt, M., Ellwanger, J., Gora, K., Sekera, M. & Sweet, J. (1998). P300 correlates of simulated malingered amnesia in a matching-to-sample task: topographic analyses of deception versus truthtelling responses. *International Journal of Psychophysiology*, **28**, 233–247.

Rosenthal, R. & DePaulo, B.M. (1979). Sex differences in eavesdropping on nonverbal cues. *Journal of Personality and Social Psychology*, **37**, 273–285.

Rosenthal, R. & Rubin, D.B. (1978). Interpersonal expectancy effects: the first 345 studies. *Behavioral and Brain Sciences*, **3**, 377–415.

Rowatt, W.C., Cunningham, M.R. & Druen, P.B. (1998). Deception to get a date. *Personality and Social Psychology Bulletin*, **24**, 1228–1242.

Rozelle, R.M. & Baxter, J.C. (1975). Impression formation and danger recognition in experienced police officers. *Journal of Social Psychology*, **96**, 53–63.

Rozelle, R.M. & Baxter, J.C. (1978). The interpretation of nonverbal behavior in a role-defined interaction sequence: the police-citizen encounter. *Environmental Psychology and Nonverbal Behavior*, **2**, 167–181.

Ruby, C.L. & Brigham, J.C. (1997). The usefulness of the criteria-based content analysis technique in distinguishing between truthful and fabricated allegations. *Psychology, Public Policy, and Law*, **3**, 705–737.

Ruby, C.L. & Brigham, J.C. (1998). Can Criteria-Based Content Analysis distinguish between true and false statements of African-American speakers? *Law and Human Behavior*, **22**, 369–388.

Ruva, C. & Bryant, J.B. (1998). *The impact of age, speech style, and question form on perceptions of witness credibility and trial outcome.* Paper presented at the AP-LS Biennial Conference, Redondo Beach, March 1998.

Saarni, C. (1984). An observational study of children's attempts to monitor their expressive behavior. *Child Development*, **55**, 1504–1513.

Saxe, L. (1991). Science and the GKT polygraph: a theoretical critique. *Integrative Physiological and Behavioral Science*, **26**, 223–231.

Saxe, L. (1994). Detection of deception: polygraph and integrity tests. *Current Directions in Psychological Science*, **3**, 69–73.

Schneider, S.M. & Kintz, B.L. (1977). The effect of lying upon foot and leg movement. *Bulletin of the Psychonomic Society*, **10**, 451–453.

Schooler, J.W., Gerhard, D. & Loftus, E.F. (1986). Qualities of the unreal. *Journal of Experimental Psychology: Learning, Memory, and Cognition*, **12**, 171–181.

Siegman, A.W. & Reynolds, M.A. (1983). Self-monitoring and speech in feigned and unfeigned lying. *Journal of Personality and Social Psychology*, **45**, 1325–1333.

Sleek, S. (1998). Psychologists debate merits of the polygraph. *Monitor*, **June**, 30.

Smith, A. (1983). Nonverbal communication among black female dyads: an assessment of intimacy, gender and race. *Journal of Social Issues*, **39**, 55–67.

Smith, H.J., Archer, D. & Costanzo, M. (1991). 'Just a hunch': accuracy and awareness in person perception. *Journal of Nonverbal Behavior*, **15**, 3–19.

Soppe, H.J.G. (1995a). Getuigenissen van kinderen in zedenzaken 1: De herinnering van kinderen en hoe hen te horen. *De Psycholoog*, **30**, 213–219.

Soppe, H.J.G. (1995b). Getuigenissen van kinderen in zedenzaken 2: Bepaling van de geloofwaardigheid. *De Psycholoog*, **30**, 261–265.

Soppe, H.J.G. (1997). Het verhoren van kinderen in zedenzaken. In P. J. Van Koppen, D. J. Hessing & H. F. M. Crombag (Eds), *Het hart van de zaak: Psychologie van het recht*. Deventer: Kluwer, 352–376.

Soppe, H.J.G. & Hees-Stauthamer, J.C. (1993). De geloofwaardigheid van getuigenissen van jeugdige slachtoffers van zedenmisdrijven. *Tijdschrift voor Ontwikkelingspsychologie*, **20**, 1–25.

Sporer, S.L. (1997). The less traveled road to truth: verbal cues in deception detection in accounts of fabricated and self-experienced events. *Applied Cognitive Psychology*, **11**, 373–397.

Steller, M. (1989). Recent developments in statement analysis. In J. C. Yuille (Ed.), *Credibility assessment*. Deventer: Kluwer, 135–154.

Steller, M. & Boychuk, T. (1992). Children as witnesses in sexual abuse cases: investigative interview and assessment techniques. In H. Dent & R. Flin (Eds), *Children as witnesses*. New York: John Wiley, 47–73.

Steller, M. & Köhnken, G. (1989). Criteria-Based Content Analysis. In D.C. Raskin (Ed.), *Psychological methods in criminal investigation and evidence*. New York: Springer-Verlag, 217–245.

Steller, M. & Wellershaus, P. (1996). Information enhancement and credibility assessment of child statements: the impact of the cognitive interview on criteria-based content analysis. In G. Davies, S. Lloyd-Bostock, M. McMurran & C. Wilson (Eds), *Psychology, law, and criminal justice: international developments in research and practice*. Berlin: de Gruyter, 118–127.

Steller, M., Haenert, P. & Eiselt, W. (1987). Extraversion and the detection of information. *Journal of Personality and Social Psychology*, **21**, 334–342.

Steller, M., Wellershaus, P. & Wolf, T. (1988). *Empirical validation of Criteria-Based Content Analysis*. Paper presented at the NATO Advanced Study Institute on Credibility Assessment in Maratea, Italy, June 1988.

Sternberg, K.J., Lamb, M.E., Hershkowitz, I., Esplin, P.W., Redlich, A. & Sunshine, N. (1996). The relationship between investigative utterance types and the informativeness of child witnesses. *Journal of Applied Developmental Psychology*, **17**, 439–451.

Sternberg, K.J., Lamb, M.E., Hershkowitz, I., Yudilevitch, L., Orbach, Y., Larson, C., Esplin, P.W. & Hovav, M. (in press). Effects of introductory style on children's abilities to describe experiences of sexual abuse. *Child Abuse and Neglect*.

Stiff, J.B. & Miller, G.R. (1986). 'Come to think of it...': interrogative probes, deceptive communication, and deception detection. *Human Communication Research*, **12**, 339–357.

Stiff, J.B., Corman, S., Krizek, B. & Snider, E. (1994). Individual differences and changes in nonverbal behavior: unmasking the changing faces of deception. *Communication Research*, **21**, 555–581.

Stiff, J.B., Hale, J.L., Garlick, R. & Rogan, R. (1990). Effect of cue incongruence and social normative influences on individual judgments of honesty and deceit. *Southern Communication Journal*, **55**, 206–229.

Stiff, J.B., Kim, H.J. & Ramesh, C.N. (1992). Truth biases and aroused suspicion in relational deception. *Communication Research*, **19**, 326–345.

Stiff, J.B., Miller, G.R., Sleight, C., Mongeau, P., Garlick, R. & Rogan, R. (1989). Explanations for visual cue primacy in judgments of honesty and deceit. *Journal of Personality and Social Psychology*, **56**, 555–564.

Streeter, L.A., Krauss, R.M., Geller, V., Olson, C. & Apple, W. (1977). Pitch changes during attempted deception. *Journal of Personality and Social Psychology*, **24**, 12–21.

Suengas, A.G. & Johnson, M.K. (1988). Qualitative effects of rehearsal on memories for perceived and imagined complex events. *Journal of Experimental Psychology: General*, **117**, 377–389.

Taylor, R. & Vrij, A. (1999). *The effects of varying stake and cognitive complexity on beliefs about the cues to deception*. Manuscript submitted for publication.

Toris, C. & DePaulo, B.M. (1985). Effects of actual deception and suspiciousness of deception on interpersonal perceptions. *Journal of Personality and Social Psychology*, **47**, 1063–1073.

Trankell, A. (1972). *Reliability of evidence*. Stockholm: Beckmans.

Tully, B. (1998). Reliability of criteria-based content analysis of child witness statements: Cohen's kappa doesn't matter. *Legal and Criminological Psychology*, **3**, 183–188.

Undeutsch, U. (1967). Beurteilung der Glaubhaftigkeit von Aussagen. In U. Undeutsch (Ed.), *Handbuch der Psychologie. Vol. 11. Forensische Psychologie*. Göttingen: Hogrefe, 26–181.

Undeutsch, U. (1982). Statement reality analysis. In A. Trankell (Ed.), *Reconstructing the past: the role of psychologists in criminal trials*. Deventer: Kluwer, 27–56.

Undeutsch, U. (1984). Courtroom evaluation of eyewitness testimony. *International Review of Applied Psychology*, **33**, 51–67.

Undeutsch, U. (1989). The development of statement reality analysis. In J. C. Yuille (Ed.), *Credibility assessment*. Dordrecht: Kluwer, 101–121.

Van Koppen, P.J., Boelhouwer, A.J.W., Merckelbach, H.L.G.J. & Verbaten, M.N. (1996). *Leugendetectie in actie: Het gebruik van de polygraaf in de praktijk*. Leiden: Nederlands Studiecentrum Criminaliteit en Rechtshandhaving.

Van Rossum, W. (1998). *Verschijnen voor de rechter: Hoe het hoort en het ritueel van Turkse verdachten in de rechtszaal*. Amsterdam: Uitgeverij duizend en een.

Volbert, R. & Van der Zanden, R. (1996). Sexual knowledge and behavior of children up to 12 years: what is age-appropriate? In G. Davies, S. Lloyd-Bostock, M. McMurran & C. Wilson (Eds), *Psychology, law, and criminal justice: international developments in research and practice*. Berlin: de Gruyter, 198–216.

Vrij, A. (1991). *Misverstanden tussen politie en allochtonen: Sociaal-psychologische aspecten van verdacht zijn*. Amsterdam: VU Uitgeverij.

Vrij, A. (1993a). Credibility judgments of detectives: the impact of nonverbal behavior, social skills and physical characteristics on impression formation. *Journal of Social Psychology*, **133**, 601–611.

Vrij, A. (1993b). *Students, prisoners and professional lie detectors' beliefs about verbal correlates of deception*. Unpublished data.

Vrij, A. (1994). The impact of information and setting on detection of deception by police detectives. *Journal of Nonverbal Behavior*, **18**, 117–137.

Vrij, A. (1995). Behavioral correlates of deception in a simulated police interview. *Journal of Psychology: Interdisciplinary and Applied*, **129**, 15–29.

Vrij, A. (1996). De rechercheur als leugendetector: Een overzicht van onderzoeken nar nonverbaal gedrag en misleiding. *Modus: Tijdschrift voor Recherche en Forensische Wetenschappen*, **5**, 4–9.

Vrij, A. (1997a). *Detecting lies in partners, friends and strangers*. Unpublished data.

Vrij, A. (1997b). *Gender differences in self-oriented and other-oriented lies*. Unpublished data.

Vrij, A. (1998a). Interviewing suspects. In A. Memon, A. Vrij & R. Bull, *Psychology and law: truthfulness, accuracy and credibility*. Maidenhead: McGraw-Hill, 124–146.

Vrij, A. (1998b). Telling and detecting lies: some future directions in research. *Forensic Update*, **54**, 14–19.

Vrij, A. (1998c). To lie or not to lie. *Psychologie*, **17**, 22–25.

Vrij, A. & Akehurst, L. (1996). *Hand movements during deception: some recent insights*. Paper presented at the Sixth European Conference on Psychology and Law. Italy, Sienna, August 1996.

Vrij, A. & Akehurst, L. (1998). Verbal communication and credibility: Statement Validity Assessment. In A. Memon, A. Vrij & R. Bull, *Psychology and law: truthfulness, accuracy and credibility*. Maidenhead: McGraw-Hill, 3–31.

Vrij, A. & Bull, R. (1992). *Beliefs about verbal correlates of deception: British students*. Unpublished data.

Vrij, A. & Fischer, A. (1995). The expression of emotions in simulated rape interviews. *Journal of Police and Criminal Psychology*, **10**, 64–67.

Vrij, A. & Graham, S. (1997). Individual differences between liars and the ability to detect lies. *Expert Evidence: The International Digest of Human Behaviour Science and Law*, **5**, 144–148.

Vrij, A. & Heaven, S. (1999). Vocal and verbal indicators of deception as a function of lie complexity. *Psychology, Crime and Law*, **5**, 203–215.

Vrij, A. & Holland, M. (1999). Individual differences in persistence in lying and experiences while deceiving. *Communication Research Reports*, **3**, 299–308.

Vrij, A. & Lochun, S. (1997). Neuro-linguïstisch verhoren. In P. J. Van Koppen, D. J. Hessing & H.F.M. Crombag (Eds), *Het hart van de zaak: Psychologie van het recht*. Deventer: Kluwer, 493–505.

Vrij, A. & Mann, S. (in press). *Lying when the stakes are high: deceptive behavior of a murderer during his police interview*. Applied Cognitive Psychology.

Vrij, A. & Mann, S. (1999). *Who killed my relative? Police officers' ability to detect real-life high-stake lies*. Manuscript submitted for publication.

Vrij, A. & Semin, G.R. (1996). Lie experts' beliefs about nonverbal indicators of deception. *Journal of Nonverbal Behavior*, **20**, 65–80.

Vrij, A. & Taylor, R. (1999). *Police officers' and students' beliefs about telling and detecting little and serious lies*. Manuscript submitted for publication.

Vrij, A. & Van Wijngaarden, J.J. (1994). Will truth come out? Two studies about the detection of false statements expressed by children. *Expert Evidence: The International Digest of Human Behaviour, Science and Law*, **3**, 78–84.

Vrij, A. & Winkel, F.W. (1990). Culturele verschillen in spreekstijl van Surinamers en Nederlanders: De relatie tussen 'zakelijkheid' en 'misleiding' bij een politieverhoor. *Recht der Werkelijkheid*, **11**, 3–15.

Vrij, A. & Winkel, F.W. (1991). Cultural patterns in Dutch and Surinam nonverbal behavior: an analysis of simulated police/citizen encounters. *Journal of Nonverbal Behavior*, **15**, 169–184.

Vrij, A. & Winkel, F.W. (1992a). Crosscultural police–citizen interactions: the influence of race, beliefs and nonverbal communication on impression formation. *Journal of Applied Social Psychology*, **22**, 1546–1559.

Vrij, A. & Winkel, F.W. (1992b). Social skills, distorted perception and being suspect: studies in impression formation and the ability to deceive. *Journal of Police and Criminal Psychology*, **8**, 2–6.

Vrij, A. & Winkel, F.W. (1994). Perceptual distortions in cross-cultural interrogations: the impact of skin color, accent, speech style and spoken fluency on impression formation. *Journal of Cross-Cultural Psychology*, **25**, 284–296.

Vrij, A., Akehurst, L. & Morris, P.M. (1997). Individual differences in hand movements during deception. *Journal of Nonverbal Behavior*, **21**, 87–102.

Vrij, A., Akehurst, L., Van Dalen, D., Van Wijngaarden, J.J. & Foppes, J. H. (1996). Nonverbaal gedrag en misleiding. *Tijdschrift voor de Politie*, **58**, 11–14.

Vrij, A., Dragt, A.W. & Koppelaar, L. (1992). Interviews with ethnic interviewees: nonverbal communication errors in impression formation. *Journal of Community and Applied Social Psychology*, **2**, 199–209.

Vrij, A., Edward, K., Roberts, K.P. & Bull, R. (1999). *Detecting deceit via Criteria-Based Content Analysis, Reality Monitoring and analyses of nonverbal behaviour*. Paper presented at the Ninth European Conference on Psychology and Law, Dublin, Ireland, July 1999.

Vrij, A., Foppes, J.H., Volger, D.M. & Winkel, F.W. (1992). Moeilijk te bepalen wie de waarheid spreekt: Non-verbaal gedrag belangrijkste indicator. *Algemeen Politie Blad*, **141**, 13–15.

Vrij, A., Kneller, W. & Mann, S. (in press). The effect of informing liars about Criteria-Based Content Analysis on their ability to deceive CBCA raters. *Legal and Criminological Psychology*.

Vrij, A., Semin, G.R. & Bull, R. (1996). Insight in behavior displayed during deception. *Human Communication Research*, **22**, 544–562.

Vrij, A., Winkel, F.W. & Akehurst, L. (1997). Police officers' incorrect beliefs about nonverbal indicators of deception and its consequences. In J. F. Nijboer & J. M. Reijntjes (Eds), *Proceedings of the First World Conference on New Trends in Criminal Investigation and Evidence*. Lelystad: Koninklijke Vermande, 221–238.

Vrij, A., Winkel, F.W. & Koppelaar, L. (1988). Culturele verschillen in nonverbaal gedrag: De persoonlijke ruimte van Nederlanders en Surinamers. *Migrantenstudies*, **4**, 40–49.

Vrij, A., Winkel, F.W. & Koppelaar, L. (1991). Interactie tussen politiefunctionarissen en allochtone burgers: twee studies naar de frequentie en het effect van aan-en wegkijken op de impressieformatie. *Nederlands Tijdschrift voor de Psychologie*, **46**, 8–20.

Wagenaar, W.A. & Groeneweg, J. (1990). The memory of concentration camp survivors. *Applied Cognitive Psychology*, **4**, 77–87.

Walkley, J. (1985). Reading the suspect. *Police Review*, **93**, 337–340.

Walters, S.B. (1996). *Kinesic interview and interrogation*. Boca Raton, FL: CRC Press.

Waltman, J.L. (1983). Nonverbal communication in interrogation: some applications. *Journal of Police and Science Administration*, **11**, 166–169.

Watson, D.C. & Sinka, B.K. (1993). Individual differences, social arousal and the electrodermal detection of deception. *Personality and Individual Differences*, **15**, 75–80.

Wells, G.L. & Leippe, M.R. (1981). How do triers of fact infer accuracy of eyewitness identification? Using memory of peripheral details can be misleading. *Journal of Applied Psychology*, **66**, 682–687.

Wells, G.L. & Loftus, E.F. (1991). Commentary: is this child fabricating? Reactions to a new assessment technique. In J. Doris (Ed.), *The suggestibility of children's recollections*: Washington, DC: American Psychological Association, 168–171.

West, I. (1992). *Decision-making in the detection of deception*. Paper presented to the British Psychology Society, Division of Criminological and Legal Psychology. Harrogate, March 1992.

Westcott, H.L., Davies, G.M. & Clifford, B.R. (1991). Adults' perceptions of children's videotaped truthful and deceptive statements. *Children and Society*, **5**, 123–135.

Wilson, D.S., Near, D.C. & Miller, R.R. (1998). Individual differences in Machiavellianism as a mix of cooperative and exploitative strategies. *Evolution and Human Behavior*, **19**, 203–212.

Winkel, F.W. & Vrij, A. (1995). Verklaringen van kinderen in interviews: Een experimenteel onderzoek naar de diagnostische waarde van Criteria Based Content Analysis. *Tijdschrift voor Ontwikkelingspsychologie*, **22**, 61–74.

Winkel, F.W., Vrij, A., Koppelaar, L. & Van der Steen, J. (1991). Reducing secondary victimisation risks and skilled police intervention: enhancing the quality of police rape victim encounters through training programmes. *Journal of Police and Criminal Psychology*, **7**, 2–11.

Woodall, W.G. & Burgoon, J.K. (1983). Talking fast and changing attitudes: a critique and clarification. *Journal of Nonverbal Behavior*, **8**, 126–143.

Young, M.J. & deTurck, M.A. (1996). *The effects of stress and coping on truthful and deceptive communication*. Unpublished manuscript.

Yuille, J.C. (1988a). *A simulation study of criteria-based content analysis*. Paper presented at the NATO advanced study institute on credibility assessment, Maratea, Italy, June 1988.

Yuille, J.C. (1988b). The systematic assessment of children's testimony. *Canadian Psychology*, **29**, 247–262.

Yuille, J.C. & Cutshall, J. (1989). Analysis of statements of victims, witnesses, and suspects. In J.C. Yuille (Ed.), *Credibility assessment*. Dordrecht: Kluwer, 175–191.

Zaparniuk, J., Yuille, J.C. & Taylor, S. (1995). Assessing the credibility of true and false statements. *International Journal of Law and Psychiatry*, **18**, 343–352.

Zuckerman, M. & Driver, R.E. (1985). Telling lies: verbal and nonverbal correlates of deception. In A.W. Siegman & S. Feldstein (Eds), *Multichannel integrations of nonverbal behaviors*. Hillsdale, NJ: Lawrence Erlbaum, 129–147.

Zuckerman, M., DeFrank, R.S., Hall, J.A., Larrance, D.T. & Rosenthal, R. (1979). Facial and vocal cues of deception and honesty. *Journal of Experimental Social Psychology*, **15**, 378–396.

Zuckerman, M., DePaulo, B.M. & Rosenthal, R. (1981). Verbal and nonverbal communication of deception. In L. Berkowitz (Ed.), *Advances in experimental social psychology. Vol. 14*. New York: Academic Press, 1–57.

Zuckerman, M., Koestner, R. & Alton, A.O. (1984). Learning to detect deception. *Journal of Personality and Social Psychology*, **46**, 519–528.

Zuckerman, M., Koestner, R. & Colella, M.J. (1985). Learning to detect deception from three communication channels. *Journal of Nonverbal Behavior*, **9**, 188–194.

Zuckerman, M., Koestner, R. & Driver, R. (1981). Beliefs about cues associated with deception. *Journal of Nonverbal Behavior*, **6**, 105–114.

Index

Related titles
of interest...

Handbook of Offender Assessment and Treatment
Edited by CLIVE R. HOLLIN
0471 988588   624pp   February 2000   Hardback

Cognitive Behavioural Treatment of Sexual Offenders
WILLIAM MARSHALL, DANA ANDERSON and
YOLANDA FERNANDEZ
0471 975664   220pp   September 1999   Paperback

Handbook of the Psychology of Interviewing
AMINA MEMON and RAY BULL
0471 974439   380pp   February 1999   Hardback

The Handbook of Forensic Psychology
2nd Edition
ALLEN K. HESS and IRVING B. WEINER
0471 177717   832pp   December 1998   Hardback

The Psychology of Criminal Conduct
RONALD BLACKBURN
0471 961752   506pp   1995   Paperback

Learning Resources